ALTERNATIVE EGYPTOLOGY

sidestonepress

ALTERNATIVE EGYPTOLOGY

Critical Essays on the Relation between Academic and Alternative Interpretations of Ancient Egypt

B. J. L. van den Bercken (ed.)

Published by Sidestone Press, Leiden
www.sidestone.com

In collaboration with the Allard Pierson – the collections of the University of Amsterdam
www.allardpierson.nl

Lay-out & cover design: Sidestone Press
Photograph cover: C. L. F. Panckoucke, *Description de l'Égypte ou Recueil des observations et des recherches qui ont été faites en Egypte pendant l'expédition de l'armée française, 1820–1830*. Detail of plate 9, showing the pyramids at Giza. Image Allard Pierson, University of Amsterdam, OL 63-999-1009

Publication manager: Paulien Retèl
Editing and translation: Noctua Text & Translation, Roek (C. L.) Vermeulen

ISBN 978-94-6426-161-5 (softcover)
ISBN 978-94-6426-162-2 (hardcover)
ISBN 978-94-6426-163-9 (PDF e-book)

DOI: 10.59641/rho5a4ij

ALLARDPIERSON
THE COLLECTIONS OF THE UNIVERSITY OF AMSTERDAM

Contents

Figure 1. Stele showing the Egyptian god Thoth, who was later equated with Hermes (Trismegistos) in three different forms: as a baboon, an ibis and an anthropomorphic image combining a human body and ibis head. Image Allard Pierson, University of Amsterdam, APM07794.

Introduction

Ben van den Bercken

Alternative interpretations of ancient Egypt

With the decipherment of the hieroglyphic script in 1822 the discipline of Egyptology was born. It is more or less the starting point from which Egyptology as a scholarly and scientific discipline started to diverge from what we now summarise as 'alternative Egyptology'. Alternative Egyptology is usually described as a different interpretation of the generally accepted scholarly interpretation of ancient Egyptian history and culture. It is an umbrella term for numerous perspectives and ideas. Lynn Picknett and Clive Prince situate the origin of the term in the 1990s, when it was used to bring together 'a loose body of competing theories about the nature and significance of Ancient Egypt that lacked a coherent identity and "label".'[1] The content of this label varies from esoteric interpretations of ancient Egypt to ideas about extraterrestrial agency in the building of the pyramids at Giza. Many of these theories had existed for some time, but were and are not always based on academic methods, reasoning or publications.

The Napoleonic expedition (fig. 2) and subsequent decipherment of the Egyptian hieroglyphs not only caused an increase in the search for ancient Egyptian objects and in visits to monuments and sites in Egypt, but also won ancient Egypt more attention from a general public. Interested amateurs or scholars from other disciplines than archaeology and Egyptology looked into aspects of ancient Egyptian culture from their perspectives. People like Ignatius Donnelly, Joseph-Alexandre Saint-Yves d'Alveydre, Helena Petrovna Blavatsky, and Edgar Cayce developed and advocated ideas that focused on esoteric and occult interpretations of ancient Egypt (fig. 3), resulting in philosophies such as theosophy and synarchy.[2]

The 1990s represent an important period in the relation between mainstream and alternative Egyptologies. With the presentation of alternative theories about the age, function and correlation of the pyramids and sphinx of Giza and the corroboration of

---

1 Picknett/Prince 2009, 175. Nielsen also uses the definition 'pseudo-Egyptology' or 'pseudo-sciences'; Nielsen 2020, X.

2 Picknett/Prince 2009, 178–181.

in Van den Bercken, B. J. L. (ed.), *Alternative Egyptology: Critical Essays on the Relation between Academic and Alternative Interpretations of Ancient Egypt*, Leiden, pp. 8–15.

Figure 2. *Bonaparte before the Sphinx*, painting by Jean-Léon Gérôme. Oil on canvas, 1886, Hearst Castle Collection. Image Wikimedia Commons.

(parts of) these theories by scientific institutions and mainstream scholars and their subsequent popularisation made it impossible for mainstream Egyptology to leave these alternative ideas unaddressed.

Parallel and/or converging lines

According to Nicky Nielsen the tenacity and continued popularity of alternative ideas about ancient Egypt, and more specifically the Giza pyramids, can be explained by people not always tending to believe experts or authorities.[3] By creating one's own alternative or pseudo-narrative to the main or generally accepted narrative, one gains a measure of control over the subject. Such narratives often use an us-v-them rhetoric. According to Nielsen mainstream Egyptology or science and scholarship in general should therefore not focus on bluntly refuting the theories or ridiculing their proponents, it should try to improve its communication and work from there. Presenting the facts that can be established on the basis of academic methods, analysis, and reasoning and presenting this not only to an academic but also to a wider public is important. The use of channels outside the standard scholarly routes can play an important role in this.

Addressing the alternative ideas and perspectives that became influential in the 1990s was a case in point. At that time it became clear, firstly, that mainstream Egyptology also had to relate to the general public in order for the scholarly perspective on Egypt to find wider acceptance.[4] With people becoming more and more dependent on (large amounts of) information (fig. 4) and at the same time susceptible for alternative interpretations in an increasingly polarised society, it is important for mainstream Egyptology to relate

3 Nielsen 2020, 151–155.

4 Picknett/Prince 2009, 190 mention the BBC Horizon science documentaries in which the legend of Atlantis played a role and which in a clear way separated fact from fiction.

Figure 3. Illustration with the *Tabula smaragdina*, from Gregorius Anglus Sallwigt (pseudonym of Georg von Welling), *Opus mago-cabalisticum et theologicum* (...), manuscript, Heidelberg 1775. Image Allard Pierson, Bibliotheca Philosophica Hermetica State Collection PH318.

Figure 4. Fantasy setting of feeding cats in an ancient Egyptian temple by British historical and fantasy illustrator Angus McBride (1931–2007). Image Bridgeman Images, LAL3641218.

to this. Secondly, there should be space for accepting the fact that ideas coming from alternative Egyptology do not always have to be fundamentally wrong or undeserving of attention. Different perspectives might help in finding new research perspectives and trying to establish facts where there were few or none before.

Symposium on alternative Egyptology

On 14 April 2021 the symposium *Alternative Egyptology* was held at the Allard Pierson in Amsterdam to mark the retirement of the curator for the Egyptian collection, Willem van Haarlem. The symposium demonstrated the diversity of the topics that alternative Egyptology encompasses. Thirteen of the contributions to the symposium are included in this volume.

Caroline Tully discusses the Hermetic Order of the Golden Dawn, which draws upon mainstream Egyptological literature but also reinterprets it. She illustrates this by discussing several prominent members of the Order who used this information to further their own agendas. Jasmine Day focuses on the (growing) divide between Egyptology and Egyptosophy in the early twentieth century. A similar split can be observed in British society at that time, and with the example of the curse of Tutankhamun's tomb Day underlines that the divide was related to the meaning that both sides attributed to ancient Egypt. Maiken Mosleth King writes on Golden Dawn protagonist Aleister Crowley and the way in which he intentionally attributed an 'otherness' to ancient Egypt which played a role in legitimising his own religious ideas. Daniel Potter describes the works and ideas of astronomer Charles Piazzi Smyth on the Great Pyramid at Giza. The case of Smyth shows how close mainstream and alternative ideas can be and at the same time how important reflection and contextualisation are.

Willem van Haarlem looks at the connection between the Giza pyramids and the Orion constellation. He summarises the discussion that took place in the 1990s, both on the pyramids and the sphinx, and where it stands today. Andrea Sinclair looks at the prolific presence of psychoactive plants in alternative Egyptology and maps how information about these plants entered the alternative discourse. The tenacity of older interpretations is partly due to dated popular works, such as several publications by Ernest A. Wallis Budge.[5] Arnaud Quertinmont discusses how and why Egyptian gods and ancient astronauts occur in comic books. He examines how mainstream Egyptology, and more specifically a museum, can relate to ideas and perspectives in comic books. Eleanor Dobson looks at how the interplay between astronomy and Egyptian archaeology led to fiction portraying ancient Egyptians as astronauts. Jean-Pierre Pätznick analyses the mysterious Paul Schliemann's quest for the lost continent of Atlantis. By reconstructing this search which also leads to Egypt and can be related to work at the Delta city of Saïs, Pätznick tries to separate fact from fiction.

Tian Tian focuses on Chinese societal elements that have contributed to the Chinese perception that ancient Egypt is in fact part of Chinese traditional history. Thomas Henrique de Toledo Stella reveals the discovery of an Egyptianising set of murals in a Freemasons' lodge in Brazil. He analyses these alternatively interpreted Egyptian tomb reliefs and explains their use in the context of the Brazilian Independence in 1822 and the change to the Republican regime in 1889. Simon Magus examines the influence of esoteric Egypt on the works of Henry Rider Haggard and in what way he combined archaeological, biblical but also imaginative narratives. Huub Pragt looks at the complicated and much-discussed exodus from Egypt by the Israelites. By comparing biblical texts with geographical markers and Egyptological interpretation he proposes a reconstruction of the route taken from Pi-Ramesses to Sinai.

One of the symposium's goals was to bring together a diverse group of researchers working on alternative Egyptological topics. Another goal was to try and map the impact of alternative interpretations of ancient Egypt on society and scholarship and assess

---

5 See also Hornung 2001, 2 on outdated Egyptological works.

how Egyptology could relate to them. With ancient Egypt and several of its main topics (pyramids, mummies) still being widely popular it is important for mainstream Egyptology to connect with what is happening in alternative Egyptology, finding channels to and relating to a wider public. Moreover, Egyptologists should be aware of the route that outdated information sometimes takes and how it enters the public domain, discussion and perspectives. Lastly, it is important to follow but also initiate public discussion and interaction on relevant topics. We hope this publication will contribute to that goal.

Bibliography

Fleischhack, M., 2015, *Narrating Ancient Egypt: The Representation of Ancient Egypt in Nineteenth-century and Early-twentieth Century Fantastic Fiction*, Frankfurt am Main

Hornung, E., 2001, *The Secret Lore of Egypt: Its Impact on the West*, Ithaca.

Nielsen, N., 2020, *Egyptomaniacs: How We Became Obsessed with Ancient Egypt*, Philadelphia.

Picknett, L., Prince, C., 2009, 'Alternative Egypts', in MacDonald, S., Rice, M., 2009, *Consuming Ancient Egypt*, London, 175–193.

About the author

Ben van den Bercken (MA) studied Egyptian archaeology at Leiden University and museum studies at the University of Amsterdam. He worked at excavations in Alexandria and was an assistant-curator at the National Museum of Antiquities in Leiden (RMO). Since 2021 he is curator of the Ancient Egypt and Sudan collection at the Allard Pierson (University of Amsterdam).

Figure 1. Image of a rose cross, a symbol connecting a rose and cross, from *Einfältig A.B.C. Büchlein. Das ist: Die Lehren der fratruum Roseae Crucis,* manuscript, [after 1785]. Image Allard Pierson, Bibliotheca Philosophica Hermetica State Collection, PH340.

Lifting the Veil of Isis

Egyptian Reception and the Hermetic Order of the Golden Dawn

Caroline Tully

The Hermetic Order of the Golden Dawn

The Hermetic Order of the Golden Dawn was a secret society in the tradition of Freemasonry that taught its members ritual magic. Entry to the Order—which was designed as a fraternal organisation—happened through elaborate initiation rituals which, along with a specific curriculum of study, provided members with access to supposed ancient wisdom. Founded in London in 1888 by Dr William Wynn Westcott (1848–1925), Samuel Liddell MacGregor Mathers (1854–1918), and Dr William Robert Woodman (1828–1891), the Golden Dawn augmented the Hermetic Egyptosophical tradition with the latest findings from academic Egyptology. 'Egyptosophy' refers to 'the study of an imaginary Egypt viewed as the profound source of all esoteric lore' and reflects the idea—prevalent since Antiquity—that the ancient Egyptians were a race of mysterious sages.[1] The academic discipline of Egyptology split from Egyptosophy in 1822 with Jean-François Champollion's decipherment of the Egyptian hieroglyphs. Once texts by the ancient Egyptians themselves could be read the centuries-old belief in a mystical Egypt was revealed to be inaccurate. The fantasy image of Egypt remained, however, in a parallel tradition alongside the scholarly one; and the two streams were utilised as complementary sources by the amateur Egyptologists of the Golden Dawn.

The Order was officially launched with the opening of the Isis-Urania Temple on 12 February 1888. New branches, the Osiris Temple in Weston-super-Mare and the Horus Temple in Bradford, both in England, were also formed later that year. By 1893 the Edinburgh Amen-Ra Temple was chartered and in 1894 the Ahathoor Temple in Paris, where Mathers and his wife had moved in 1892, was founded. As the Order was designed as a school that would expound Western esoteric systems such as alchemy, astrology, tarot, kabbala, geomancy and ritual magic through elaborate initiation rituals, its ceremonies were infused with Egyptian content. Utilising the long-accessible Classical literature about Egypt as well as the latest research from academic Egyptology, the Golden Dawn interpreted both types of material through a Hermetic lens.

1 Hornung 2001, 1, 3.

in Van den Bercken, B. J. L. (ed.), *Alternative Egyptology: Critical Essays on the Relation between Academic and Alternative Interpretations of Ancient Egypt*, Leiden, pp. 16–27.

The Hermetic tradition is based on pseudo-epigraphic texts purporting to explain ancient Egyptian wisdom and believed during the Renaissance to date to the time of Moses.[2] Although the French classical scholar and theologian Isaac Casaubon (1559–1614) in 1614 exposed it as dating to the early centuries AD and it was subsequently abandoned in intellectual circles, the Hermetic presentation of Egypt as a repository of ancient wisdom retained its importance within European secret societies such as Rosicrucianism and Freemasonry.[3] In these organisations ancient Egypt was considered to be the source of all religion, knowledge and architecture—'not an ancient dead culture but a living tradition that could be inherited and carried on.'[4]

The Golden Dawn's ritual programme was infused with aspects of Egyptian religion. Members were initiated into the Order through the Neophyte Ceremony, which combined echoes of Apuleius' description of the initiation into the Isis cult in his *Metamorphoses* dating from the second century AD and vignettes from the recently translated Egyptian New Kingdom *Book of the Dead*.[5] Higher-degree members encountered the myth of Isis and Osiris, as told in Plutarch's *De Iside et Osiride* (13–19), in symbolic form through the mystical 'L.V.X. signs.'[6] These physical gestures symbolically encapsulated the story of Osiris' murder by Typhon (the Egyptian god Seth), the subsequent mourning of Isis, and Osiris' eventual resurrection, syncretising these Egyptian deities with Christianity by associating Osiris with the crucified Christ. Another set of gestures, known as the 'Portal Sign,' enabled initiates to rend and see beyond the 'veil of Isis,' a prerequisite to entering the 'tomb of Osiris' in which, after experiencing a symbolic death, they were reanimated through a version of the ancient Egyptian Opening of the Mouth ceremony.[7] The Order's biannually enacted Equinox Ritual incorporated the Isian myth of Pharaonic succession; the officer who had for the previous six months played the role of Hierophant in Golden Dawn ceremonies, representing Osiris who in Egyptian religion signified the deceased pharaoh, vacated his position in favour of a new officer representing Horus, the new pharaoh.[8]

MacGregor and Moina Mathers

Samuel Liddell MacGregor Mathers and his wife Moina (1865–1928)[9] were the creative geniuses of the Order. They met in 1887 in the British Museum, where MacGregor was undertaking a self-directed study of magic, alchemy, symbolism and ancient Egyptian religion while Moina, an artist, was sketching statues in the Egyptian Sculpture Gallery.[10] The following year MacGregor co-founded the Golden Dawn and Moina became the first initiate of the Order, and later the only female member to attain the highest degree in its graded system of advancement. MacGregor himself would become sole leader of the Order in 1893.

---

2 Ebeling 2007, 60–3.
3 Ebeling 2007, 91–2; Assmann 2007, vi–xiii.
4 Hornung 2001, 118; Curl 2005, 230.
5 Regardie 1990, vol. 6, 5–22; vol. 8, 62–6; vol. 3, 2, 10; Faulkner 1985, 44–50.
6 Regardie 1990, vol. 7, 53.
7 Regardie 1990, vol. 7, 151; vol. 8, 17–19.
8 Regardie 1990, vol. 8, 1–13; vol. 6, 84; Tully 2010, 37.
9 Greer 1995, 41–2.
10 Greer 1995, 55.

In 1892 MacGregor and Moina had moved permanently to Paris, where a flourishing occult scene existed.[11] Mathers' years of amateur Egyptological studies in the British Museum meant that when visiting the Louvre's substantial Egyptian collection he could confidently pontificate on the meanings of ancient Egyptian statuary to his students; but he did this through a Hermetic lens and his interpretations were coloured by an unwarranted belief in occult meanings.

By 1896 the couple was heavily involved in the exploration of what they termed 'the Egyptian Mysteries.' By 1898 they were 'restoring the Mysteries,' while 1899 saw them putting on public performances of 'Rites of Isis' at the Théâtre Bodinière in Paris, having been 'converted to the strange and passionate mysticism of the worship of Isis during their travels in Egypt,' a claim that was almost certainly untrue.[12] In 1900 this led to their establishment of private initiations into the 'Mysteries of Isis.'[13] Like the Golden Dawn rituals, the Rites of Isis were constructed from Classical and Pharaonic sources filtered through the Hermetic tradition, combined with the couple's supposed 'memories' of past lives lived in Egypt.[14]

The main problem with the Matherses' attempt at creating this initiatory system was that there were no 'Egyptian Mysteries' to begin with. While there certainly were Graeco-Roman mysteries of the Hellenised Isis, the idea that there were ancient Egyptian 'mysteries' originated with Greeks like Herodotus misunderstanding the Egyptian cult of Osiris at Abydos and interpreting it as a mystery religion because it was carried out by a specially consecrated priesthood, unlike the part-time priests of Greece.[15] Only Apuleius' description of the initiation of a priest of Isis can be considered to be an Egyptian ritual with some of the characteristics of a Greek mystery cult; in subsequent European history it was perceived as the 'Egyptian initiation' par excellence. Perhaps the actual revelation of the 'mystery' in the Matherses' ritual was the unveiling of a statue of Isis, inspired by Plutarch's description of the statue of Saite Isis 'I am all that has been and is and will be; and no mortal has ever lifted my veil' (*De Iside* 9); the Freemasonic tradition interprets the veiled Isis as a symbol of the hidden secrets of nature.[16]

Florence Farr

The British actor Florence Farr (1860–1917) joined the Hermetic Order of the Golden Dawn in 1890, becoming Praemonstratrix in 1893 (in charge of all rituals, invocations and teachings), as well as being MacGregor Mathers' representative in England. She was elevated to the role of 'Chief in Anglia,' or head of the Order in England, in 1897.[17] In 1895, five years after joining the Golden Dawn, whilst researching material for her book *Egyptian Magic* in the British Museum, Farr 'made contact' with what she described as 'an Egyptian Adept' whom she would subsequently introduce to a secret group formed within the Golden Dawn.[18] This 'Adept' was a long-dead ancient Egyptian mummy.[19]

---

11 McIntosh 1972; Webb 1974, 153–90; Churton 2016; Greer 1995, 102.
12 Greer 1995, xviii, 155, 207; Colquhoun 1975, 86.
13 Gaucher 1900; Lees 1900.
14 Tully 2009a, 64–8; Tully 2020; Young 1945, 105; Greer 1995, 200, 314; Lefkowitz 1997, 93.
15 Burkert 1987, 39–40.
16 Hornung 2001, 134–5.
17 Greer 1995, 130.
18 Greer 1995, 195.
19 Tully 2009b; Tully 2018.

Figure 2. Samuel Liddell MacGregor Mathers in ceremonial regalia relating to ritual magic, *c.*1895, by Moina Mathers. Image Bridgeman Images, RGL212682.

Figure 3. Sketch of Moina Mathers in the role of the High Priestess Anari, working in the rites of Isis, Paris, 1899. Image Bridgeman Images, RGL212685.

The mummy with which Farr formed a psychic relationship was acquired by the British Museum in 1835. Like other museum attendees, Farr would have been under the impression that this ostensibly female mummy was that of Mutemmenu, 'a lady of the college of the God Amen-Ra at Thebes,' as described in the museum guidebooks for many years.[20] X-rays of the mummy undertaken in the 1960s and more recent CT scans

20 Budge 1898.

Figure 4. Florence Farr. Reworked after Marley 2017.

show, however, that this description is only half correct. While the coffin is indeed that of Mutemmenu, a Chantress of Amun, dating from the 19th (1295–1186 BC) or 20th (1186–1069 BC) Dynasties, the mummy associated with the coffin dates from the Roman period (30 BC–AD 395) and is actually that of a man whose wrappings are padded and swathed in such a manner as to appear to imitate feminine features such as breasts and rounded thighs.[21] The fact that the mummy dates from the Roman period but came to the

21 Taylor/Antoine 2014, 142.

British Museum in a coffin belonging to a Chantress of Amun from the Ramesside period can be explained by the fact that Roman-period burials in the Theban Necropolis, where this mummy probably originated, often reused earlier tombs and funerary goods such as coffins and shrouds.[22]

Farr came to believe that she had actually *been* Mutemmenu in one of her past lives.[23] She also had another ancient Egyptian contact who, like Mutemmenu, was (and is) part of the Egyptian collection in the British Museum: Nenkheftka. This provincial official is shown in the form of a painted limestone statue from Deshasha, dating to the 5th Dynasty (*c*.2450 BC), at the height of the Old Kingdom. The British Museum acquired it in 1897 as a gift from the Egypt Exploration Fund.[24] Farr considered him to be her *ka* (life force).[25] She interpreted the *ka* as the celestial double of a person, the real ego or self, whose mission was to grow and develop through 'celestial evolution' just as physical bodies evolve in the material world. Farr may have either associated the last syllable of Nenkheftka's name with the idea of the *ka*, or thought she had been the *wife* of Nenkheftka in a previous incarnation.[26]

Aleister Crowley

Aleister Crowley (1875–1947) joined the Golden Dawn in 1898. Advancing rapidly through the grades, he had completed the Outer Order curriculum by 1899.[27] Although qualified to be initiated into the Second Order, Farr, as Chief in Anglia, decided not to allow him to advance to the higher degrees because of his reputation of 'sex intemperance,' so Crowley went to Paris and was initiated by Mathers instead.[28] In 1903 Crowley embarked on a long overseas honeymoon to Ceylon and Egypt with his new wife, Rose Kelly. As a Golden Dawn student it must have been exciting for him to visit the land that ostensibly supplied the Order with much of its spiritual authority. As he explained: 'My gods were those of Egypt.'[29]

Crowley performed Golden Dawn rituals in Egypt, including a ritual inside the Great Pyramid of Khufu.[30] At the spring equinox of 1904 he performed a ritual to the Egyptian god Horus and received what he felt was a startling revelation: 'I was told that "The Equinox of the Gods had come;" that is, a new epoch had begun. I was to formulate a link between the solar-spiritual force and mankind (...) the Secret Chiefs (...) had sent a messenger to confer upon me the position which Mathers had forfeited.'[31]

As explained above, the Golden Dawn equinox ritual involved the participants changing roles.[32] Crowley's 'Equinox of the Gods' followed this structure but on a cosmic scale, signifying the shift from an 'aeon' (a time period of about 2000 years) ruled by Osiris to the new 'Aeon of Horus'.[33] On an earthly level this provided a way for Crowley to break

22 Taylor/Antoine 2014, 142; Riggs 2005, 180–1; Riggs 2003, 190.
23 Greer 1995, 169; Toomey 1997, 111–2.
24 Strudwick 2006, 58; Bednarski 2007, 235.
25 Gould 1997, 167.
26 Gould 1997, 170.
27 Howe 1972, 192, 16.
28 Howe 1972, 206.
29 Symonds/Grant 1969, 357.
30 Crowley 2000, xxxv.
31 Symonds/Grant 1969, 394.
32 Crowley 1974, 137–8; Regardie 1990, vol. 6, 54; Symonds/Grant 1969, 399.
33 Symonds/Grant 1969, 399; Crowley 1936, 134.

Figure 5. Aleister Crowley in ceremonial robes with an Egyptian-style *nemes* headcloth. Aleister Crowley, 1910, *The Rites of Eleusis*, n.p.

with his former mentor Mathers, identifying the latter with the 'old king', Osiris, and himself with the 'rightful heir,' Horus.[34]

In order to support the genuineness of this revelation, Crowley and his wife Rose went to the Egyptian Museum, where she led him to 'an image of Horus in the form of Ra Hoor Khuit painted on a wooden stele of the 26th Dynasty—*and the exhibit bore the number 666!*'[35] This was an exciting confirmation for Crowley who, steeped in both the Egyptophilia of Hermeticism and the kabbalistic symbolic attribution of numbers, in addition to having come from a strict Christian background, had always associated himself with the biblical 'Beast of Revelation' whose number was 666. The antiquity was a double-sided, painted wooden stele belonging to the Theban priest Ankhefenkhons I from the late Third Intermediate Period. He served Montu, the falcon-headed god of war and his stele dates from the overlapping 22nd, 23rd and 24th Dynasties, around 716 BC (see also Mosleth King's contribution, pp. 42–52).[36]

Crowley had the hieroglyphic texts of the stele translated into French by the assistant curator of the museum, Georges Émile Jules Daressy (1864–1938).[37] He then made poetic paraphrases of the texts in English, believing that they contained 'a certain secret ritual of the highest rank' that the original ancient Egyptian author had recorded especially for him.[38] Back at his Cairo apartment Crowley performed a one-hour ritual on three consecutive days during which he clairaudiently heard and transcribed a voice belonging to a being called Aiwass, who described himself as 'the minister of Hoor-paar-kraat.'[39] The three one-hour dictation instalments would become the basis for a text called *The Book of the Law*.[40] In the sixty-one pages of *The Book of the Law* all the Egyptian deities on the obverse of the stele—Nut, Behdet, and Re-Horakhty—'reveal' themselves and command particular types of action to be performed by the reader. More interested in viewing the gods through Hermetic symbolism than history, Crowley modified their names and characteristics and spent time trying to understand them via kabbalistic numerology rather than through Egyptology. He also recalled being Ankhefenkhons in a previous life. Crowley had 'sent' this stele to himself in a future life, back when he was an ancient Egyptian.[41]

Although by this time (1904) Crowley was able to resort to scientific Egyptology in order to discover what the hieroglyphs on Ankhefenkhons' stele actually said, he ignored the original intention of its author—that the priest Ankhefenkhons might successfully traverse the underworld and maintain life after death—, re-interpreting and appropriating the stele for his project of the inauguration of a 'New Aeon' with himself as its prophet. The hieroglyphic text on the stele had nothing to do with the contents of *The Book of the Law*: the only link was the museum catalogue number 666, which had piqued Crowley's interest in the object in the first place.

---

34 Crowley 2000, xl.

35 Crowley 2000, 412.

36 Kitchen 1973, 190–1 and 255, places him in the 25th Dynasty, *fl.* c.725 BC; Zayed 1968, 149–52, and Plate 7; Crowley 2000, 745. note 257; Wilkinson 2003, 203–4.

37 Crowley 1936, 114; Crowley 2001, 745, note 258.

38 Crowley 1974, 101 and 275; Crowley 2000, 412.

39 Crowley 1936, 118; Symonds/Grant 1969, 610; Wilkinson 2003, 132; Hornung 2001, 66; Regardie 1990, vol. 6, 17.

40 Symonds/Grant 1969, 395.

41 Crowley 1936, 126; Crowley 1974, 275.

Legitimation and power

MacGregor and Moina Mathers, Florence Farr and Aleister Crowley all utilised ancient Egypt as a source of legitimation and power within the competitive environment of the Hermetic Order of the Golden Dawn in order to distinguish their own spiritual prowess. The Matherses acquired spiritual authority, social credibility, students, media attention, notoriety and modest financial gain through their claims to be priests of Isis. Farr's apparent intimacy with ancient Egypt provided a prestige commensurate with her roles in the Golden Dawn and supplied precedents for female spiritual competence, even superiority. Crowley's accurate assessment of the spiritual clout possessed by ancient Egypt in the eyes of his peers meant that regardless of the actual function and meaning of Egyptian material culture, the simple fact of its Egyptian nature provided him with spiritual credibility and sanctioned his assumption of the role of prophet of the New Aeon. For these members of the Golden Dawn, Egypt was both a source and an endorsement of magical power, and one of the ways this could be obtained was through Egyptian antiquities in museums.

Bibliography

Assmann, J., 2007, Foreword, in Ebeling, F., 2007, *The Secret History of Hermes Trismegistus*, Ithaca, vi–xiii.

Bednarski, A., 2007, 'Deshasheh, Dendereh, and Balabish', in Spencer, P. (ed.), 2007, *The Egypt Exploration Society: The Early Years*, London, 232–254.

Burkert, W., 1987, *Ancient Mystery Cults*, Cambridge.

Churton, T., 2016, *Occult Paris: The Lost Magic of the Belle Époque*, Rochester.

Colquhoun, I., 1975, *The Sword of Wisdom: Macgregor Mathers and the Golden Dawn*, New York.

Crowley, A., 1974, *Magical and Philosophical Commentaries on The Book of the Law*, Montreal.

Crowley, A., 1991, *The Equinox of the Gods*, Scottsdale.

Crowley, A., 2000, *Magick Liber ABA: Book Four, Part IV*, Maine.

Curl, J., 2005, *The Egyptian Revival: Ancient Egypt as the Inspiration for Design Motifs in the West*, London.

Ebeling, F., 2007, *The Secret History of Hermes Trismegistus*, Ithaca.

Faulkner, R., 1985, *The Ancient Egyptian Book of the Dead*, New York.

Gaucher, A., 1900, 'Isis à Montmartre', in *L'Echo du merveilleux*, 446–9.

Gould, W., 1997, '"The Music of Heaven": Dorothea Hunter', in Toomey, D., 1997, *Yeats Annual No. 9: Yeats and Women*, Houndmills, 132–188.

Greer, M., 1995, *Women of the Golden Dawn: Rebels and Priestesses*, Rochester.

Hornung, E., 2001, *The Secret Lore of Egypt: Its Impact on the West*, Ithaca.

Howe, E., 1972, *The Magicians of the Golden Dawn*, London.

Kitchen, K., 1973, *The Third Intermediate Period in Egypt (1100–650 B.C.)*, Warminster.

Lees, F., 1900, 'Isis Worship in Paris: Conversations with the Hierophant Rameses and the High Priestess Anari', in *The Humanitarian* 16: 2, n.p.

Lefkowitz, M., 1997, *Not Out of Africa: How Afrocentrism Became an Excuse to Teach Myth as History*, New York.

McIntosh, C., 1972, *Eliphas Lévi and the French Occult Revival*, London.

Marley, R., 2017, *Farr from the Magical Crowd: On why the Brilliance of Florence Farr is as Timeless as it is Evocative*, published on https://medium.com/@missrhiannonmarley/farr-from-the-magical-crowd-on-why-the-brilliance-of-florence-farr-is-as-timeless-as-it-is-98452980d223 (accessed: 24/4/2022).

Regardie, I., 1990, *The Complete Golden Dawn System of Magic*, Scottsdale.
Riggs, C., 2003, 'The Egyptian Funerary Tradition at Thebes in the Roman Period', in Strudwick, N., Taylor, J. (eds.), 2003, *The Theban Necropolis: Past, Present and Future*, London, 189–99.
Riggs, C., 2005, *The Beautiful Burial in Roman Egypt: Art, Identity, and Funerary Religion*, Oxford.
Strudwick, N., 2006, *Masterpieces of Ancient Egypt*, London.
Symonds, J., Grant, K. (eds.), 1969, *The Confessions of Aleister Crowley*, London.
Taylor, J., Antoine, D., 2014, *Ancient Lives New Discoveries: Eight Mummies, Eight Stories*, London.
Toomey, D., (ed.), 1997. *Yeats Annual No. 9: Yeats and Women*, Houndmills.
Tully, C., 2020, 'Celtic Egyptians: Isis Priests of the Lineage of Scota', in Dobson, E., Tonks, N. (eds.), 2020, *Ancient Egypt in the Modern Imagination*, London, 145–60.
Tully, C., 2018, 'Egyptosophy in the British Museum: Florence Farr, the Egyptian Adept and the Ka', in Ferguson, C., Radford, A., *The Occult Imagination in Britain, 1875–1947*, London, 131–45.
Tully, C., 2010, 'Walk Like an Egyptian: Egypt as Authority in Aleister Crowley's Reception of *The Book of the Law*', in *Pomegranate: International Journal of Pagan Studies*, 12, 20–47.
Tully, C., 2009a, 'Samuel Liddell MacGregor Mathers and Isis', in Evans, D., Green, D. (eds.), *Ten Years of Triumph? Academic Approaches to Studying Magic and the Occult: Examining Scholarship into Witchcraft and Paganism Ten Years after Ronald Hutton's Triumph of the Moon*, Harpenden, 62–74.
Tully, C., 2009b, 'Florence and the Mummy', in Williams, B. (ed.), *Women's Voices in Magic*, Stafford, 15–23.
Wallis Budge, E., 1898, *A Guide to the First and Second Egyptian Rooms: Predynastic Antiquities, Mummies, Mummy-Cases, and Other Objects Connected with the Funeral Rites of the Ancient Egyptians*, London.
Webb, J., 1974, *The Occult Underground*, Illinois.
Wilkinson, R., 2003, *The Complete Gods and Goddesses of Ancient Egypt*, London.
Young, E., 1945, *Flowering Dusk: Things Remembered Accurately and Inaccurately*, New York.
Zayed, A., 1968, 'Painted Wooden Stelae in the Cairo Museum', in *Revue d'égyptologie* 20, 149–52.

About the author

Caroline Tully (PhD) is a lecturer in the School of Historical and Philosophical Studies at the University of Melbourne, Australia. She is an archaeologist who specialises in the Bronze Age Aegaean and eastern Mediterranean as well as in the reception of ancient religion and its use in the magical revival of the late nineteenth and early twentieth centuries. Tully's publications include: 'Celtic Egyptians: Isis Priests of the Lineage of Scota' in *Ancient Egypt in the Modern Imagination* (2020), 'Egyptosophy in the British Museum: Florence Farr, the Egyptian Adept and the Ka' in *The Occult Imagination in Britain 1875–1947* (2018), and 'Walk Like an Egyptian: Egypt as Authority in Aleister Crowley's Reception of The Book of the Law' in *Pomegranate* (2010).

Figure 1. Howard Carter and Lord Carnarvon at the opening of the door to the burial chamber of Tutankhamun's tomb on 16 February 1923. Image reproduced with permission of the Griffith Institute, University of Oxford (colourised by Dynamichrome).

'Someone Who Has Power and Who Understands'

Egyptology, Egyptosophy, and the 'Truth' about Ancient Egypt

Jasmine Day

Introduction[1]

The death of the fifth Earl of Carnarvon, financier of the excavation of Tutankhamun's tomb, on 5 April 1923 gave superstitious people all the proof they needed that Egyptian tombs were cursed. Some had already experienced forebodings from the moment they first heard about the discovery of a pharaoh's tomb. On 13 January 1923, perturbed by claims about storms plaguing the excavation, an Irish magician, Ella Young, telegraphed the archaeologist Howard Carter: 'If trouble continues reseal tomb / pour milk oil wine at / threshold'.[2] On 8 April, three days after the Earl's death, she warned him:

> I believe that Lord Carnarvon owes his death to the fact that the tomb of Tutankhamen was opened without any ceremonies calculated to placate any Ka or Kas that might be in the sepulchre. [...] Such entities have [...] power to influence the weather & to [have caused] the death of Lord Carnarvon [...] [G]reat dangers may result from the re-opening of the sealed tomb—and <u>it is possible to avert the dangers</u>. The Ka [...] can be placated by proper ceremonies [...][3]

1 I am grateful to William Joy of the Peggy Joy Egyptology Library and staff at the Griffith Institute, University of Oxford, for access to their collections.

2 Young 1923a.

3 Young 1923b.

in Van den Bercken, B. J. L. (ed.), *Alternative Egyptology: Critical Essays on the Relation between Academic and Alternative Interpretations of Ancient Egypt*, Leiden, pp. 28–41.

Reading press claims that Carter had been taken ill[4], Young wrote again on 13 April:

> If you have any reason to think your illness connected with an occult source, I would urge you to take instant steps to avert the anger of a Ka disturbed in the tomb [...] [T]he really important thing is to get the assistance of someone [...] who is able to communicate with a Ka. [...] The ordinary medium would be useless, it must be some one who has power & who understands: [ideally] a native of Egypt [...][5]

Young probably learned about funeral libations from Egyptology books, not occult sources. Yet she, not Carter, saw reason to revive the practice. What archaeologists deemed a scientific discovery, the magician regarded as a sacred site. Young's letters exemplify belief that science cannot fully access the truth, which requires occult knowledge of supernatural phenomena. Qualification to enter Egyptian tombs is attained not through academic study, but by initiation in sacred rites.

Egyptologists have long disputed esoteric interpretations of ancient Egypt, termed 'Egyptosophy'.[6] Their failure to supplant these unscientific paradigms is a consequence not only of their initial dismissal of them, but also of more recent insistence on engagement with them in incompatible scientific terms. 'Truth' is an object to be constructed via negotiation in today's pseudoscientific communities, in contrast to scientific understandings of it as fixed and evidence-based.[7] A century ago, Egyptology and Egyptosophy were often indistinguishable;[8] Egyptologists' current difficulties in discrediting pseudoscience are a consequence of their discipline's professionalisation during the interwar period, when it divorced Egyptosophy, losing the means to communicate with its followers in their own language. The legend of Tutankhamun's curse encapsulates the formation of this gulf between professional and popular visions of ancient Egypt.

The 'truth'

Victorians' knowledge of the Middle East was deemed authentic when gained through personal experience, whether by Orientalists immersing themselves in its cultures[9] or by occultists practising ancient Egyptian religion as 'revealed' to them by 'ancient spirits'. Non-academics in the 1920s devised their own, spiritual terms in which to understand ancient Egypt,[10] including belief that a curse on Tutankhamun's tomb would punish anyone who defiled it. Roger Luckhurst traces the origins of 'Tut's curse' to rumour-based Victorian curse mythology.[11] Magical explanations for incidents in the lives of Victorian collectors developed as these stories circulated between the press and the public. The formation of Egyptian curse lore coincided with British working-class struggles for improved conditions; unable to comprehend how elites acquired wealth, the poor explained it as

---

4 Luckhurst 2012, 11.
5 Young 1923c.
6 Hornung 2002, 3.
7 Flemming 2006.
8 An objection can therefore be made to distinguishing between the two, Magus 2017, 484. In the long term, however, they have become distinguishable, even though they did not originate as two distinct categories.
9 Said 1991, 187–8.
10 Frayling, 1992, 46.
11 Luckhurst 2012.

'luck' and delighted in millionaires' misfortunes, which were 'bad luck'—namely curses.[12] Since archaeology was an elite pastime then, Egyptologists were curses' prime targets.

Like rumour, contemporary pseudoarchaeology regards truth as negotiable. N. C. Flemming explains that pseudoscientific visions of past civilisations exchange arduous examination of evidence and tentative conclusions[13] for confident announcements of sensational findings[14], attacking scientific authority by portraying pseudoscience as the heroic underdog.[15] Pseudoscience weaponises language to undermine experts, eschewing a neutral tone for a dramatic one derived from fiction and religious or autobiographical genres.[16] This emotional engagement is a 'structure of persuasion'[17] that thwarts scientists, who do not speak in esoteric or emotive terms. Pseudoscientists seek public debates with scientists so that they can control the terms of debate;[18] Howard Carter's psychic correspondents demanded his response.

Flemming's observations provide insight into rumour-driven responses to Egyptology a century ago, notwithstanding that the occult paradigm of that period has been largely superseded today by one of aliens and misapplied scientific theory. Pseudoscience and rumour share an idea that truth can be created and adapted and is not fixed. Rumour theory and pseudoscience theory, not usually discussed in conjunction, can both be applied to curse lore. Barbara Suczek linked studies of pseudoscience and rumour by suggesting that (quasi-)religions can originate via rumour;[19] as Egyptianising occult ideas are a kind of religion, they evolve and manifest through rumour just as they also contain pseudoscientific ideas. What archaeologists have dismissed as pseudoscience or rumour could be nascent or unrecognised religious cults—which explains why they cannot be understood or dismantled by scientific reasoning.

Curses and magic: manufacturing truth

The first inklings of guilt about stripping mummies were expressed through nineteenth-century poetry, plays and fiction.[20] Female-authored American curse fiction of the 1860s punished male characters who despoiled female mummies with deadly contagions or with transformation of their fiancées into debilitated living 'mummies'.[21] This literature was mined by male late-Victorian authors, notably Arthur Conan Doyle in 'Lot N°. 249'.[22]

---

12 Ibid., 23 (after Thorstein Veblen). Frayling adds that the inaccessibility of Egyptological knowledge to most members of the public enhanced the appeal of occult explanations: they were more enjoyable and easier for non-academics to understand, Frayling 1992, 47.

13 Flemming 2006, 58.

14 Ibid., 60.

15 Ibid., 56.

16 Ibid., 54.

17 Ibid., 48.

18 Ibid., 52.

19 Suczek 1972.

20 Day 2013, 199-202, 211–4; Day 2020, 25–8, 34; Hawthorne 1993, 723–7.

21 Day 2006, 43–7; Day 2008.

22 Doyle 1892. The earliest known ambulatory mummy character—a mummy come back to life—featured in Jane Webb Loudon's novel *The Mummy! A Tale of the Twenty-second Century* (1827); it was followed by others in Edgar Allan Poe's short story *Some Words with a Mummy* (1845) and the anonymously authored short story *The Mummy's Soul* (1862), but these pieces never attained the fame of Doyle's work, which must derive directly or indirectly from them. As the most famous ambulatory mummy of late nineteenth-century literature, the creature in 'Lot N°. 249' probably inspired Hollywood's mummy monsters decades later.

Fiction buttressed rumours that mummies were cursed, especially a mummy board[23]—mistaken for a mummy proper—in the British Museum. Reconstructing the formation of this tale about the 'Unlucky Mummy' of a priestess, Roger Luckhurst notes its 1860s acquisition by Thomas Douglas Murray, 1889 donation to the British Museum, reportage of the curse by journalist and fiction writer Bertram Fletcher Robinson in 1904, Robinson's premature death in 1907 (attributed to the curse by the press), 1909 publication of the story in *Pearson's Magazine*,[24] and international syndication by journalist and spiritualist William T. Stead.[25] When Stead perished on the *Titanic* and was recalled by a survivor as having told a curse tale during the ship's final dinner, the priestess mummy was claimed to have been on board.[26] Further iterations declared that it was retrieved, only to sink the *Empress of Ireland* and the *Lusitania*,[27] and kill associates of its purchaser and people who photographed or mocked the mummy at the British Museum.[28]

Ernest Wallis Budge, Keeper of Egyptian Antiquities at the British Museum, retold the Unlucky Mummy tale to the novelist Henry Rider Haggard,[29] whose publication of the story along with Budge's refutation of it[30] only fed its growth (fig. 2). While blaming the spiritualists Murray and Stead for circulating curse rumours, Budge left out his friendship with Murray, including a visit in 1904[31] to Murray's associates at the Ghost Club[32]—a private dining group where wealthy men discussed their supernatural experiences[33] confidentially, to avoid censure since some were scientists.[34] Murray was chided for inviting Budge, who denied that a curse rested on the Unlucky Mummy or any other mummy.[35]

The professionalisation championed by Budge ultimately cost Egyptology its former communication with Egyptosophy, but during Budge's last years, rogue practitioners postponed a final delineation between what was, and was not, 'proper' Egyptology. After Howard Carter's resignation from Egypt's Antiquities Service in 1905[36] his colleague Arthur Weigall (fig. 3) took over his position. Later ejected under suspicion of antiquities theft reported by Carter,[37] Weigall returned to London during World War I, worked as a stage set designer and novelist, then moved into journalism. The *Daily Mail* dispatched him to Egypt to cover Tutankhamun but, frustrated by the press blockade caused by the

23 British Museum catalogue number EA22542.
24 St. Russell 1909.
25 Luckhurst 2012, 27–9.
26 Ibid., 40. Although the *Titanic*'s very brief cargo manifest does not mention any Egyptian antiquities, in the opinion of Dominic Montserrat (pers. comm.) it is highly probable that they were on board because some of the wealthy passengers had been wintering in Egypt and probably acquired items for donation to American museums. Thus, the possibility that there was at least one mummy on board the *Titanic* cannot be ruled out.
27 Ibid., 41.
28 Ibid., 32–33.
29 Ibid., 35.
30 Ibid., 26, 36–37.
31 Ibid., 53.
32 Ibid., 39.
33 Ibid., 46.
34 Ibid., 47.
35 Ibid., 53–54.
36 Carter, a British inspector in the French-administered Antiquities Service, ejected drunken French tourists from the Serapeum in Saqqara and was pressured by French government representatives to apologise; he resigned instead, Frayling 1992, xv.
37 Luckhurst 2012, 11.

Figure 2. 'Quiz' (Powys Evans), E. A. Wallis Budge caricature. Budge had become synonymous with the Unlucky Mummy by the time he gave press interviews about the Tutankhamun discovery. *The Saturday Review*, 24 February, 1923. Peggy Joy Egyptology Library.

Figure 3. Arthur Weigall. Studio portrait used by Weigall for publicity. 1923. Peggy Joy Egyptology Library.

Earl of Carnarvon's exclusive *Times* contract and the slow progress of excavation news, Weigall published claims that Carnarvon's death had been caused by a curse.[38]

This sensational story was elaborated upon by other journalists and convinced many readers—familiar by now with curse lore—that ancient magic was potent. Arguably, Weigall did not endorse the curse myth, but left readers to make their own judgement.[39] Mentioning a curse, however, raises the possibility of its existence;[40] pseudoscience is a 'structure of persuasion'[41] that exploits the emotive language of novels[42]—most especially in the hands of a novelist! The writer, if not a believer, is a cynic manipulating the public; Weigall said of his story, '[S]ee how the public will lap it up!'[43] He had previously published an account of his attempt in 1909 to stage a play in the Valley of the Queens, which was fraught with bad weather and aborted when several performers became ill.[44] Was this another manipulation of readers' credulity, or an indication that a creative writer—even if also an Egyptologist—may not be entirely devoted to scientific rationale and is inclined to wish, if not believe, that magic can happen?

The apparent existence of a curse discouraged a search for its inventor. Carter had no doubts about its authorship:[45]

> I have not [any kind] sentiments [about] Weigall. [...] [H]is death is a real blessing. For although he was a clever writer, he was cunning. His inventions had no basis and thus [were] a menace to Archaeology. Most of them for temporary excitement and amusement at the expense of others. The 'Tut Ankh Amen Curse' was his invention, invented out of pique—a sort of vengeance—towards his loyal friend Lord Carnarvon, who, because Weigall came out solely as correspondent of the Daily Mail, was obliged to treat him like the other newspaper correspondents. [...] But enough of this venom [...][46]

Carter's pique was hypocritical. He had collaborated with Percy White (fig. 4), a novelist and professor of English at Cairo University, to convert his diary into more evocative prose; White ghostwrote *The Tomb of Tutankhamun*.[47] Carter insisted that White preserve the facts—'Try and make [a] good a thing out of it [...], providing the meaning is not lost.

---

38 Sales/Mota 2020, 575; Tyldesley 2012, 226.

39 Fritze 2016, 236.

40 Luckhurst 2012, 13.

41 Flemming 2006, 48.

42 Ibid., 54.

43 Hankey 2007, 5.

44 Weigall 1912.

45 Rumours grow incrementally and via consensus. Weigall's invented curse was a development of Victorian curse lore, itself derived from Victorian fiction, the legend of the mummy's curse being circulated and developed continuously between authors of printed works (not all of which were deemed fiction in their era) and verbal rumourmongers (Day 2006, 19–63; Luckhurst 2012, 23).

46 Carter 1934. One of two letters Carter addressed to Miss Helen Euphrosyne Ionides (1871-1967), the sixth child of Constantine Ionides, a wealthy collector and philanthropist.

47 Carter/Mace 1923. This book and its subsequent two volumes did not constitute conventional excavation reports about Tutankhamun's tomb, which Carter never produced. It is probable that White rewrote Carter's imprecisely recorded remark upon first gazing into the tomb as 'Yes, wonderful things', Carter/Mace 1923, 96. According to Carnarvon, Carter said, 'There are some marvellous objects here', Carnarvon 1922, 13. Carter himself recalled saying, 'Yes, it is wonderful', Carter 1922–1923, 26 November.

Figure 4. Percy White and Howard Carter. Press photo taken aboard the *Berengaria* entering New York harbour at the beginning of an American Tutankhamun lecture tour by White (left) and Carter (right). April 19, 1924. Peggy Joy Egyptology Library.

Change the wording into nice flowing English'[48]—but conceded to some embroidery. 'I hope to expand the narrative', wrote White, '"embellish" some might call it'.[49] Carter and White collaborated on *The Tomb of the Bird: Death of the White Canary,*[50] an account of the incident in which Carter's canary was allegedly swallowed by a cobra. White's framing narrative insinuated a supernatural explanation,[51] while Carter played the sober scientist, objecting to superstitious nonsense.[52] This oscillation between scientific and fantastic perspectives[53] betrayed tension between them. Carter was no more commercially motivated than Weigall, and no less inclined to flights of fancy.[54] Eventually though, a tentatively supernatural tone gave way to a scientific, secular[55] one in Egyptology.

It was not so elsewhere. While Tutankhamun's curse originated in poor public-relations management by Carnarvon in his *Times* exclusive[56], the perpetual growth of this legend was a consequence of public interest, if not outright faith, in supernatural phenomena. Letters to Carter from self-proclaimed psychics and magicians demonstrate how faith in curses was proclaimed and knowledge about them obtained.

On 4 July 1923, Rosa Atkins of Nottingham, England reported to Carter a vision locating Tutankhamun's mummy:

> I saw a man coming down [...] by a rope with a big C on his back [...] I see a heap of money & jewels about the tombs [...] I have no fancy to court illness or death [...] & I can't afford to come & find wealth for the Egyptian government [...] [E]very care must be taken for your safety as there are [so] many pitfalls which you will meet.[57]

On 8 June 1924, Marie Coleman of Columbus, Ohio warned Carter:

---

48 Carter 1925.

49 White 1925.

50 Carter/White 1923.

51 Namely that the cobra embodies the spirit of a dead pharaoh, Tutankhamun, who takes symbolic revenge against those who have violated his tomb by attacking their mascot bird.

52 Dobson 2021.

53 An oscillation to which Weigall was also inclined, Luckhurst 2012, 12.

54 Novelists were often consulted in preference to Egyptologists as curse 'experts', Dobson 2021; Frayling 1992, 46. Therefore, it was tempting for archaeologists to toy with popular psychology. Frayling mentions a curse story Carter told to a tourist in the tomb of Amenhotep II in 1900, and lists instances in which Carter invented stories for the press about non-existent objects he claimed to have found in Tutankhamun's tomb and his 'discovery' of the tomb of Alexander the Great, Frayling 1992, 51–52.

55 Luckhurst views spiritualist beliefs, like those of the Ghost Club members, as a response to the growing challenge of scientific discoveries to Christian dogma by those who were reluctant to abandon religious concepts that they recognised as being increasingly untenable, Luckhurst 2012, 45. Concepts like curses appealed to them by offering some alternative form of religiosity, perhaps one that might be borne out by scientific proof of curses' and other psychic powers' existence.

56 Sales/Mota 2020, 576.

57 Atkins 1923.

> [I]f I had been able to get a message to your mate I could have saved his life. King Tut told me he was going to control this insect[58] and make it sting the Earl, and why. [...] [N]ow I've a warning for you [to] prevent your and other e[x]cavators' death [...] If you will give me one hundred dollars I will give you this message from [Tutankhamun]. Lord Carnarvon beseech you to get this [...] poem of 13 verses [...][59]

Young, Atkins and Coleman were anxious to protect Carter, eager to vicariously participate in his discovery yet determined to assert their own kind of authority over it. Unable to visit Egypt, they resorted to emphatic phrases and repeated attempts to contact Carter. Their concern may have arisen from frustration that they could not shoehorn themselves into the unfolding Tutankhamun narrative, the headline of the century. 'The pseudo loves the limelight'.[60]

The most concerted campaign to sway Carter was conducted by a European psychic, Margit Labouchere, through fifteen letters (*c.*1924–1928).[61]

> You won't find Tot-ench-Amon in his tomb. / He is not there.[62]
> Tot-ench-Aton[63] was much older, when he was murdered. / His son Tot died before him, 14 years old. / Your poor mummy was never the king.[64]

Labouchere hinted at some psychically ascertained alternative history of Tutankhamun's family. Carter stood accused of feigning ignorance of this history,[65] a strategy to draw him into a debate in which Labouchere determined the terms of discourse to control events from afar.

Carter's correspondents gave inconsistent accounts of the supernatural powers of Tutankhamun's tomb; Labouchere even denied the existence of a curse.[66] Yet all agreed that the resident spirits could be contacted to determine the correct course of action. Like later pseudoscientists, occultists attempted to draw an archaeologist away from scientific terms of debate into supernatural ones[67] of which Carter would, they presumed, be ignorant. They were wrong but, inundated with mail—and perhaps apprehensive about further forays into supernaturalism after receiving so many 'crank' letters—Carter never replied to his psychic correspondents.

58 The Earl of Carnarvon died from blood poisoning after cutting a mosquito bite on his cheek while shaving, Frayling 1992, 38; Luckhurst 2012, 8.

59 Coleman 1924.

60 Flemming 2006, 49.

61 Labouchere's letters, which were among Howard Carter's effects auctioned at Bonhams in 2012, are now held by the Peggy Joy Egyptology Library. Given the repetitiveness of Labouchere's remarks throughout her correspondence, it makes no difference to my interpretation of her statements if the placement of several undated letters within the chronological sequence errs.

62 Labouchere 1925a, MSS4.

63 Labouchere refers to Tutankhamun alternately by his Amarna (Aton) and post-Amarna (Amun) names as if she has some knowledge of 18th-Dynasty history, but this is mere name-dropping to buttress her authority, as the names are traded randomly through the series of letters.

64 Labouchere 1926, MSS10.

65 'Listen to your inward voice.' Labouchere 1925b, MSS5. 'The mummy is not Tot ench Aton, and you know it too.' Labouchere 1927, MSS14.

66 'It is not the vengeance of Tot-ench-Amon!' Labouchere *c.*1924, MSS1. 'There is no danger for you!' Labouchere *c.*1925, MSS6.

67 Flemming 2006, 52.

Conclusion

While curse lore critiqued imperialism,[68] its portrayal of archaeologists as fools oblivious to ethereal powers suggests that esoteric interpretations of ancient Egypt also sought to invest it with spiritual meaning to counter secular interpretations that seemed dry and distant. Thus, the conflict between Egyptology and Egyptosophy rests not upon truth per se, but upon construction of the *meaning* of ancient Egypt, which the former reads from material evidence while the latter creates and negotiates to make it contemporary, immediate and personal. The popular consensus is that ancient Egypt must be known not simply for its own sake, but for ours; it should be engaged to serve our needs. This is a lesson that Egyptology must incorporate.

Egyptologists could adopt ethnography to study adherents of pseudoscience and rumour. Ethnographers represent, rather than reject, their subjects' worldviews. Many Orientalist studies reflected contempt for their subjects;[69] Egyptologists have only perpetuated Orientalism by condemning rather than comprehending pseudoscientists and occultists. A conversation between Egyptologists and Egyptosophists is needed for the latter to gain appreciation of the knowledge produced by Egyptologists and for Egyptologists to understand the cultural applications of their work. A battle to attain control of discourse must yield to mutual recognition of the validity, or at least the motivations, of each perspective.

Bibliography

Anonymous, 1862, 'The Mummy's Soul', in *The Knickerbocker; or New York Monthly Magazine*, 59 (5), 435–46.

Atkins, R., 1923, Letter to Howard Carter, 4 July, Peggy Joy Egyptology Library.

Carnarvon, C., 1922, 'The Egyptian Treasure. Story of the Discovery. A Graphic Account by Lord Carnarvon', in *The Times*, 11 December, 13.

Carter, H., 1922–1923, *Notes, Diary, and Articles, Referring to the Theban Royal Necropolis and the Tomb of Tutankhamen* (Season I), Griffith Institute, (accessed via http://www.griffith.ox.ac.uk/discoveringTut/journals-and-diaries/season-1/journal.html on 20 April 2022).

Carter, H., 1925, Letter to Percy White, 7 December, Peggy Joy Egyptology Library.

Carter, H., 1934, Letter to Helen Euphrosyne Ionides, 21 January, sighted on collector's market, 2021 (image supplied by William Joy, Peggy Joy Egyptology Library).

Carter, H., Mace, A., 1923, *The Tomb of Tut-Ankh-Amen, Discovered by the Late Earl of Carnarvon and Howard Carter*, vol. 1, London, New York, Toronto & Melbourne.

Carter, H., White, P., 1923, 'The Tomb of the Bird: Death of the White Canary', in *Pearson's Magazine*, Volume 56, 335 (November), 433–37.

Coleman, M., 1924, Letter to Howard Carter, 8 June, Peggy Joy Egyptology Library.

Day, J., 2006, *The Mummy's Curse: Mummymania in the English-speaking World*, London & New York.

---

68 I have noted that the mummy's-curse legend condemned patriarchy, Day 2006, 171, 178. Roger Luckhurst explores its use to attack upper-class privilege in Britain, Luckhurst 2012. Scott Trafton observes its condemnation of racism in the United States, Trafton 2004. We agree that these various rebukes denounced their common imperial cause and context; colonial conquest creates and works through intersecting inequalities of gender, class and race.

69 Said 1991, 209.

Day, J., 2008, 'The Rape of the Mummy: Women, Horror Fiction and the Westernisation of the Curse', in Peña, P., Martin, C. and Rodriguez, A. (eds.), 2008, *Mummies and Science – World Mummies Research: Proceedings of the VI World Congress on Mummy Studies*, Santa Cruz de Tenerife, Academia Canaria de la Historia, 617–21.

Day, J., 2013, 'The Maid and the Mummy', in Dann, R., Exell, K. (eds.), *Egypt: Ancient Histories, Modern Archaeologies*, New York, 193–232.

Day, J., 2020, 'Allamistakeo Awakes: the Earliest Image of an Ambulatory Mummy', in Dobson, E. (ed.), *Victorian Literary Culture and Ancient Egypt*, Manchester, 20–42.

Dobson, E., 2021, *'Whatever Happened to Carter's Canary?': Facts, Fictions and the Tutankhamun Excavations*, Egyptology Scotland (Zoom lecture), 20 March.

Doyle, A., 1892, 'Lot N°. 249', in *Harper's Monthly Magazine*, 24, 525–44.

Flemming, N. C., 2006, 'The Attraction of Non-Rational Archaeological Hypotheses: The Individual and Sociological Factors', in Fagan, G. G. (ed.), *Archaeological Fantasies: How Pseudoarchaeology Misrepresents the Past and Misleads the Public*, Abingdon & New York, 47–61.

Frayling, C., 1992, *The Face of Tutankhamun*, London & Boston.

Fritze, R. H., 2016, *Egyptomania: A History of Fascination, Obsession and Fantasy*, Chicago.

Hankey, J., 2007, *A Passion for Egypt: Arthur Weigall, Tutankhamun and the 'Curse of the Pharaohs'*, London, New York.

Hawthorne, M., 1993, 'Dis-Covering the Female: Gautier's Roman de la Momie', in *The French Review*, (66) 5, 718–29.

Hornung, E., 2002, *The Secret Lore of Ancient Egypt: Its Impact on the West* (trans. David Lorton), Ithaca & London.

Labouchere, M., *c.*1924, Letter to Howard Carter, n.d., Peggy Joy Egyptology Library (MSS1).

Labouchere, M., 1925a, Letter to Howard Carter, 6 January, Peggy Joy Egyptology Library (MSS4).

Labouchere, M., 1925b, Letter to Howard Carter, 21 January, Peggy Joy Egyptology Library (MSS5).

Labouchere, M., *c.*1925, Letter to Howard Carter, n.d., Peggy Joy Egyptology Library (MSS6).

Labouchere, M., 1926, Letter to Howard Carter, 12 March, Peggy Joy Egyptology Library (MSS10).

Labouchere, M., 1927, Letter to Howard Carter, 13 April, Peggy Joy Egyptology Library (MSS14).

Loudon, J., 1827, *The Mummy! A Tale of the Twenty-second Century*, London.

Luckhurst, R., 2012, *The Mummy's Curse: The True History of a Dark Fantasy*, Oxford.

Magus, S., 2017, 'A Victorian Gentleman in the Pharaoh's Court: Christian Egyptosophy and Victorian Egyptology in the Romances of H. Rider Haggard', in *Open Cultural Studies*, 1, 483–92.

Poe, E. A., 1845, 'Some Words with a Mummy', in *The American Review: A Whig Journal of Politics, Literature, Art and Science*, 1, 63–70.

Said, E., 1991, *Orientalism: Western Conceptions of the Orient*, London.

Sales, J., Mota, S., 2020, 'Tutankhamun in Portugal: Reports in the Portuguese Press (1922–1939)', in *Aegyptiaca: Journal of the History of Reception of Ancient Egypt*, 5, 565–609.

St. Russell, G., 1909, 'The Mysterious Mummy', in *Pearson's Magazine*, vol. 28, 164 (August), 162–72.

Suczek, B., 1972, 'The Curious Case of the "Death" of Paul McCartney', in *Urban Life and Culture*, 1, 61–76.; reprinted in Reeve., A. J., 2004, *Turn Me On, Dead Man: the Beatles and the 'Paul-Is-Dead' Hoax*, Bloomington, 271–81.

Trafton, S., 2004, *Egypt Land: Race and Nineteenth-Century American Egyptomania* (New Americanists), Durham, NC & London.

Tyldesley, J., 2012, *Tutankhamen's Curse: The Developing History of an Egyptian King*, London.

Weigall, A., 1912, 'The Ghosts of the Valley of the Tombs of the Queens', in *Pall Mall Magazine* (June), 766.

White, P., 1925, Letter to Howard Carter, 11 December, Peggy Joy Egyptology Library.

Young, E., 1923a, Telegram to Howard Carter, 13 January, Griffith Institute (TAA.ii.3).

Young, E., 1923b, Letter to Howard Carter, 8 April, Griffith Institute (TAA.ii.3.23).

Young, E., 1923c, Letter to Howard Carter, 13 April, Griffith Institute (TAA.ii.3.24).

About the author

Dr Jasmine Day, author of *The Mummy's Curse: Mummymania in the English-speaking World* (Routledge 2006), is an anthropologist and Egyptologist specialising in mummymania, the 'mummy's curse', and ethics of mummy displays. She has published papers in *Egypt: Ancient Histories, Modern Archaeologies* (2013), *Histories of Egyptology: Interdisciplinary Measures* (2014), *Victorian Literary Culture and Ancient Egypt* (2020), and academic and popular Egyptology journals. She has contributed to the International Congress on Mummy Studies, *Tea with the Sphinx* and documentaries including *Egypt's Unexplained Files* (2019). Day is president of the Ancient Egypt Society of Western Australia Inc.

Figure 1. Aleister Crowley in England, *c.*1912, with a replica of the Stele of Revealing and other occult attributes. Image Underwood Archives/UIG/Bridgeman Images, UIG1582176.

Aleister Crowley's Egypt: The Stele of Revealing

Maiken Mosleth King

Introduction

In 1904 Aleister Crowley travelled to Egypt with his first wife, Rose Edith Kelly.[1] During their stay in Cairo they encountered the 26th-Dynasty funerary stele of the priest Ankhefenkhonsu (see also Tully's contribution in this volume) in the Boulaq Museum, which Crowley termed 'the Stele of Revealing' (fig. 2a and 2b)[2]. It became a central object in Crowley's religious movement of Thelema.[3] He had previously been initiated into the Hermetic Order of the Golden Dawn in 1898, and under the guidance of his mentor Charles Henry Allan Bennett had learned how to perform magical rituals and use ceremonial drugs.[4] Crowley's involvement with the Order was short-lived, however, as his bisexuality and feuds with other prominent members caused tension in the group.[5] He was evicted from the Order in 1900 after unsuccessfully attempting a coup in London, wearing Highland dress and an Osiris mask.[6]

In this paper I explore how he used the stele and drew on the discipline of Egyptology, contemporary Egyptomania and Orientalism to legitimise his personal religious practices.[7] As I demonstrate in this paper, Crowley operated in a framework that was both Orientalist and Hermetic, conceptualising Egypt as a mystical cradle of 'Eastern' wisdom whilst largely overlooking academic research; he also drew on contemporary spiritualism and Judaeo-Christian traditions in order to render his ideas more recognisable to his intended

1 Churton 2011, 94.
2 Sutin 2000, 120–22.
3 Treating decontextualised ancient objects as significant in themselves is also a driving force in pseudo-archaeology, frequently fuelled by racist agendas and anti-indigenous biases; Moshenska 2017, 126; Andersson 2012, 132–33.
4 Booth 2000, 98–103.
5 Kaczynski 2010, 64–67.
6 Booth 2000, 118–23; Kaczynski 2010, 75–80.
7 Crowley was also an influential figure in the development of the religious movement of Wicca; Hutton 2012, 285–306.

in Van den Bercken, B. J. L. (ed.), *Alternative Egyptology: Critical Essays on the Relation between Academic and Alternative Interpretations of Ancient Egypt*, Leiden, pp. 42–53.

a.

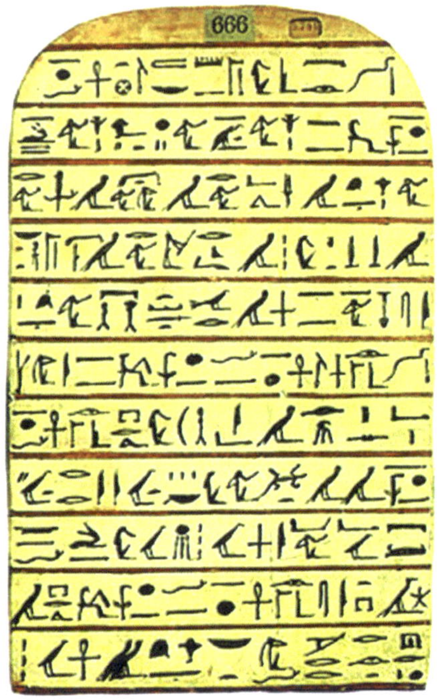

b.

Figure 2a and b. Stele of Ankhefenkhonsu in the Cairo Museum. The object had the accession number 666 in the Bulaq Museum. Image in the public domain, via Wikimedia Commons.

audience; finally, by crafting an 'Egyptian' persona, Crowley actively participated in a discourse on gender and sexuality, challenging contemporary mores and ideals.

The stele of Ankhefenkhonsu

Crowley viewed the stele's museum accession number, 666, as a portent and personal message due to its association with the Antichrist of Christian eschatology, with whom Crowley identified.[8] Following his encounter with the stele, Crowley began his composition of *Liber AL Vel Legis: The Book of the Law*, which he presented as a divine revelation from the Egyptian deities Nut and Horus.[9] This text became the central 'scripture' in Thelema, the religion Crowley founded following his alleged revelation in Cairo. He describes his encounter with the stele as follows:

> Fra. P.[10] advanced to the case. There was the image of Horus in the form of Ra Hoor Khuit painted upon a wooden stele of the 26th dynasty – and the exhibit bore the number 666! (666 had been taken by Fra. P. as the number of His own Name (The Beast) long years before, in His childhood.[11]

---

8 'This calls for wisdom. Let the person who has insight calculate the number of the beast, for it is the number of a man. That number is 666'; Rev. 13: 18; NIV.

9 Originally published privately in 1909 through A.∴A.∴, the Thelemic order Crowley had founded in 1907. Numerous editions have been published in the century since.

10 Frater Perdurabo; referring to himself in the third person is characteristic of Crowley's writings. He assumed this alias upon initiation into the Golden Dawn; Kaczynski 2010, 60–61.

11 Crowley 1936, ch. 6.

Having obtained a French translation from the assistant of curator Émile Brugsch[12], Crowley created his own 'paraphrased' English adaption of the text:

Above, the gemmèd azure is
The naked splendour of Nuit;
She bends in ecstasy to kiss
The secret ardours of Hadit.
The wingèd globe, the starry blue
Are mine, o Ankh-f-n-Khonsu.

I am the Lord of Thebes, and I
The inspired forth-speaker of Mentu;
For me unveils the veiled sky,
The self-slain Ankh-f-n-Khonsu
Whose words are truth. I invoke, I greet
Thy presence, o Ra-Hoor-Khuit!

Unity uttermost showed!
I adore the might of Thy breath,
Supreme and terrible God,
Who makest the gods and death
To tremble before Thee: —
I, I adore Thee!

Appear on the throne of Ra!
Open the ways of the Khu!
Lighten the ways of the Ka!
The ways of the Khabs run through
To stir me or still me!
Aum! let it kill me!

The Light is mine; its rays consume
Me: I have made a secret door
Into the House of Ra and Tum,
Of Khephra, and of Ahathoor.
I am thy Theban, o Mentu,
The prophet Ankh-f-n-Khonsu!

By Bes-na-Maut my breast I beat:
By wise Ta-nech I weave my spell.
Show thy star-splendour, O Nuit!
Bid me within thine House to dwell,
O winged snake of light, Hadit!
Abide with me, Ra-Hoor-Khuit!

---

12 Crowley 1936, ch. 7.

Saith of Mentu the truth-telling brother
Who was master of Thebes from his birth:
O heart of me, heart of my mother!
O heart which I had upon earth!
Stand not thou up against me as a witness!
Oppose me not, judge, in my quest!
Accuse me not now of unfitness
Before the Great God, the dread Lord of the West!
For I fastened the one to the other
With a spell for their mystical girth,
The earth and the wonderful West,
When I flourished, o earth, on thy breast!
The dead man Ankh-f-n-Khonsu
Saith with his voice of truth and calm:
O thou that hast a single arm!
O thou that glitterest in the moon!

I weave thee in the spinning charm;
I lure thee with the billowy tune.
The dead man Ankh-f-n-Khonsu
Hath parted from the darkling crowds,
Hath joined the dwellers of the light,
Opening Duant, the star-abodes,
Their keys receiving.
The dead man Ankh-f-n-Khonsu
Hath made his passage into night,
His pleasure on the earth to do
Among the living.[13]

This version, which places much emphasis on rhyming due to Crowley's love of poetry, can be contrasted with a direct translation by the author:

> Spoken words by the Osiris, the priest of Montu Lord of Thebes, the Opener of the Doors of Heaven in Karnak, Ankhefenkhonsu, the justified: O exalted one! May he be praised; the one whose powers are great! The Great Ba whom the gods fear has appeared upon his Great Throne. Create the ways for the Ba, for the Akh, and for the Shadow. I am equipped so that I might shine there as an equipped one. Create for me the way to the place in which Ra-Atum-Khepri and Hathor are. The Osiris, the priest of Montu Lord of Thebes, Ankhefenkhonsu, son of the equally (titled) Basenmut, born of the Chantress of Amun-Ra, the Lady of the House, Ta-Neshet.
>
> Spoken words by the Osiris, the priest of Montu Lord of Thebes, Ankhefenkhonsu, the justified: My heart of my mother, my heart of my mother, my heart of my existence on earth—do not stand up against me as my witness, do not oppose me in

13 Crowley 1936, The Comment.

the Tribunal, do not act against me in the presence of the Great God, the Lord of the West. I have united the great Western land and the sky which are in Heaven, so that I may flourish upon earth.

Spoken words by the Osiris, the Stolist of Thebes, Ankhefenkhonsu, the justified: O sole one who shines in the moon, may the Osiris Ankhefenkhonsu go forth amongst this multitude of yours through the Two Gates of Heaven; releaser of those who are in the sunshine, open the Duat for him when the Osiris Ankhefenkhonsu goes forth by day in order to do everything he desires upon the earth amongst the living.

The text of the stele includes Spells 2, 30B and 91 of the Book of the Dead; this seemingly went unnoticed by Crowley.[14] His adaptation of the text suggests that his engagement with Egyptological scholarship was minimal, and that his understanding of the ancient Egyptian language and religion was rudimentary. Instead, he drew on the Hermetic Order of the Golden Dawn's writings on ancient Egypt; these centre on the notion of Egypt as the cradle of wisdom and source of Hermetic authority, with academic scholarship playing a more peripheral role.[15] This view of Egypt has been termed 'Egyptosophy', distinct from the scientific Egyptology that emerged in the nineteenth century.[16] Caroline Tully has previously demonstrated that the library of Golden Dawn founder William Wynn Westcott included Egyptologist Henry Salt's linguistic book Essay on Dr. Young's and M. Champollion's Phonetic System of Hieroglyphics (1823), and that the writings of the founding members also drew on Samuel Birch's 1867 translation of the Book of the Dead; they also frequented the Egyptological collections in the British Museum.[17]

In Crowley's translation of Ankhefenkhonsu' stele, he inserts the term *Khabs*, likely taken from the Golden Dawn mantra *Khabs Am Pekht*, where the original text says 𓋺𓏤 *šwt*, 'shadow'. *Khabs Am Pekht* was understood by Samuel Liddell MacGregor Mathers to mean 'Light in extension'.[18] Crowley explains his understanding of *Khabs* as follows: 'Khabs is the secret Light or L.V.X.; the Khu is the magical entity of a man. I find later (Sun in Virgo, An VII) that Khabs means star.'[19]

Crowley's translation is semantically distinct from the original text; this allows him to use the text as a vehicle for his own religious ideas and philosophy without being constrained by the ancient Egyptian religious framework.[20]

---

14 E. A. Wallis Budge's *Book of the Dead* was published in 1895, but Crowley's version bears few traces of influence by this famous work.

15 Tully 2010, 20–47. Crowley's spelling of Hathor's name as Ahathoor is a convention of the Golden Dawn, whose Paris affiliate was called the Ahathoor Temple, founded by Samuel Liddell MacGregor Mathers in 1893; King 1989, 43.

16 Hornung 2001, 1.

17 Tully 2010, 26–8.

18 Brodie-Innes/Mathers 1983, 50. 'Khabs' is likely the word *ḫꜣbs*, 'lamp', from which the meaning 'light' is produced in a somewhat contrived manner; Lesko 2002, 348. The title of Crowley's publication *Konx Om Pax* (1907) is a variant of the phrase.

19 Crowley 1909, § 1.8, The Old Comment. The meaning 'star' is likely derived from the phonetically similar word *ḫꜣbꜣs*, 'starry sky'; Faulkner 1962, 184.

20 It is also possible that Crowley confused the term *Khabs* with *khaibt*, an erroneous reading of 𓋺𓏤 *šwt* employed by early Egyptologists such as E. A. Wallis Budge; in Florence Farr's Golden Dawn treatise *Egyptian Magic* (1896) the term *khaibt* is understood to mean 'aura'.

Thelema and *The Book of the Law*

The name Thelema comes from the Greek word θέλημα ('will'), and the central doctrine is summarised in the following statement: 'Do what thou wilt shall be the whole of the Law.'[21] Whilst Crowley presented this as an 'Egyptian' revelation, the concept itself was taken from François Rabelais' 1532 novel *Gargantua et Pantagruel*; in this fictional narrative, the so-called Abbey of Thélème had a single rule: 'Do what you will'.[22] Crowley understood 'will' to be separate from ego and desire[23], and taught that an individual's True Will is a type of destiny that can only be discovered through spiritual work and magical rituals.[24] He conceptualised the annihilation of the ego as 'the crossing of the Abyss', alluding heavily to the Buddhist doctrine of Nirvana.[25] In Thelema, the guardian of the Abyss is the female deity Babalon,[26] based on the female eschatological figure Babylon from the New Testament;[27] in the Thelemic framework she is elevated to sacred status.[28]

The revelation described in *The Book of the Law* is presented as coming from the Egyptian goddess Nut, conceptualised as the female element in a divine triad with Ra-Harakhty ('Ra-Hoor-Khuit') and 'Hadit'; the latter is based on the French translation's erroneous reading of Horus' epithet Behdety as Houdit.[29] This conceptual triad is based on the iconography on Ankhefenkhonsu's stele, which depicts a seated Ra-Harakhty, the winged sun-disk Horus Behdety and an arching Nut; in the Egyptian religious framework, however, Harakhty and Behdety are merely different aspects of Horus rather than two distinct deities.[30]

Despite the polytheistic nature of Thelema, Crowley operates with a religious framework largely drawn from the Judaeo-Christian tradition: he functions like a prophet similar to Biblical figures such as Moses, Isaiah and Ezekiel; he also places himself firmly in the Judaeo-Christian tradition through his self-identification with the Beast of the Book of Revelation.[31] The biblical framework serves to render Crowley's ideas more recognisable to his contemporaries, removing some of the 'Eastern otherness' of Orientalist fantasy.[32]

---

21 Crowley 1909, § 1.40.

22 Wilson 2005, 73. Crowley established his own 'Abbey of Thelema' on the island of Sicily in 1920, but was evicted by Mussolini's government in 1923; Churton 2011, 263–64.

23 'From these considerations it should be clear that "Do what thou wilt" does not mean "Do what you like." It is the apotheosis of Freedom; but it is also the strictest possible bond'; Crowley 1916, 2.

24 'The obvious practical task of the magician is then to discover what his will really is, so that he may do it in this manner, and he can best accomplish this by the practices of Liber Thisarb or such others as may from one time to another be appointed'; Crowley 1916, 3.

25 Djurdjevic 2019, 222–23. 'The conception is, therefore, of an eternal motion, infinite and unalterable. It is Nirvana, only dynamic instead of static – and this comes to the same thing in the end'; Crowley 1916, 3.

26 'And for this is BABALON under the power of the Magician, that she hath submitted herself unto the work; and she guardeth the Abyss'; Crowley 1911: Cry of the 3rd Aethyr.

27 'Babylon the Great, the Mother of Prostitutes and of the Abominations of the Earth'; Rev. 17:4–6, NIV.

28 'Glory unto the Scarlet Woman, BABALON, the Mother of Abomination, that rideth upon the Beast, for She hath spilt their blood in every corner of the earth, and lo! She hath mingled it in the cup of Her whoredom'; Crowley 1911, Cry of the 12th Aethyr.

29 Churton 2012, 183.

30 Shonkwiler 2014, 63–70.

31 Crowley published several essays and monographs under the alias Master Therion, using the Greek word Θηρίον ('beast').

32 On Orientalism, see Said 1978, 57–59.

Crowley and Orientalism

Ankhefenkhonsu is presented in the text as a spiritual messenger acting on behalf of the Egyptian gods, and the text also implies that Crowley is the reincarnated Ankhefenkhonsu:

> Now ye shall know that the chosen priest & apostle of infinite space is the prince-priest the Beast; and in his woman called the Scarlet Woman is all power given. They shall gather my children into their fold: they shall bring the glory of the stars into the hearts of men.[33]

> My scribe Ankh-af-na-khonsu, the priest of the princes, shall not in one letter change this book; but lest there be folly, he shall comment thereupon by the wisdom of Ra-Hoor-Khuit.[34]

By identifying himself with Ankhefenkhonsu, Crowley in effect creates an 'Egyptian' persona for the purpose of legitimising his ideas; several extant photographs of Crowley also depict him wearing both 'ancient Egyptian' costume, derived from cinematic tropes, and contemporary Egyptian dress (see fig. 4 in Tully's contribution, p. 22).[35] Despite his Egyptian persona, Crowley's knowledge of the ancient Egyptian language was minimal.[36] In his writings Egyptian words and phrases are used sparingly, primarily serving as a vehicle for deliberately enigmatic utterances, thereby reinforcing its status as a mystical and mysterious language.[37]

Crowley also adopted another 'Eastern' persona, this time Persian, for his homoerotic poetry volume *Bagh-i-Muattar: The Scented Garden of Abdullah the Satirist of Shiraz*, published in 1910.[38] He was openly bisexual and non-monogamous in an era when non-normative sexualities were stigmatised,[39] and the adoption of 'Oriental' personae constituted part of Crowley's discourse on sex and sexuality. It is likely that he drew on Orientalist ideas of a sexually permissive and erotic East, inhabited by seductive odalisques and effeminate men,[40] in his attempt to challenge contemporary sexual norms.[41]

The word Aum (alternatively spelled Om) is employed in Crowley's version of Ankhefenkhonsu's stele; this is a sacred syllable in Asian religious traditions, uttered before and during prayers and the recitation of sacred texts.[42] In the Hindu tradition

---

33 Crowley 1909, § 1.15.

34 Crowley 1909, § 1.36.

35 The *nemes*-headdress worn by Crowley in some photographs was a royal emblem in ancient Egypt, but served as a visual trope signifying 'ancient Egypt' in the silent films of Crowley's time; Lant 2015, 53–54. Crowley also had himself depicted wearing the leopard-skin dress of an ancient Egyptian *sem* priest during his time in the Golden Dawn; extant images of Samuel Liddell Macgregor Mathers also depict him in such Egyptianising dress (see p. 24).

36 By contrast, Crowley claimed to have acquired Greek and Latin with 'great facility' in his youth; Crowley 1936, ch. 1.

37 'The Khabs is in the Khu, not the Khu in the Khabs. Worship then the Khabs, and behold my light shed over you'; Crowley 1909, § 1.8–9.

38 Prof Ronald Hutton: personal communication.

39 Homosexuality was decriminalised in England with the passing of the Sexual Offences Act 1967, twenty years after Crowley's death.

40 Loshitzky 2000, 53–55; McLeod 2000, 45–46; Said 1978, 166–67.

41 'Sex magick' formed an important part of Crowley's writings and religious rituals, through which he circumvented contemporary taboos on extramarital sex, masturbation and homosexuality; Urban 2006, 11.

42 Moebus/Wilke 2011, 435–56.

Figure 3. Aleister Crowley in England, *c.*1925. Image Underwood Archives/UIG/Bridgeman Images, UIG1582177.

the syllable is conceptualised as the primordial sound of the universe[43]; the Buddhist mantra *Om Mani Padme Hum* ('Jewel in the Lotus Flower') invokes the compassionate Boddhisattva Avalokiteshvara,[44] and is believed to contain the *mahavidya* ('Great Wisdom') required to achieve Nirvana.[45] Crowley's writings represent an eclectic mix of distinct religious traditions; to a certain extent he conflated the ancient Egyptian religion with Asian traditions, essentially creating a monolithic 'Eastern' religious framework.

The spiritual entity Aiwass is stated to be the messenger of Crowley's revelation, functioning as an intermediary between him and the Egyptian gods.[46] He is presented as simultaneously Egyptian, Persian, Assyrian and Sumerian,[47] thus acting as a stereotypical 'Oriental wise man' from an imagined monolithic and timeless Middle East (fig. 3).[48] It was Crowley's first wife who named the entity, and he speculated that she based the name on *aywa*, the Egyptian Arabic word for 'yes'.[49] Aiwass is presented as both audible

---

43 Beck 1993, 42–48.

44 Lopez 1998, 331.

45 Studholme 2002, 68 and 108. Crowley included the mantra in his essay *Berashith: An Essay in Ontology* (1903), in which he discussed the concept of Nirvana.

46 'On April 8, 9 and 10, 1904, e.v. this book was dictated to 666 (Aleister Crowley) by Aiwass, a Being whose nature he does not fully understand, but who described Himself as "the Minister of Hoor-Paar-Kraat" (the Lord of Silence)'; Crowley 1936, The Summons.

47 Crowley 1936, ch. 7.

48 This trope, exemplified through the Egyptian priest, can be traced back to Roman literature; Frankfurter 1998, 233–37.

49 Crowley 1936, ch. 7.

and physically visible, thus being 'spirit made flesh'. The notion of manifesting spirits in the flesh was a popular idea in Victorian and Edwardian spiritualism, with many mediums claiming the ability to do this.[50] As such, it is likely that Crowley was inspired by contemporary spiritual practices, whilst also drawing on the Orientalist notion of a mysterious and timeless 'East' filled with arcane wisdom. The stele of Ankhefenkhonsu functions within the Thelemic framework as an embodiment of this idea; as such, the historical and cultural context of the stele is seen as irrelevant, and Egyptological research unimportant.

Conclusion

The examination of the 'Stele of Revealing' demonstrates that Egypt is presented in Crowley's writings as 'Eastern', timeless and mystical, conflated with various Asian religious traditions. Presenting different Middle Eastern and Asian religions and cultures as a monolithic unity despite great geographical and temporal distances is an Orientalist trope that serves to emphasise the otherness of 'the Orient'. In Crowley's conceptual framework, the otherness of ancient Egypt serves to imbue it with mystical qualities; at the same time, there is a perceived need to reduce some of the otherness by drawing on Judaeo-Christian traditions.

For Crowley's purposes, academic Egyptological research was peripheral and largely irrelevant; instead, the contemporary writings of the Hermetic Order of the Golden Dawn were more instrumental in shaping his views on ancient Egypt. In this framework, the stele of Ankhefenkhonsu functioned as a visual and conceptual representation of the 'essence' of ancient Egypt. Drawing on Hermetic ideas of Egypt as the source of arcane wisdom, Crowley adopted an Egyptian persona in order to legitimise his religious ideas and practices; this was done through his self-identification with Ankhefenkhonsu, by claiming contact with Egyptian deities, and by dressing in Egyptianising costume for photographs. This persona also served as a subversive tactic intended to challenge contemporary ideas regarding gender and sexuality. For Crowley, Egypt simultaneously represented mystical knowledge and personal freedom.

Bibliography

Andersson, P., 2012, 'Alternative Archaeology: Many Pasts in Our Present', in *Numen* 59 (2/3), 125–37.

Beck, G. L., 1993, *Sonic Theology: Hinduism and Sacred Sound*, Columbia.

Booth, M., 2000, *A Magick Life: The Biography of Aleister Crowley*, London.

Brodie-Innes, J. W., Mathers, S. L. M., 1983, *The Sorcerer and His Apprentice: Unknown Hermetic Writings of S. L. MacGregor Mathers and J. W. Brodie-Innes*, Northamptonshire.

Churton, T., 2011, *Aleister Crowley: The Biography*, London.

Churton, T., 2012, 'Aleister Crowley and the Yezidis', in Bogdan, H., Starr, M. P. (eds.), *Aleister Crowley and Western Esotericism*, Oxford, 81–208.

Crowley, A., 1909, *Liber AL Vel Legis: the Book of the Law*, London.

Crowley, A., 1911, *The Vision and the Voice: Liber 418*, London.

Crowley, A., 1916, *Liber II: The Message of Master Therion*, London.

50 Female mediums were considered to be particularly adept at manifesting, and mediumship offered a source of autonomy and empowerment for women; Tromp 2006, 21–47.

Crowley, A., 1936, *Equinox of the Gods*, London.
Djurdjevic, G., 2019, '"Wishing You a Speedy Termination of Existence": Aleister Crowley's views on Buddhism and Its Relationship with the Doctrine of Thelema', *Aries Journal for the Study of Western Esotericism*, 19, 212–30.
Faulkner, R. O., 1962. *A Concise Dictionary of Middle Egyptian*, Oxford.
Frankfurter, D., 1998, *Religion in Roman Egypt: Assimilation and Resistance*, Princeton.
Hornung, E., 2001, *The Secret Lore of Egypt: Its Impact on the West*, Ithaca.
Hutton, R., 2012, 'Crowley and Wicca', in Bogdan, H., Starr, M. P. (eds.), Aleister Crowley and Western Esotericism, Oxford, 285–306.
Kaczynski, R., 2010, *Perdurabo: The Life of Aleister Crowley*, Berkeley.
King, F., 1989, *Modern Ritual Magic: The Rise of Western Occultism*, Bridport.
Lant, A., 2015, 'Cinema in the Time of the Pharaohs', in Michalakis, P., Wyke, M. (eds.), *The Ancient World in Silent Cinema*, Cambridge, 53–73.
Lesko, L., 2002, *A Dictionary of Late Egyptian*, Fall River.
Lopez, D. S., 1988, *Prisoners of Shangri-la: Tibetan Buddhism and the West*, Chicago.
Loshitzky, Y., 2000, 'Orientalist Representations: Palestinians and Arabs in Some Postcolonial Film and Literature', in Hallam, E., Street, B.V. (eds.), *Cultural Encounters: Representing 'Otherness'*, Abingdon, 51–71.
McLeod, J., 2000, *Beginning Postcolonialism*, Manchester.
Moebus, O., Wilke, A., 2011, *Sound and Communication: An Aesthetic Cultural History of Sanskrit Hinduism*, New York.
Moshenska, G., 2017, 'Alternative Archaeologies', in Moshenska, G. (ed.), *Key Concepts in Public Archaeology*, London, 122–37.
Said, E., 1978, *Orientalism: Western Conceptions of the Orient*, London.
Shonkwiler, R. L., 2014, *The Behdetite: A Study of Horus the Behdetite from the Old Kingdom to the Conquest of Alexander*, University of Chicago (unpublished PhD thesis).
Studholme, A., 2002, *The Origins of Om Manipadme Hum: A Study of the Karandavyuha Sutra*, Albany.
Sutin, L., 2000, *Do What Thou Wilt: A Life of Aleister Crowley*, New York.
Tromp, M., 2006, *Altered States: Sex, Nation, Drugs, and Self-Transformation in Victorian Spiritualism*, Albany.
Tully, C. J., 2010, 'Walk Like an Egyptian: Egypt as Authority in Aleister Crowley's Reception of The Book of the Law', in *The Pomegranate: International Journal of Pagan Studies*, 12/1, 20–47.
Urban, H., 2006, *Magia Sexualis: Sex, Magic, and Liberation in Modern Western Esotericism*, Berkeley.
Wilson, C., 2005, *Aleister Crowley: The Nature of the Beast*, London.

About the author

Maiken Mosleth King has a BA and MA in Egyptology from the University of Liverpool and is a PhD student in the Department of Classics and Ancient History at the University of Bristol. Her thesis focuses on Egyptian funerary stelae from the Roman Period and how they construct and express ethnicity, gender, and religious identity. Her research interests include cross-cultural contact in Antiquity; Hellenism and Greek language in Egypt and the Near East; religion in the ancient Mediterranean and Near East; the reception of ancient Egypt in visual media; and the reception of Egypt in contemporary esoteric spirituality.

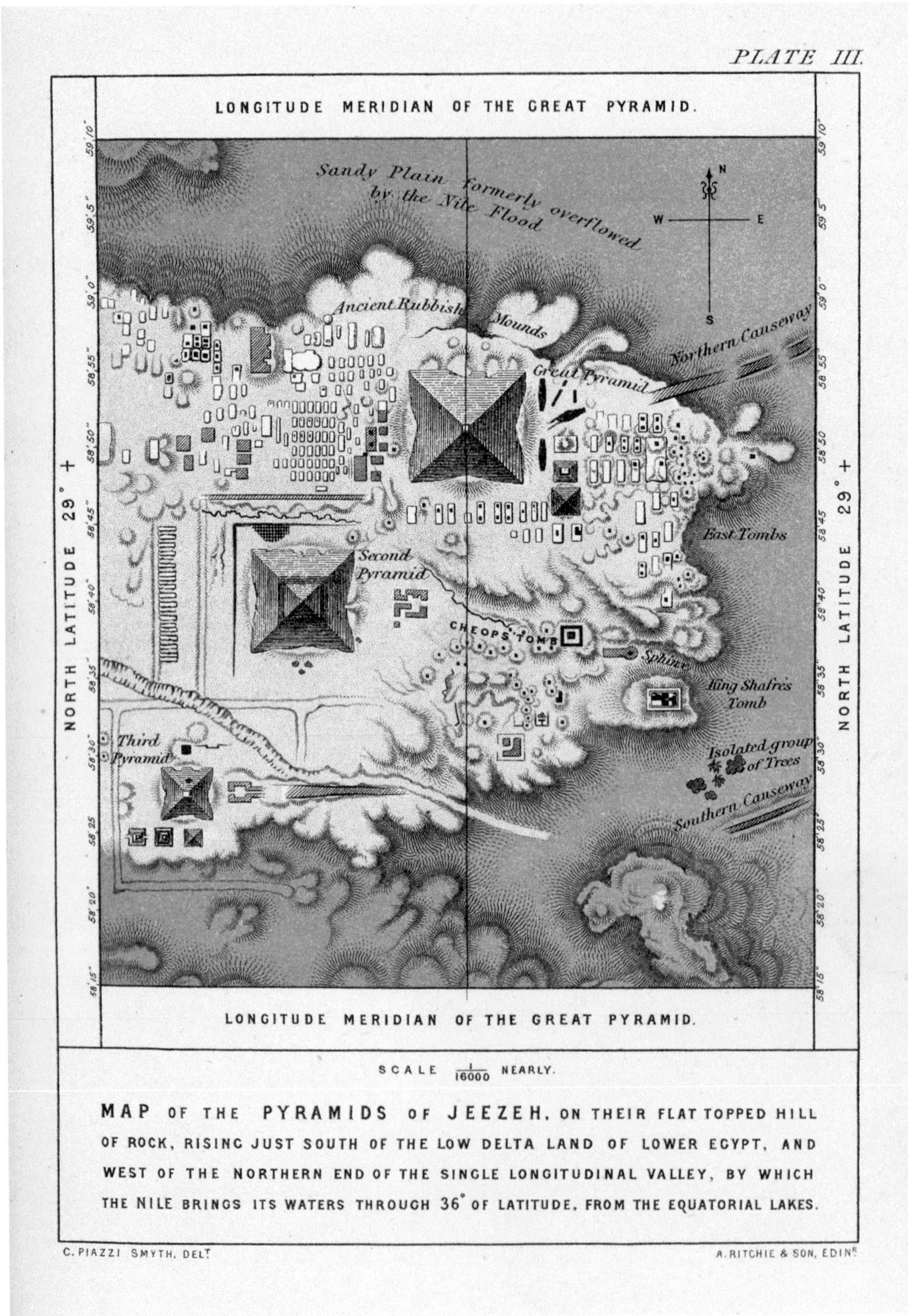

Figure 1. Map of the Giza plateau from Charles Piazzi Smyth, *Life and Work at the Great Pyramid*, plate III. Image National Museums of Scotland.

Measurement Standards and Double Standards

Reassessing Charles Piazzi Smyth's Egyptological Reputation

Daniel M. Potter[1]

> The Pyramids baffle the minds of men of intelligence, and (their most extravagant) dreams become insignificant compared with their magnitude.
> Ibn ʿAbd al-Ḥakam (*c.* AH 187–257/AD 803–871)[2]

In 1864–5, the Astronomer Royal for Scotland, Charles Piazzi Smyth (1819–1900),[3] his wife Jessie (1812–1896),[4] and a small team of Egyptian archaeological workers conducted an extensive survey of the Great Pyramid of Giza. Smyth had become interested in the structure as he read John Taylor's *The Great Pyramid: Why Was It Built—And Who Built It?*, in which Taylor argued that the pyramid was not a tomb, but rather a divinely inspired metrological monument, essentially serving as a biblical time capsule of weights and

1 This contribution stems from presentations I have given at *Stars, Pyramids and Photographs: Charles Piazzi Smyth, 1819–1900*, Edinburgh, 2–3 September 2019 and *Alternative Egyptology*, Allard Pierson Museum, 14 April 2021. My thanks to the participants of both events who provided helpful contributions, questions and thoughts. I would also like to thank Tacye Phillipson (National Museums Scotland), Andy Lawrence (University of Edinburgh), Margaret Maitland (National Museums Scotland), Clive Davenhall (Royal Observatory Edinburgh), and Meira Gold (York University) for sharing their thoughts and expertise. Great thanks also to the Royal Observatory Edinburgh, particularly to Karen Moran, who provided invaluable access to the CPS archives. Much of my work on Smyth originated in the preparation of the *Discovering Ancient Egypt* touring exhibition, which could not have been put together without the hard work of Natalia Ostrowska, Cassia Pennington, Fiona Thornton, and Jilly Burns.

2 al-Ḥakam, *Futūh Misr (Conquest of Egypt)* quoted in translation: al-Suyūṭī/Nemoy 1939, 21.

3 Brück/Brück 1988; Brück *ODNB*. Smyth usually went by the name Piazzi rather than Charles as an adult.

4 Jessica 'Jessie' Piazzi Smyth, née Duncan (1812–1896): Brück 2007, 331.

in Van den Bercken, B. J. L. (ed.), *Alternative Egyptology: Critical Essays on the Relation between Academic and Alternative Interpretations of Ancient Egypt*, Leiden, pp. 54–67.

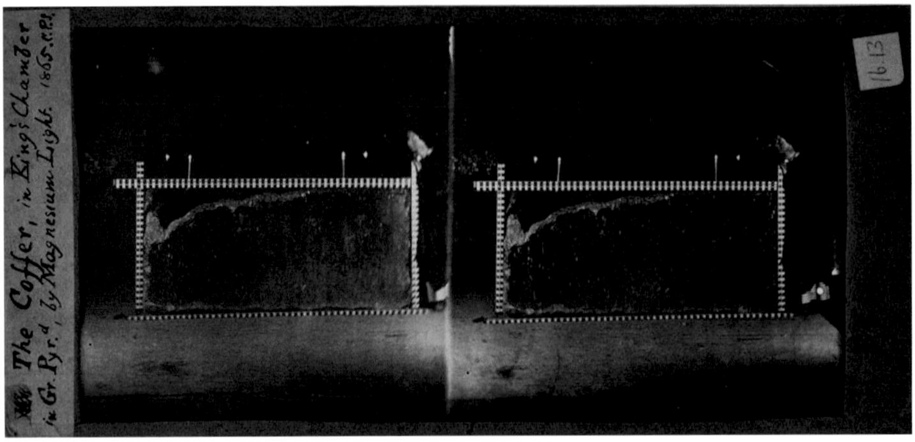

Figure 2. Stereoscopic plate titled 'The Coffer, in King's Chamber in Gr. Pyr.[d], by Magnesium Light. 1865. C.P.S.' showing the sarcophagus of King Khufu with measuring rods and candles. Jessie Smyth is standing to the right. Royal Observatory Edinburgh CPS Archives.

measures built by Noah. In its measurements the 'pyramid inch', a hidden ancestor of the fractionally larger Imperial inch, could be identified.[5]

Smyth was initially sceptical about Taylor's work, and notably dissatisfied by his omission of the works of Lepsius and von Bunsen.[6] His scepticism dissipated though, and he began to plan a survey to confirm the pyramid-inch theory and reveal hidden chronological prophecies.[7] This would support Smyth's Anglo-Israelism, and in turn confirm British links to the lost tribes of Israel and Britain's colonial supremacy.[8] It would also ensure that the new French metric system was discarded. Smyth was certain he could build on the work of the Napoleonic *savants*, Taylor, and Howard Vyse,[9] even though his venture was entirely self-funded.[10]

Over several months the team took thousands of measurements and made geological, astronomical, and meteorological observations. Smyth also took dozens of photographs of the site, including the first of the interior of the pyramid (fig. 2 and 3).[11] Upon his return to Edinburgh, he published his results and data in multiple popular editions (reprinted later at his own expense), received large amounts of related correspondence, and was well received in the press.[12] Despite this initial popularity, Smyth's diversion into pyramid metrology is often described as a blemish on his otherwise well-regarded scientific career, 'obscuring his

---

5 1 pyramid inch = 1.00106 Imperial inch. A difference of *c*.30 microns, or as Smyth 1874, 35 states 'half a hair's breadth'. 25 pyramid inches equate to 1 sacred cubit.

6 Brück/Brück 1988, 99. The works of interest to Smyth were von Bunsen 1859 and Lepsius 1849–1859.

7 Brück/Brück 1988, 99–100; Barany 2010, 48–9; Moshenska 2008, 8.

8 Moshenska 2008, 5–16.

9 Major-General Richard William Howard Vyse (1784–1853); Bierbrier 2019, 476.

10 Schaaf 1979, 337; Smyth 1870, 13 '[I had to] pay all expenses there out of my very slender salary'; Smyth 1867–68, 343 states that his salary was £300 p.a. and the costs of the survey could be up to £10,000.

11 Schaaf 1979, 331–54; Smyth 1870, 13. Schaaf 1979, 342–3 notes that Smyth experimented with early flash-powder, potentially making him the first true flash photographer.

12 Brück/Brück 1988, 125 and 130.

Figure 3. Photographic plate showing the 'Base of Niche in Queen's Chamber, Gt. Pyramid', taken with magnesium light. Smyth (1877, 6) states that the quality of the masonry at this entrance supported his metrological-monument hypothesis. Royal Observatory Edinburgh CPS Archives.

real merit'.[13] By the time of his death he had held the respectable post of Astronomer Royal for Scotland for 42 years, instituted the One O'Clock Gun in Edinburgh, pioneered high-altitude astronomy with his 1856 'Tenerife Experiment', contributed to the development of photography and produced a solar spectrum map amongst much else.

Despite these achievements, he has received conflicting treatment within Egyptology. The Smyths' work is often omitted from histories of the discipline,[14] while Piazzi is included solely as the inspiration for the often heroically portrayed Sir William Matthew Flinders Petrie (1853–1942).[15] Elsewhere Smyth has been typified as a 'pyramidiot', 'cultist'

13 Brück/Brück 1988, 256.

14 e.g. Thompson 2015, 191–2 discusses other pyramid researchers, such as Vyse, Perring and Petrie, but not Smyth.

15 Lehner 1997, 56–57; Petrie 1932, 13. For Sir William Matthew Flinders Petrie (1853–1942) see Bierbrier 2019, 363–5 and Drower *ODNB*. Henceforth referred to simply as Flinders Petrie.

or 'crank' worthy of 'no further mention'.[16] Notably, despite the intense popularity and pioneering nature of his photographs,[17] very few of these have been reproduced in Egyptological literature, possibly reducing the impact of this facet of his work. This paper examines Smyth's reception and reputation up to the present and seeks to reassess his contributions to Egyptology.

The scientific reception

In January 1868 the Royal Society of Edinburgh awarded Smyth its highest honour, the Keith Medal, for 'the energy, self-sacrifice, and skill' he displayed conducting the 'vast series of measurements'.[18] The award was tempered by the chairman's remark 'that the Council offered no opinion' on his theories,[19] echoed in the same session by A. Diedrich Wackerbarth as he commended Smyth's zeal, diligence and effort but questioned the logic of some of his calculations.[20] While Wackerbarth showed respect to Smyth in his paper, the same audience of the Royal Society of Edinburgh (RSE) were also witness to Sir James Young Simpson's[21] open attempt to ridicule Smyth's calculations by comparing the sacred cubit of 25 pyramid inches as 'one ten-millionth of the earth's semi axis of rotation'[22] to measurements of the brim of his hat and other arbitrary measurements to illustrate the contrast between Smyth's exact measurements worthy of the Keith Medal and his subsequent inexact reasoning.[23] This shade of *ad hominem* critique would not be the last directed at Smyth for his pyramid researches, with one public review of his work describing him as an 'insane person'.[24]

Smyth was affronted by the papers presented at the RSE and defended himself vigorously, angry that these individuals who had not surveyed Giza could confront him so openly, going so far as alleging libel![25] Disagreements over his pyramid theories and the vicious public feud with Simpson resulted in his resignation from the RSE; a further disagreement with Sir Henry James, director of the Ordnance Survey,[26] later precipitated Smyth's resignation from the Royal Society of London.[27] Both resignations were viewed as premature by colleagues who supported his work and grievances. Reinforced by his growing Evangelical Christianity, Smyth doubled down on his theories and results, ensuring that he would be regarded as a 'pyramidologist' from then on.

---

16 Wheeler 1935, 292–93, 304; Wortham 1971, 78–80; Reisner 1931, 4.
17 Schaaf 1979, 345f. for details of the images licensed as slides to publisher J. S. Pollitt.
18 [Royal Society of Edinburgh] 1867–68, 227.
19 [Royal Society of Edinburgh] 1867–68, 228. The Keith Medal was awarded every two years, with Smyth's awarding period April 1865 to April 1867.
20 Athanasius Diedrich Wackerbarth (1813–1884). Wackerbarth 1867–68, 235–8.
21 Sir James Young Simpson, 1st Baronet Simpson of Strathavon and Edinburgh (1811–1870), physician and obstetrician best known for his experiments with chloroform as a medical anaesthetic: Nicolson *ODNB*.
22 Simpson 1867–68, 259. One pyramid inch is described as 'One 500 millionth of Earth's Axis of Rotation Or Dist[ance] from Pole to Pole' on a set of wooden measures made by Bryson, Edinburgh in 1881 for Smyth: National Museums Scotland T.1983.205 and Whipple Museum of the History of Science Wh1155.
23 Simpson 1867–68, 264, 247; Brück/Brück 1988, 121.
24 [Newcomb] 1877, 400.
25 Smyth 1867–68, 344–55.
26 Lieutenant-Colonel Sir Henry James (1803–1877): Vetch (Baigent) *ODNB*.
27 Brück/Brück 1988, 122, 177–9.

It is worth noting that in the face of these critiques, not only that Smyth's deductions were supported by the polymath Sir John Herschel,[28] but that Smyth's figures were not simply picked from the air. Smyth's focus on the Earth's axis was likely echoing the metre's division as one ten-millionth of the distance between the North Pole and the Equator through Paris.[29] Smyth would not be the last person to attempt to find an ancient origin for metrology and was followed not only by young Flinders Petrie, but also by Ludovic Mann and others.[30]

Metrology as a political issue has often been tied to questions of national identity. In Britain, Smyth's support of an ancient origin for the Imperial inch is echoed today by arguments for the use of imperial weights and measures put forward as an 'ancient liberty'.[31] Xenophobic or exceptionalist arguments around styles of measurement persist; as Smyth described the centimetre as a 'hearty aid' of Satan, today right-wing commentators describe the metric system as 'weird, utopian, inelegant, [and] creepy'.[32]

Long before Flinders Petrie's refutation of Smyth's theories, the two families were closely acquainted, Smyth having struck up a friendship with Flinders' father, William Petrie, during their time in South Africa.[33] Smyth described a visit he and Jessie made to the Petries in 1869, receiving a tour of the British Museum from William's 16-year-old son, 'Willie' (Flinders), and indulging in 'much Pyramid talk, prayer and Scripture expounding' with William and other members of the Plymouth Brethren.[34] Inspired by Smyth's writing and theories, William and Flinders began producing their own related work.[35] Seeking to prove Smyth's theories, Flinders conducted his own survey at Giza from 1880 to 1882. In print, Flinders Petrie acknowledged Smyth and utilised some of his measurements,[36] stating that his main aim was to triangulate the site, something Smyth did not attempt.[37] Though Smyth's theory was given a 'decent burial',[38] it had already been questioned and rejected by many, meaning Flinders Petrie's 1883 book may not have been the coffin nail it is often reported to be.[39] Not all of Flinders Petrie's new measurements were 'far beyond' Smyth's, despite *The Athenaeum*'s claim promoting the second edition.[40] Across the work, differences highlighted by Flinders Petrie include 11 arc seconds (0.009166667°), 0.14" (3.556mm), an average 0.55" (13.95mm) and a shortfall of 1" (25.4mm).[41] The most conspicuous difference is a 71" (2m) disparity in the length of the base of the pyramid,

---

28 Sir John Frederick William Herschel, 1st Baronet Herschel of Slough (1792–1871): Crowe *ODNB*.

29 Smyth 1880, 54–5; Brück/Brück 1988, 125.

30 Henty 2020, 52–64.

31 'Brexit: Government to Launch Study on Economic Benefits of Reintroducing Imperial Units', J. Stone, *The Independent* https://www.independent.co.uk/news/uk/politics/brexit-imperial-measurements-economic-benefit-study-b2021304.html (accessed: 23/02/2022).

32 Smyth 1874, 185; *'Video: Fox Host Tucker Carlson Attacks "Inelegant, Creepy" Metric System that the U.S. Alone Has Resisted', Newsweek* https://www.newsweek.com/fox-tucker-carlson-attacks-metric-system-1442485 (accessed: 10/02/2022).

33 William Petrie (1821–1908). Petrie 1932, 3–4; Brück/Brück 1988, 123.

34 Brück/Brück 1988, 136.

35 Smyth 1874, 150; Drower 1985, 27–30; Petrie 1874; Petrie 1877.

36 Petrie 1883, xi, 2 and 22.

37 Petrie 1883, 2.

38 Petrie 1883, xii.

39 For the reception of Smyth, see Brück/Brück 1988, 116–34.

40 Petrie 1883, 96.

41 Petrie 1883, 34, 197, 57 and 56.

Figure 4. Photographic plate showing the measuring of one of the corner sockets of the Great Pyramid. Smyth (1877, 11) identifies the individuals as 'Mr. Inglis, engineer, the two Sheiks [*sic*] of the Great Pyramid, and Alee Dobre [*sic*]'. Royal Observatory Edinburgh CPS Archives.

due to their differing interpretations of the corner sockets rather than any error in measurement (fig. 4).[42]

Smyth 'expected and desired' that increasingly detailed measurements would be conducted following his, but viewed the 'smart young scientist['s]' work as 'mischief intending'.[43] He praised the quality of Flinders Petrie's work but continued to prefer the measurements he himself had taken.[44]

An Egyptological network

When tracing the religious and cultural influences on the development of Egyptology, Gange described a 'seamless link' between Smyth and others 'outside Egyptology' to the *inside* Egyptological work of Flinders Petrie and the Egypt Exploration Fund (Society).[45]

42 Petrie 1932, 36.
43 Smyth 1884, 16 and 83.
44 Smyth 1884, 83 and 16.
45 Gange 2013, 128.

The search for biblical illustrations or proofs greatly influenced archaeology, leading to the foundation of the Society of Biblical Archaeology and to the search for the store city of Pithom by the EEF.[46] The influence of biblical study continued in Egyptology for several decades after Smyth's death in 1900,[47] and still continues today.

In this context, Smyth was not a true outsider and his Egyptological network reflected this. Piazzi's father, Admiral William Henry Smyth,[48] was an active archaeologist, acquainted with the Wāli Mohammed Ali *Pasha* from his time in the Royal Navy.[49] His most fruitful relationships were with Dr John Lee of Hartwell House and Joseph Bonomi (the younger).[50] In W. H. Smyth's *Aedes Hartwellianae*, devoted to Lee and his collections, the author lists several 'excellent friends'[51] as correspondents in addition to Dr Lee and Bonomi: 'W. R. Hamilton',[52] 'Colonel Leake',[53] 'the Duke of Northumberland',[54] 'Sir Gardner Wilkinson',[55] 'Mr Salt',[56] 'Mons Drovetti',[57] and 'Signor Belzoni'.[58] W. H. Smyth's enthusiasm for the subject is perhaps best reflected in his daughter Georgina's middle name, Rosetta.[59] Piazzi could easily call on the scholarship of these individuals, and in the case of Bonomi a friendship.[60] Samuel Birch, a friend of his father, also invited Piazzi to join the Society of Biblical Archaeology and to present at the 1874 Oriental Congress.[61]

As noted above, William Petrie, the father of William Matthew Flinders Petrie, was a friend and supporter of Smyth, who planned to join him in Egypt 1872, and contributed to his publications.[62] The proposed second Giza survey envisioned by William Petrie and Smyth was instead undertaken by the physician Dr James Grant *Bey*[63] and the engineer Wayman Dixon,[64] both of whom corresponded with Smyth.[65] Grant *Bey* was an influential collector and facilitator for archaeologists in Egypt, who discovered the Queen's chamber of the Great Pyramid and the so-called 'Dixon Relics' with Dixon. Wayman and his brother John were later instrumental in the transport of 'Cleopatra's Needle' to the UK. In an intersection of social groups over time, both William Petrie and W. H. Smyth had lobbied for the transport of the obelisk.[66]

---

46 Bierbrier 2019, 51–2; Dodson 2021, 103 and 108; published by Naville 1885.

47 Gange 2013, 322–3.

48 Admiral William Henry Smyth (1788–1865): Laughton (Morris) *ODNB*.

49 Brück/Brück 1988, 97.

50 Dr John Lee [formerly Fiott] (1783–1866): Bierbrier 2019, 270; McConnell *ODNB*. Joseph Bonomi (1796–1878): Bierbrier 2019, 58; Meadows *ODNB*.

51 Smyth 1851, 57–8.

52 William Richard Hamilton (1777–1859): Bierbrier 2019, 204; Anderson (Jones) *ODNB*.

53 Lieutenant-Colonel William Martin Leake 'Colonel Leake' (1777–1860): Bierbrier 2019, 268; Wagstaff *ODNB*.

54 Admiral (Lord) Algernon Percy, Fourth Duke of Northumberland (1792–1865): Bierbrier 2019, 359; Thompson *ODNB*.

55 Sir John Gardner Wilkinson (1797–1875): Bierbrier 2019, 491–3; Thompson *ODNB*.

56 Henry Salt (1780–1827): Bierbrier 2019, 409–10; Manly/Rée *ODNB*.

57 Bernadino Michele Maria Drovetti (1776–1852): Bierbrier 2019, 136.

58 Giovanni Battista Belzoni (1778–1823): Bierbrier 2019, 45–6; Rée *ODNB*.

59 Brück/Brück 1988, 136. Lady Georgina Rosetta Flower née Smyth (1835–1923).

60 Brück/Brück 1988, 136.

61 Brück/Brück 1988, 130.

62 Drower 1985, 29; Brück/Brück 1988, 124.

63 Dr James Andrew Sandilands Grant *Bey* (1840–1896): Bierbrier 2019, 188.

64 Waynman Dixon (1844–1930): Bierbrier 2019, 130–1.

65 Smyth 1874, 489–96, Gold 2019, 78–9.

66 Brück/Brück 1988, 97; Drower 1985, 31; Wilson 1878, vii.

Smyth's connection to the Egyptological community was not limited to the UK; during his time in Egypt 1864–5,[67] his actions and treatment by others demonstrate that he was considered a colleague, not an outsider. His application to conduct work at Giza received approval and assistance from the Khedive Ismail *Pasha* in the presence of the Governor of Cairo, Zeki *Bey*, following support from the Consul-General in Egypt[68] after an introduction by the Secretary of State for Foreign Affairs, Lord John Russell.[69] This was enacted by the Director of Antiquities, Auguste Mariette *Pasha*[70], who also gave Smyth a tour of the Boulaq Museum, drawing attention to the statue of King Khafre, which Smyth thought to have Anglo-Saxon features.[71] Before moving to Giza, Smyth visited the Armenian-Turkish engineer and archaeologist Yusuf/Joseph Hekekyan *Bey* in Ezbekeyah,[72] likely knowing that they shared theories about the sarcophagus of Khufu as a 'stone coffer' which encoded metrological data.[73]

Smyth's survey was supervised by Luigi Vassali, who visited every 3–4 days.[74] Appointed by Mariette as 'superintendent of excavations',[75] in charge of arranging a workforce (taken from the government excavations in Saqqara),[76] ensuring that Smyth followed his permissions and communicating with the viceroy about the work, he was still cautious of conducting certain work in Mariette's absence.[77] Smyth's Egyptian team was headed up by Ali Gabri, the already experienced archaeologist and dealer who would later work with Flinders Petrie after negotiations by Grant *Bey*.[78] Gabri was also responsible for finding a suitable piece of hard stone to be made into a new reference scale of five British inches, after the 100-inch reference scale had been affected by the heat.[79] Having initially considered an unvarnished wooden scale, Smyth approached Mariette and Vassali to provide a fragment of hard stone, suggesting one of the large number of basalt sarcophagus fragments present at the Boulaq Museum; they acquiesced but failed to deliver.[80] The scale was ground and marked ready for use, ensuring that Smyth's measurements had an immovable reference point for his work. [81]

67 This was Smyth's only visit to the country.

68 Sir Edward Baldwin Malet, 4th Baronet of Wilbury (1837–1908).

69 Smyth 1867 I, ix and 29; Brück/Brück 1988, 104. John Russell, 1st Earl Russell (1792–1878).

70 François Auguste Ferdinand Mariette *Pasha* (1821–1881): Bierbrier 2019, 304–5.

71 JE 10062 = CG14; Smyth 1867 I, 7, and 13–4; Smyth 1864–65, Journal 16, 20 (17/12/1864).

72 Joseph Hekekyan *Bey* (1807–1875): Bierbrier 2019, 214–15.

73 Smyth 1864, 134–5; Smyth 1864–65, Journal 16, 11 (10/12/1864). Smyth 1877, 5–6 states that the lack of hieroglyphic inscription on the sarcophagus was influential in his interpretation of the 'coffer' as a metrological object modelled on the Ark of the Covenant.

74 Luigi Vassalli *Bey* (1812–1887): 'M. Vassalis' in Smyth 1867 I, 65f; Bierbrier 2019, 471; a sketch of Vassali by Smyth may be identified in Smyth 1864–65, Journal 17, 16 (8/11/1865).

75 Smyth 1867 I, 63.

76 Smyth 1867 I, 67.

77 For example, the lifting of the King's sarcophagus, Smyth 1867 I, 366.

78 Ali Gabri (1833/34–1904): Hagen/Ryholt 2016, 195–6. Called 'Alee Dobree' by Smyth 1867 I, 61; Petrie 1880–81, 29–30.

79 These measures made from organ pipes had bowed beyond use in the heat, Smyth 1867 I, 283; Barany 2010, 50.

80 Smyth 1867 I, 286–7 and 293–4. Hard stone such as granite or basalt was preferred as it was difficult to mark, necessitating the use of Jessie's diamond ring, meaning that the measures could not be affected by rough handling. Vassali (presumably) suggested a measure could be made from glass, but Smyth refused, see Smyth 1867 I, 288.

81 Now preserved in the Whipple Museum of the History of Sciene, Cambridge as Wh.1155. For a ful discussion of the scale, see Barany 2010, 45–60.

Figure 5. Stereoscopic plate titled 'Alee Dobree [*sic*] at East-Tombs, Gr. Pyr.d 1865'. This image was not included in Smyth's published catalogue or album. Royal Observatory Edinburgh CPS Archives.

Smyth's posthumous reputation

Upon Smyth's death, the mathematician Augustus De Morgan described Smyth's metrological obsession with the Great Pyramid as a 'paradox of a very high order', at odds with his character.[82] Such paradoxical thought or cognitive dissonance is apparent in other scientists as well, although their shortcomings have not always been the focus of posthumous treatment. Sir Isaac Newton, for example, proposed the existence of a sacred cubit based upon the work of John Greaves[83] and dedicated large amounts of time to alchemical research. When some of his pyramid notes surfaced for sale in 2020, however, his search for biblical units of measurements and alchemical secrets were put forward as one element of his 'genius'.[84] Flinders Petrie, 'the father of Egyptian archaeology', was not simply the refuter of Smyth but had originally been a keen supporter, although he later omitted his earlier pyramid research from his autobiography, describing Smyth's theories as 'hallucination[s]'.[85]

Flinders Petrie held repugnant racist views, was a supporter of eugenics and clung to his own 'new race' theory despite evidence to the contrary,[86] but his data has not been discarded from the study. Smyth thus seems to be an example of Egyptological double standards in historiography. If we were to examine other early scholars, then we could easily identify inconsistencies in opinion, incorrect assumptions and contradictions made apparent by recent research or subsequent discoveries. The influence of Flinders Petrie in the development of UK Egyptology has made him a key

---

82 *The Times*, 24/2/1900, 11.

83 Newton 1737.

84 Revealed: Isaac Newton's Attempts to Unlock Secret Code of Pyramids, *The Guardian*, https://www.theguardian.com/science/2020/dec/06/revealed-isaac-newtons-attempts-to-unlock-secret-code-of-pyramids (accessed: 28/2/2022).

85 Petrie 1932, 35.

86 Petrie/Quibell 1896, vii and Chapters III–V.

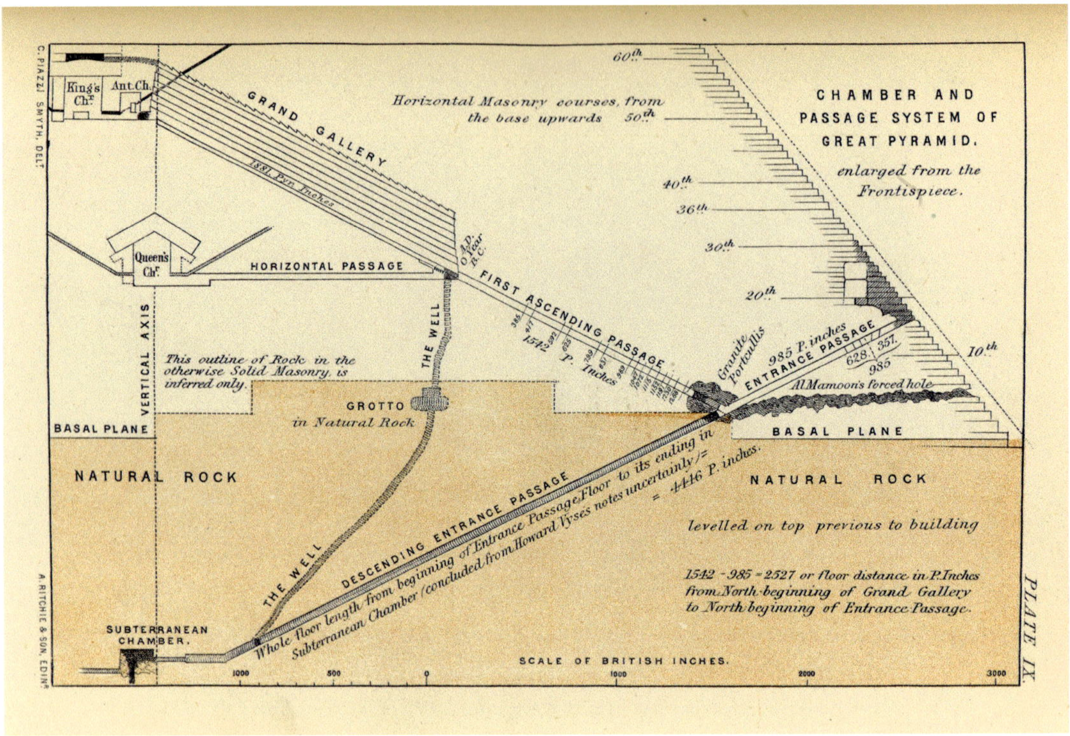

Figure 6. Cross-section of the interior of Khufu's pyramid including a scale in both British and pyramid inches, from Charles Piazzi Smyth, *Life and Work at the Great Pyramid*, plate IX. Image National Museums of Scotland.

figure; it is unsurprising that his first achievement, disproving Smyth, has often been used as a point of departure for histories of the subject. This departure may also reflect the development of archaeology more broadly, as it moved away from a search for biblical evidence towards 'material facts'.[87]

Ostentatious rejection of Smyth, as a stereotype of non-scientific Egyptology, may have become a way of distancing the discipline from some of its unwelcome researchers. Smyth's Egyptological work reflected his involvement in the broader 'Battle of the Standards', heavily influenced by issues of science, national identity and religion (fig. 6).[88] Similar nationalist and religious motivations colour the continuing history of Egyptology and cannot simply be ignored. By excising Smyth from Egyptological historiography, treating him purely as an alternative Egyptologist, calling him a 'pyramidiot' or downplaying his contributions, while extolling Flinders Petrie, we ignore the broader context of his work within nineteenth-century scholarship. Smyth was part of the Egyptological milieu; he produced popular books, took pioneering photographs and made impressive measurements, for which he was recognised by many of his contemporaries. He was, however, unwilling to give up his theories, which became a defining part of his religiosity, nationalism and scientific personality. Smyth simultaneously engaged and connected with his peers, whilst also believing that the pyramid was not a burial monument of

87 Stevenson 2019, 31–2.

88 Reisenauer 2003; Kramper 2019, 392–3.

'idolatrous Egyptians'.[89] In other ways, he could also be forward-thinking, arguing against the 'barbarism' of breaking pieces off standing monuments and encouraging their return to Egypt for display in the Boulaq Museum.[90]

Smyth represents an intersection in Egyptological history, straddling the 'outside' and the 'inside' of Egyptology. He provided inspiration for both the alternative and the mainstream in the same way Isaac Newton, Flinders Petrie and others have also produced scientific and non-scientific legacies.[91] The modern reception of Smyth in Egyptology is a reminder of the importance of context, and of the need to acknowledge and address incorrect theories and their influence on the history of the subject.

Bibliography

Barany, M. J., 2010, 'Great Pyramid Metrology and the Material Politics of Basalt', in *Spontaneous Generations: A Journal for the History and Philosophy of Science*, 4/1, 45–60.

Bierbrier, M. L. (ed.), 2019, *Who Was Who in Egyptology* (5th edition), London.

Brück, H. A., Brück, M. T., 1988, *The Peripatetic Astronomer: The Life of Charles Piazzi Smyth*, Bristol.

Brück, M. T., 2007, 'Smyth, Jessica Piazzi (Jessie)', in Ewan, E., Innes, S., Reynolds, S. (eds.), 2007, *The Biographical Dictionary of Scottish Women*, Edinburgh, 331.

Bunsen, C. C. J. von, 1859, *Egypt's Place in Universal History* (5 vols.)

Dodson, A., 2021, 'The British Isles', in Bednarski, A., Dodson, A., Ikram, S. (eds.), 2021, *A History of World Egyptology*, Cambridge, 91–135.

Drower, M. S., 1985, *Flinders Petrie: A Life in Archaeology*, London.

Gange, D., 2013, *Dialogues with the Dead: Egyptology in British Culture and Religion, 1822–1922*, Oxford.

Gold, M., 2019, *Victorian Egyptology and the Making of a Colonial Field Science, 1850–1906*, unpblished PhD thesis, University of Cambridge.

Hagen, F., Ryholt, K., 2016, *The Antiquities Trade in Egypt 1880–1930: The H. O. Lange Papers*, Copenhagen.

Henty, L., 2020, 'Ludovic McLellan Mann's Place in the History of Prehistoric Metrology', in *Scottish Archaeological Journal*, 42, 52–64.

Kramper, P., 2019, *The Battle of the Standards: Messen, Zählen und Wiegen in Westeuropa 1660–1914*, Berlin.

Lehner, M., 1997, *The Complete Pyramids*, London.

Lepsius, K. R., 1849–1859, *Denkmäler aus Ägypten und Äthiopien*, Berlin.

Moshenska, G., 2008, '"The Bible in Stone": Pyramids, Lost Tribes and Alternative Archaeologies', in *Public Archaeology*, 7/1, 5–16.

Naville, E., 1885, *The Store-City of Pithom and the Route of the Exodus*, London.

[Newcomb, S.], 1877, Review of C. P. Smyth 'Our Inheritance in the Great Pyramid', in *Nation*, 25, 27/12/1877, 400.

Newton, I., 1737, 'A Dissertation upon the Sacred Cubit of the Jews and the Cubits of the Several Nations', in Greaves, J., 1737, *Miscellaneous Works of Mr. John Greaves, Professor of Astronomy in the University of Oxford*, vol. 2, London, 405–33.

89 Smyth 1874, 193.

90 Wilson 1878, 194; Smyth 1867, I and 15.

91 Dodson 2021, 104 notes the continued popularity of Smyth's work, even when refuted.

ODNB = *Oxford Dictionary of National Biography*, https://www.oxforddnb.com/ (accessed: 17/03/2022).
Petrie, W. M. F., 1874, *Researches on the Great Pyramid, or Fresh Connections, Being a Preliminary Notice of Some Facts and a Fuller Statement*, London.
Petrie, W. M. F., 1877, *Inductive Metrology: Or, The Recovery of Ancient Measures from the Monuments*, Cambridge.
Petrie, W. M. F., 1880–81, Journal MSS 1.1, Griffith Institute, Oxford.
Petrie, W. M. F., 1883, *The Pyramids and Temples of Gizeh*, London.
Petrie, W. M. F., 1932, *Seventy Years in Archaeology*, New York.
Petrie, W. M. F., Quibell, J.E., 1896, *Naqada and Ballas*, London.
Reisenauer, E. M., 2003, '"The Battle of the Standards": Great Pyramid Metrology and British Identity, 1859–1890', in *The Historian*, 65/4, 931–78.
Reisner, G.A., 1931, *Mycinerus: The Temples of the Third Pyramid at Giza*, Cambridge MA.
[Royal Society of Edinburgh], 1867–68, 'On the Antiquity of Intellectual Man: From a Practical and Astronomical Point of View. By Professor C. Piazzi Smyth', in *Proceedings of the Royal Society of Edinburgh*, 6, 226–228.
Schaaf, L., 1979,' Charles Piazzi Smyth's 1865 Conquest of the Great Pyramid', in *History of Photography*, 3/4, 331–54.
Simpson, J. Y., 1867–68, 'Pyramidial Structures in Egypt and Elsewhere; And the Objects of their Erection', in *Proceedings of the Royal Society of Edinburgh*, 6, 243–68.
Smyth, C. P., 1864–65, Journals 14–19, Royal Observatory Edinburgh CPS Archive.
Smyth, C. P., 1864, *Our Inheritance in the Great Pyramid*, 1st Edition, London.
Smyth, C. P., 1867, *Life and Work at the Great Pyramid*, 3 vols., London.
Smyth, C. P., 1867–68, 'Remarks on two Pyramid Papers in the Last Published Number of the "Proceedings" of the Royal Society of Edinburgh. By Prof. Piazzi Smyth', 20 April 1868, *Proceedings of the Royal Society of Edinburgh*, 6, 316 –78.
Smyth, C. P., 1870, *A Poor Man's Photography at the Great Pyramid in the Year 1865*, London.
Smyth, C. P., 1877, *Descriptive Catalogue of Photographs of the Great Pyramid taken by Professor C. Piazzi Smyth in connection with his three vol. book 'Life and work at the Great Pyramid'*, Manchester.
Smyth, C. P., 1874, *Our Inheritance in the Great Pyramid*, 2nd edition, London.
Smyth, C. P., 1880, *Our Inheritance in the Great Pyramid*, 4th edition, London.
Smyth, C. P., 1884, *New Measures of the Great Pyramid, by a New Measurer*, London.
Smyth, W. H., 1851, *Aedes Hartwellianae; or, Notices of the Manor and Mansion of Hartwell*, London.
Stevenson, A., 2019, *Scattered Finds: Archaeology, Egyptology and Museums*, London.
al-Suyūṭī, J. al-Dīn, Nemoy, L., 1939, 'The Treatise on the Egyptian Pyramids (Tuḥfat al-kirām fī khabar al-ahrām)', in *Isis*, 30, 17–37.
Taylor, J., 1859, *The Great Pyramid: Why Was It Built—And Who Built It?*, London.
Thompson, J., 2015, *Wonderful Things: A History of Egyptology, I: From Antiquity to 1881*, Cairo.
Wackerbarth, A. D., 1867–68, 'On the Great Pyramid of Gizeh, and Professor C. P. Smyth's Views Concerning it', in *Proceedings of the Royal Society of Edinburgh*, 6, 235–38.

Wheeler, N. F., 1935, 'Pyramids and their Purpose', in *Antiquity*, 9/33, 5–21.
Wilson, E., 1877, *Cleopatra's Needle: With Brief Notes on Egypt and Egyptian Obelisks*, London.
Wortham, D., 1971, *The Genesis of British Egyptology, 1549–1906*, Newton Abbott.
1900, Obituary: Charles Piazzi Smyth, *The Times*, 24/2/1900, 11.

About the author

Daniel M. Potter is assistant-curator of the Ancient Mediterranean at National Museums Scotland. He has conducted research focusing on the Ramesside language of religion, prosopography and the history of Egyptological collecting and museum display. He was the lead curator of *Discovering Ancient Egypt*, a 2019–2021 National Museums Scotland touring exhibition. He is the principal investigator in the AHRC-funded *Buying Power: The Business of British Archaeology and the Antiquities Market in Egypt and Sudan 1880–1939*.

Figure 1. The pyramids of Giza seen from the southwest. Image Bildarchiv Steffens/Bridgeman Images, STF146861.

The Orion Correlation Theory: Past, Present, and Future?

Willem van Haarlem

In 1964, Egyptologist Alexander Badawy and British astronomer Virginia Trimble were the first to suggest that the enigmatic so-called air shafts in the Khufu pyramid at Giza were aligned with constellations such as Orion.[1] The ascension of the king to the circumpolar stars and Orion as described in the Pyramid Texts (such as PT 539) should constitute an ideological foundation for this (fig. 2). Several attempts to explore the shafts in the so-called Queen's Chamber with robot cameras seem to have reached results that contradict this theory.[2] It was already established before that the Queen's Chamber shafts did not reach the outer surface of the pyramid, which made their interpretation as 'air shafts' unlikely in any case.[3] It is a different matter for the shafts extending from the King's Chamber; these do reach the surface.

Thirty years later, and building upon Badawy and Trimble's work, Robert Bauval and Adrian Gilbert developed the theory that the three Giza pyramids were the reflection on earth of the three stars in the so-called Belt of the Orion constellation.[4]

Bauval and Gilbert do not contest the conventional date for the construction of the pyramids in the third millennium BC. Orion's orientation towards the pyramids, however, does not correspond to its relative position on a date in the third millennium, but rather to the position of Orion 10,000 years earlier (fig. 3).[5] Bauval and Gilbert claim to have solved this discrepancy with the theory that the Giza pyramids were built according to a masterplan devised by an advanced civilisation 10,000 years before their actual construction. No convincing explanation is given why it took so long to realise the plan and build the pyramids, or how this plan was handed down over the ages. Although it is not really mentioned as such, the authors silently imply that this advanced civilisation

1 Badawy 1964, 189–206.
2 See, for example, Bauval 1993.
3 Belmonte/Shaltout 2010, 308–11.
4 Bauval/Gilbert 1994, *passim*.
5 The orientation changes over time due to precession, fluctuations in the position of the earth's axis.

in Van den Bercken, B. J. L. (ed.), *Alternative Egyptology: Critical Essays on the Relation between Academic and Alternative Interpretations of Ancient Egypt*, Leiden, pp. 68–75.

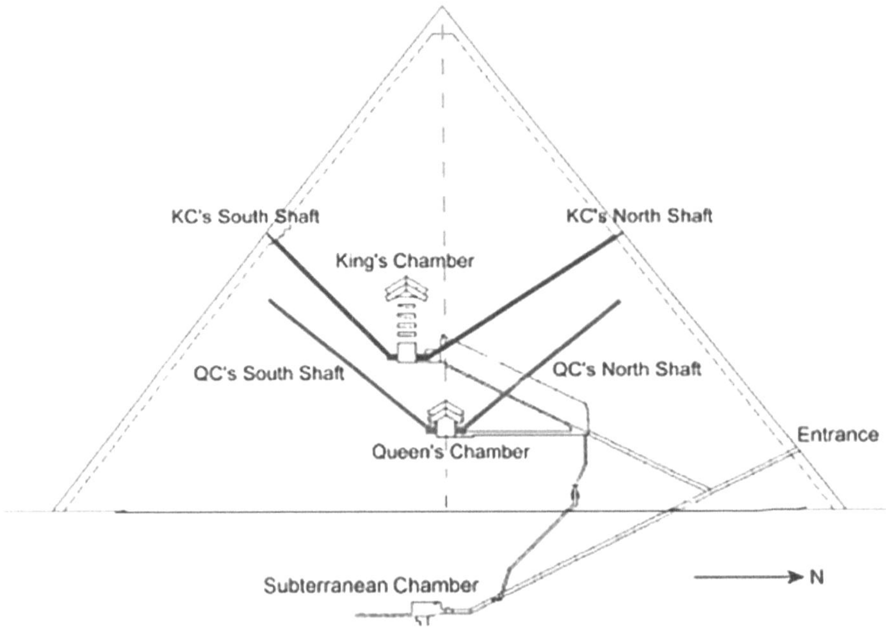

Figure 2. The air shafts as defined by Badawy (reproduced with permission from L. Miatello).

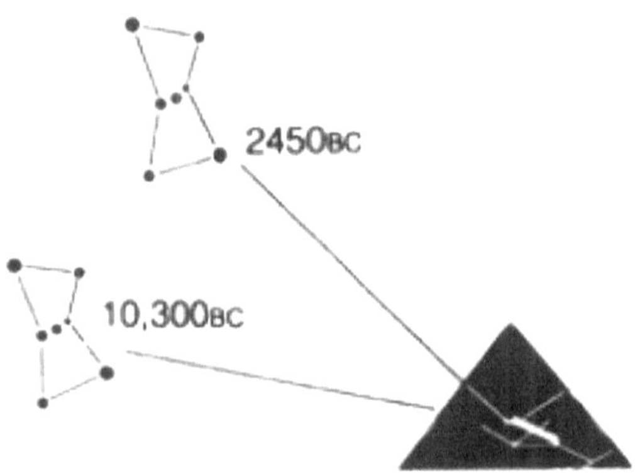

Figure 3. The change in Orion's orientation towards the air shafts through the ages (after Bauval/Gilbert 1994).

is otherwise known as Atlantis. Apparently, the name 'Atlantis' has too many doubtful connotations to be used without reservations in this context. The theory would be more coherent if the actual construction date of the pyramids were set 10,000 years earlier as well, but Bauval and Gilbert do not consider this. Their theory is based on assumptions that are not clarified.[6]

Expanding this theory, Bauval attempted to link other 4th-Dynasty pyramids, such as those at Dahshur and Abu Roash, to other stars in the Orion constellation.[7] He interpreted these pyramids as reflections on earth of the stars Saiph and Bellatrix, at least at first sight. Unfortunately for this hypothesis, upon closer examination they do match the general

6 Belmonte/Shaltout 2010, 318–20.

7 Bauval/Gilbert 1994, *passim*.

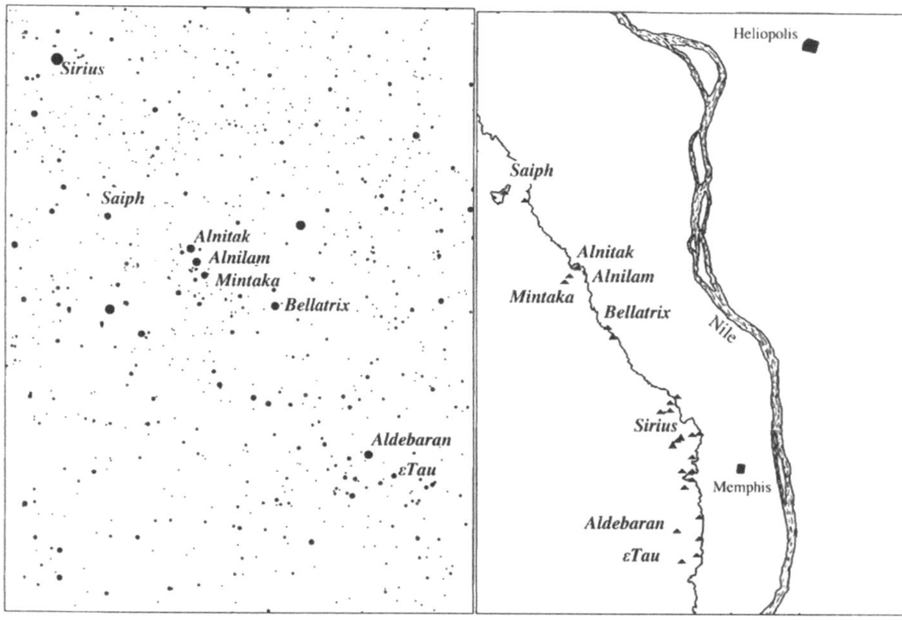

Figure 4. Positions of the Orion stars and pyramid locations compared (after Bauval/Gilbert 1994).

position of the stars, but the relative distances are quite different between the stars on the one hand, and the pyramids on the other. Additionally, a number of stars in Orion have no corresponding pyramids at all. These lacunae were interpreted as evidence that the masterplan was never completed, or that modern research simply has not discovered them yet. This does not increase the plausibility of the theory (see also 'A recent development' below) (fig. 4).[8] Then again, absence of proof is no proof of absence.

The Sphinx

A related issue concerns the theory that the original Giza Sphinx *was* produced in the period of this alleged early civilisation, as opposed to the conventional construction date of the pyramids around 2500 BC. It is argued that the Sphinx shows traces of erosion caused by extensive rainfall (fig. 5), which must have taken place during a much longer period than the conventional date allows for.[9] There are also arguments, though, that a shorter period (from 2500 BC to the present) seems enough for this erosion of the Sphinx' body to have taken place.[10] Long periods of heavy rainfall are, moreover, not attested for the period of 12000–2000 BC; on the contrary, a gradual drying up of the Sahara area is a more valid hypothesis.[11] Apart from that, it is plausible that the Sphinx was almost completely buried by desert sand most of the time, and not exposed to the elements.

---

8 Bauval's fellow researcher Graham Hancock (Hancock 1998) expanded the theory with more temple complexes such as Angkor Wat (Cambodia), as an effigy of the firmament on earth as well (although much later, twelfth century AD). Even Indonesia's Borobudur temple (seventh century AD) is referred to as such.

9 Schoch 1992, *passim.*

10 Hawass/Lehner 1994, *passim.*

11 Bader/Dallmeyer/Claussen 2017, *passim.*

More related theories claim that the Sphinx looked different in earlier times as suggested by the disproportionally small head, which is supposed to have been recut from an earlier, larger version as a lion's head,[12] or even as the head of Anubis. This discrepancy can be explained by reversing the argument: the head actually is not too small for the body, but the body too big for the head.[13] The fragility of the rock forming the body forced the stonecutters to elongate it, making the already finished head disproportionally small in relation to the body.

In the 1990s these alternative theories on the Sphinx received a lot of attention in the media, and consequently acquired much popular support. It was accompanied by expectations about the opening of the alleged 'Hall of Records' under the Sphinx as envisioned by a clairvoyant, Edgar Cayce.[14] Even more momentum came with the supposed apocalyptical revelation records hidden in this Hall, to be disclosed in anticipation of the arrival of the new millennium.[15] Unfortunately, nothing of the kind happened on or near the Sphinx at 00:00 hours on 1 January 2000 (beside a concert by Jean-Michel Jarre).

No traces of a 'Hall of Records' were ever found. By using ground-penetrating radar, anomalies were discovered, but so far appeared to be nothing more than natural fissures and cavities in the unstable bedrock structure below the Sphinx. And thus, attention for all these theories began to diminish as the new millennium proceeded.

A recent development

Recently though, Larry Pahl, director of The American Institute of Pyramid Research, launched the Egyptian New Orion Connection Hypothesis, or ENOCH,[16] and dusted off the old theory again, stating once more that *all* the stars of Orion *are* represented by pyramids in Egypt. Pahl also argues that this 'project' was possibly never finished or that these 'missing' pyramids are presently buried deep under the desert surface, which still remains to be confirmed. Some Orion stars have their supposed counterpart pyramids projected in the fertile zone along the Nile, or far into the desert: one of the flaws of the original theory (see above).[17] Whether this is really a new perspective or a recapitulation of the old hypothesis is not clear.

Some questions remain unanswered: why, of all the dozens of pyramids, is only the pyramid of Khufu provided with shafts? Is the fact that it is the largest pyramid a sufficient answer? If the three pyramids of Giza are so important for the Orion Correlation Theory, why are none of them provided with any of the Pyramid Texts, essential for this interpretation? The first pyramid with any Pyramid Texts is the one attributed to Unas, who reigned at least a hundred years later.

12 Reader 1999, *passim*.
13 Lehner 1997, 127.
14 Hancock/Bauval 1996, *passim*.
15 Lawton/Ogilvie-Herald 1999, 493–503.
16 Pahl 2019.
17 Bauval seems to have silently abandoned this theory of more corresponding pyramids, but has limited it to the Giza pyramids and the Orion Belt (compare Bauval/Gilbert 1994 to Hancock/Bauval 1996).

Figure 5. Traces of erosion on the body of the Sphinx of Giza (detail of a photograph by the author).

Bibliography

Badawy, A., 1964, 'The Stellar Destiny of Pharaoh and the So-called Air-shafts of Cheops' Pyramid', in *Mitteilungen des Instituts für Orientforschung,* 10, 189–206.

Bader, J., Dallmeyer, A., Claussen, M., 2017, 'Theory and Modeling of the African Humid Period and the Green Sahara', in *Oxford Research Encyclopedia of Climate Science,* 1.

Bauval, R., 'The Upuaut Project. New Findings in the Southern Shaft of the Queen's Chamber in Cheops' Pyramid', in *Discussions in Egyptology,* 27, 5–7.

Bauval, R., Gilbert, G. A., 1994, *The Orion Mystery,* New York.

Faulkner, R. O., 1969, *The Ancient Egyptian Pyramid Texts,* Oxford.

Hancock, G., 1998, *Heaven's Mirror. Quest for the Lost Civilization,* New York.

Hancock, G., Bauval, R., 1996, *The Message of the Sphinx. A Quest for the Hidden Legacy of Mankind,* New York.

Hawass, Z., Lehner, M., 1994, 'Remnant of a Lost Civilization?', in *Archaeology,* 47, 45–7.

Lawton, I., Ogilvie-Herald, C., 1999, *Giza—The Truth,* London.

Lehner, M., 1997, *The Complete Pyramids,* London.

Magli, G., Belmonte, J. A., 2010, 'Pyramids and Stars. Facts, Conjectures and Starry Tales', in Belmonte, J. A., Shaltout, M., 2010, *In Search of Cosmic Order*, 307–21.

Pahl, L., 2019, *Enoch: Egyptian New Orion Connection Hypothesis.*

Reader, C. D., 1999, *Khufu Knew the Sphinx*, published on https://www.academia.edu/7046492/Khufu_Knew_the_Sphinx (accessed 11/4/2023).

Schoch, R. M., 1992, 'Redating the Great Sphinx of Giza', in *KMT, A Modern Journal of Ancient Egypt*, vol. 3 no. 2 (1992) 52–59.

Trimble, V., 1964, 'Astronomical Considerations concerning the so-called Air Shafts of Cheops' Pyramid', in *Mitteilungen des Instituts für Orientforschung* 10, 183–87.

About the author

Willem van Haarlem graduated in Egyptology at the University of Amsterdam and obtained his PhD at Leiden University. Between 1990 and 2014 he worked as field director of the excavations at Tell Ibrahim Awad. From 1999 to 2003, he was assistant-director of the Dutch-Flemish Institute in Cairo. Van Haarlem is the author of a number of publications on ancient Egypt. He retired from his post as curator of the Egyptian Department of the Allard Pierson (University of Amsterdam) in 2021.

Figure 1. A mourner kneels at the feet of a mummy in front of a bouquet of lotus, poppy and mandrake. Detail of a painting of a funeral ceremony from the tomb of Nebamun and Ipuky (TT181). Facsimile painting by Charles K. Wilkinson, 1920–21. Image in the public domain, Metropolitan Museum of Fine Art, Rogers Fund, 1930, accession no. 30.4.108.

High Times in Ancient Egypt

Andrea Sinclair

Introduction

The identifications of psychoactive[1] plants that may be claimed for ancient Egypt in alternative Egyptology[2] are various and include such substances as mandrake, lettuce, *Nymphaea* lotuses, cocaine, opium, and cannabis. Within Egyptology, discussion of the former three plants is well attested[3] while the latter three are either disputed or unattested, yet still have substantial followings beyond the discipline.[4] Nonetheless, citations of psychoactives and intoxicants represent a large subculture that is rarely addressed by academia, apart from the plants for which we have empirical evidence, for perfectly sound reasons. This does nothing, however, to dispel the proliferation of misinformation in the public sphere. The intention of this paper is to track this process as it is interpreted from academic sources. Therefore, it begins early, with the poet Homer.

In the nineteenth century identification of ancient flora depended on that part of Antiquity that was familiar to scholars: Classical texts. For this reason we begin with the *Odyssey*, where Helen lulls the grief of her husband and his companions by slipping into the wine a remedy described as *nepenthes*,[5] causing forgetfulness of all ills.[6] The

1 I avoid using the term 'entheogen', as this was introduced by Ruck et al. in 1979 as a solution to the negative baggage carried by 'hallucinogen' and 'psychedelic'. 'Entheogen' is applied to ritual and shamanistic use of psychoactives, whereas this paper is concerned with a wider context.

2 'Alternative' is used here out of deference to the theme of this volume, with awareness of the ambiguity of terms associated with non-academic research. In English 'alternative' is used to describe the possibility of a different manner of approaching an issue or topic. In this paper, it is a convenient yet unsatisfactory umbrella term that has wide application ranging from neo-pagan and entheogen studies to pseudo-science.

3 The extent of the psychoactive impact and usage of these is subject to debate. See Samorini 2019, 68; Merlin 2003, 316–17; Counsell 2008, 208, 215.

4 Counsell 2008; Buckland/Panagiotakapolu 2001; Feagans 2018; Kearney 2019.

5 νη-πενθής is an adjective meaning 'banishing pain', Liddell/Scott 2000, 532; *adj.* [privatv. prfx. + πένθος] (of a drug) 'banishing sorrow', Diggle 2021, 966. It is the description of the drug, and not a name.

6 *Odyssey* IV, 219-32, 'Then Helen, born of Zeus, deliberated, and at once she threw into the wine from which they drank a remedy to remove sorrow, allay anger and cause one to forget all evils (...) the daughter of Zeus possessed such all-wise drugs, effective ones, that Polydamna, wife of Thon, had given her, a woman of Egypt,' author's translation.

in Van den Bercken, B. J. L. (ed.), *Alternative Egyptology: Critical Essays on the Relation between Academic and Alternative Interpretations of Ancient Egypt*, Leiden, pp. 76–95.

identity of this drug[7] has been a matter of debate for millennia.[8] The term is otherwise unconfirmed, except as an epithet of Apollo. Therefore, it cannot be excluded that it is a poetic construct, and it is worth noting that both opium and cannabis are identified in Classical texts.[9] Diodorus is also cited for this topic, as he repeated the anecdote about Helen and introduced the idea that the women of Egyptian Thebes were known to brew a powerful remedy that drives away grief.[10]

These few phrases have provided the foundation for the identification of two of the plants discussed here;[11] moreover, both Homer and Diodorus are staples of academic literature and alternative culture when referencing these topics.

Poppies

Papaver somniferum is an annual herb with pink or white flowers that after flowering produces large pods containing edible seeds.[12] The pods extrude a latex (milky fluid) containing morphine when they are slit.[13] In Europe this plant has been domesticated since the Neolithic and was exploited by humans for the sap and for food.[14] Contrarily, evidence for poppies from pharaonic Egypt appears to be *Papaver rhoeas*, the bright red corn poppy.[15] Apart from this the only archaeological evidence for the opium poppy in Egypt before the Classical period is disputed[16] and possibly provided by imported Cypriot juglets dating from the late 18th Dynasty.[17]

---

7 *Pharmakon* may be translated as 'medicine', 'potion', 'remedy', 'treatment' or 'drug', Diggle 2021, 1454; for a discussion see Arata 2004, 34; Jouanna 2012, 8.

8 *Nepenthes* has also been argued to be magical speech (Plutarch and Eustathius), a root from the island of Aegina (Galen), a clay otherwise called *miltos* (Eutecnius), a mixture of herbs (Psellus), or a type of wine (Rufus of Ephesus, via Oribasius). See Arata 2004, 37–9.

9 The poppy, μήκων, is also mentioned in Homer's *Iliad* to describe the death of Gorgythion (XVIII.306).

10 *Bibliotheca Historica* 1.97.7, 'For it is manifest that the poet had acquired exact knowledge of the *nepenthic* drug which he says Helen brought from Egyptian Thebes, given her by Polydamna the wife of Thon; for, they allege, even to this day the women of this city use this powerful remedy, and in ancient times, they say, a drug to cure anger and sorrow was discovered exclusively among the women of Diospolis,' Oldfather 1933.

11 Jouanna 2012, 8–9; as opium see Lewin 1998, 29; Rosso 2010, 81; Brownstein 1993, 5391; Carod-Artal 2013, 31; as cannabis see Reichardt 1859, 149; Brotteaux 1967, 12; Arata 2004; Bennett 2021; Bennett 2013, 57; a mixture of opium, cannabis and datura, Dorie 1968, 35.

12 The wide range of colours among *P. somnifera* in gardens today will be due to modern hybridisation.

13 This latex contains alkaloids inclusive of morphine, codeine and thebaine, but the sap is psychoactive predominantly in relation to morphine, causing drowsiness and euphoria; it is neurotoxic if taken in a larger quantity, Germer 2008, 310; Carod-Artal 2013, 31; Chovanec 2019.

14 Cultivation is first attested archaeologically from Central Europe (*c.*5600–3200 BC). In the Aegean and Cyprus it is documented later, Middle Bronze to Late Bronze Age, Merlin 2003, 302; Sherratt 2007, 28; Samorini 2019, 64, 69; Guerra-Doce 2015, 753.

15 *Rhoeas* seeds are attested in the archaeological record in Egypt at Memphis as early as the 12th Dynasty, Middle Kingdom, de Varvatan et al. 2010, 175. The plant was a popular floral element in New Kingdom visual rhetoric, Counsell 2008, 198; Loeben & Kappel 2009, 180–1. There is often confusion between identifying the red pomegranate fruit and the poppy pod in New Kingdom iconography.

16 Two dried poppy pods were allegedly found by Bruyére in an 18th-Dynasty tomb at Deir el Medina in the early twentieth century, but the identification of the variety of *Papaver* has never been confirmed and the current location of the pods is unknown, de Varvatan et al. 2010, 115, Germer 2008, 45.

17 Bunimovitz and Lederman 2016; Chovanec et al. 2015. More recently, a study of residue from a Cypriot juglet has confirmed opioid residues, but the identity of the contents and their intended usage are disputed, see Smith et al. 2018. The finding of opium in a study by Bisset et al., 1996, is critiqued in that paper.

Nonetheless, the earliest identification of *somniferum* in Egyptology is from Heinrich Brugsch in 1880,[18] who proposed the terms *Xsaī.t, Xsa* and *Xsī.t*[19] would apply to a calming, sleep-inducing plant, from an association with the verb *Xs*, 'to be tired'.[20] Before that time, it was considered doubtful whether opium was known in Egypt, with the quotes from Homer and Diodorus being considered the only clues.[21] In the late 1880s an alternative identification was proposed that was based on the Ebers medical papyrus.[22] This had been acquired by Georg Ebers in 1872–73 and translated two years later, without him identifying opium.[23] In a study of Egyptian medical knowledge, however, Henrich Lüring concluded that the terms *šepennu n šepen*[24] from this papyrus must indicate a variety of poppy, on the basis of a remedy for calming a distressed child.[25] This lexical identification was then adopted by Adolf Erman,[26] while other Egyptologists remained more cautious.[27]

Shepen/špn

Lüring's interpretation was subsequently reinforced in Heinrich Joachim's translation of the papyrus in 1890. Although, to be correct, Joachim referred to both Brugsch and Lüring, and therefore he identified five terms as meaning poppies: *šepen, šepnen, Xesaīt (chesayt), Xasīt (khasyt),* and *Xesau* (*khesau*).[28] Another forty years later an English translation of Joachim's book was published by Cyril Bryan, in which the reading of opium poppy was similarly flexible and applied to any remedy employing *shepen, shepenen, khesau,* and *khasyt*.[29] Not to mention the fact that he provided additional quirky commentary that was not in the original translation.[30] Most problematic, however, is that Bryan's translation is easily accessed digitally today while later academic translations are not,[31]

---

18 Brugsch 1880, 896.

19 These are Brugsch's transliterations, now written as *ḫꜣs.yt* (*khasyt*) and *ḫsꜣ.yt (chesayt).*

20 *ḫs/ hz (ches)* is now translated as 'weak' or 'feeble', Faulkner 1981, 204; 'be wretched, miserable, vile', Allen 2014; 'elend; schwach' ('miserable; weak'), *TLÄ Lemmata.*

21 '... ist es zweifelhaft, ob diese Pflanze den alten Ägyptern bekannt war.' Reichardt 1859, 150.

22 Purchased from Edwin Smith, the text is dated to the New Kingdom reign of Amenhotep I, *c.*1515 BC, but it contains copies of earlier recipes, Nunn 2006, 30–34; Scholl 2021, 17; Popko 2021, 34.

23 Ebers 1875.

24 '«Mohn-kapseln» Papaver setigerum oder somniferum,' Lüring 1888, 45.

25 Spell 782: 'Remedy for eliminating the plaintive cries (of a child): špnn part from a špn plant, propolis (?) that is on the wall. To be made into a homogenous mass; (then) squeezed out. To be drunk over 4 days so that (it) immediately ceases,' Popko 2022, *SAE* website (Sinclair translation).

26 Erman 1894, 362 'the poppy'; Erman/Grapow 1921, 181 'špnn - Mohnkörner?'

27 Wönig 1897, 25 'no evidence'; Budge 1920, 736 'a plant used in medicine'; Lefebvre 1956, 110 'Pavot (?)'; Breasted 1980, 564 'špnn, an unidentified drug'; Deines/Grapow 1959, 490 'diese Deutung ist nicht gesichert'; Ghalioungui 1987 'poppy (?)' / 'poppy seeds (?)'; Hannig/Vomberg 1999, 541 '"Mohn" (unsicher)'; Manniche 2006, 130 (?); Nunn 1996, 154-5 'less certain'. More recently Germer 1979, 236; 2008, 132, and Popko 2022, *SAE Ebers Papyrus*; 2021, 280, reject the identification.

28 'špn n špnn as 'Kapseln von der Mohnpflanze (?)' for Ebers Spell 782 for a crying child, and 'Mohnpflanze' for remedies using 'šepnen, *Xesīt, Xesau, Xasīt'*, Joachim 1890, 102–3, 169.

29 Bryan 1930, *khasyt*: 40, 45, 62, 113, 114 and 139, *shepen*: 162, *shepenen*: 60, *khesau*: 83. He does not number the spells, so it was difficult to confirm recipes involving *chesayt*.

30 For Spell 782, for example, he wrote, 'This is startling! No other word can convey the amazement with which one finds that the means employed to quell a squalling infant five thousand years ago are identically the same as many a modern mother employs today.' Bryan 1930, 162.

31 Ebbell 1937; Deines et al. 1958; Ghalioungui 1987; the papyrus is available to read in German and English at the *SAE* and the Albertina Library, University of Leipzig, websites, see link in Bibliography.

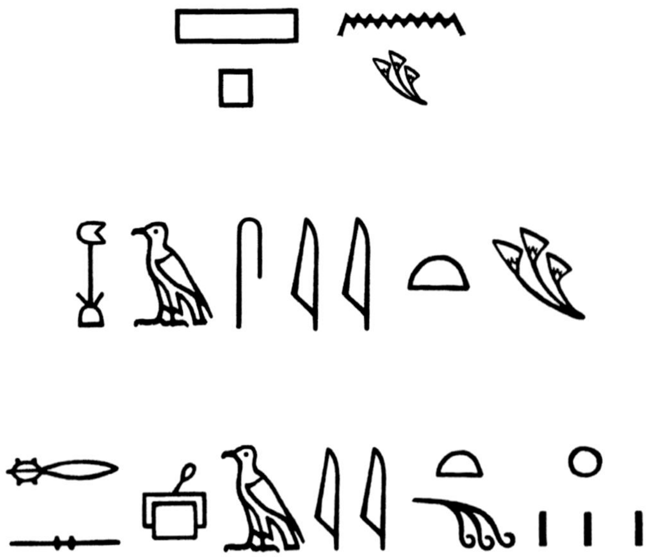

Figure 2. *Shepen* (above), *khasyt* (centre) and *chesayt* (below). Image A. Sinclair.

with the outcome that citations for opium in ancient Egypt are able to cherry-pick his text, with varying results.[32]

In addition, the opium rationale for *shepen* is not supported by the three remedies from the Ebers Papyrus that use *shepenen* as an ingredient. These are pastes and a powder that were applied to the head.[33] While it is unconfirmed but possible that these were poppy seeds, this does little to support an argument for medical opium[34], nor is there any confirmation from other sources that might clarify the issue. Equally, if opium was available in medicine in 1515 BC one would expect more examples from a treatise containing around 875 remedies. The Edwin Smith Papyrus[35] incidentally also contributes two spells employing red *shepennu*, applied externally as a dressing for wounds.[36] Nonetheless, the descriptive 'red'[37] also does little to argue for opium, although it has been used to argue that this was *P. rhoeas*.[38]

The other proposals from Brugsch that identified *khesau, chesayt* and *khasyt* were never supported by further evidence and have subsequently disappeared from discourse,[39] with many now citing white bryony[40] as the likely identification for the

32 History.com 2017; Pomeroy 2012; Rosso 2010, 82; Dormandy 2012, 10 and 17; Duarte 2005, 141; Halpern/Blistein 2019, 19-21; Kapoor 1995, 2–3.

33 Possibly for hair loss and a skin condition, Ebers Papyrus Spells 440, 443 and 445.

34 *Somniferum* seeds contain low levels of opiates, Carlin et al. 2020, 2; Chovanec 2019.

35 Acquired by Edwin Smith in 1862 at Luxor, it is dated to *c.*1550 BC, Nunn 2006, 25–30.

36 Breasted 1980, Case 41, 379, Case 46, 411.

37 *dšrw*, lit. 'orange/red'.

38 Gabra 1956, 51 and 54.

39 *Khesau* (*ḫsꜣw*) remains unidentified, but may refer to a part of a tree that was used as burning material; *chesayt* (*ḫsꜣ.yt*) is an aromatic resin, Popko 2021, 272; Germer 2008, 101 and 105–6, Hannig and Vomberg 1999, 234 and 485–86.

40 *Bryonia dioica.*

latter, from a proposal by Warren Dawson in 1934.[41] Nonetheless, this has not prevented *khasyt* from being cited for opium by alternative sources, predominantly using Bryan's version of Spell 247, where Isis heals Re of an illness in his head.[42] More concerning however is the fact that *khasyt* as opium in this spell has also become embedded as fact in academic publications beyond Egyptology.[43] In these, the Homeric reference to *nepenthes*, Diodorus, the Ebers Papyrus, and the terms *shepen* or *khasyt* are often cobbled together and embellished creating elaborate false narratives.[44] Yet to sum up the available evidence, we have no confirmation from medical texts of a term for *Papaver somniferum*, either as poppy seeds or as genuine opium. We similarly have no undisputed archaeological confirmation of the plant in Egypt before the Ptolemaic period. Thus there is no evidence of the recreational or ritual use of the drug opium.

Cannabis

Cannabis sativa is an annual herb of medium height with distinctive leaves that grow palmately. It is dioecious, meaning separate plants produce male or female flowers, the female being most psychoactive due to the cannabinoid tetrahydrocannabinol (THC).[45] Humans have exploited the plant for the fibre, resin, seeds and oil since the Neolithic period,[46] and in Antiquity it appears heating the seeds may have been the favoured method in fumigation.[47] The earliest evidence for use of cannabis as an intoxicant is from

---

41 Dawson 1934, 45; see Deines/Grapow 1959, 392; Faulkner 1981, 185 'bryony (?)'; Ghaliounghui 1987, 272 'bryony / balsamodendron kafal'; Manniche 2006, 81, Hannig/Vomberg 1999, 234; Nunn 2006, 152. This identification is based on the parts of this plant that were ingredients in Egyptian medicine, such as the bark, roots, fruits, seeds, and 'tails'.

42 'Another remedy which the goddess Isis prepared for the god Ra to drive out the pains that are in his head: Berry-of-the-coriander, Berry-of-the-poppy-plant, Wormwood, Berry-of-the-sames-plant, Berry-of-the-juniper-plant, Honey,' Bryan 1930, 40. Now more accurately: 'Another, sixth (remedy) that Isis has made for Re himself, in order to eliminate the illness that was situated in his head: Coriander seeds, fruit/seeds of a ḫꜣs.yt plant, sꜥꜣm plant, fruit/seeds of a šꜣms plant, Phoenician juniper berries, honey,' Popko 2022 (Sinclair translation, numerals omitted from both).

43 See e.g.: Wink 1998, 36; Schiff 2002, 198; Escohotado 2010, 104; Flascha 2011; Saunders 2013, 15.

44 E.g.: 'Undoubtedly the success that attended the headache-cure compounded by Isis was due to the Opium it contained in the guise of Berry-of-the-Poppy-plant, and it may well be that it was her success with this drug that led that other woman-pioneer of medicine, Helen of Troy, in a later age to produce her nepenthe and to use it with the startling results that Homer records', Bryan 1930, 40-1. Stefano et al. 2017, 2891: 'The Ebers Papyrus from 1552 BC describes a blend of substances, including opium, which was used to sedate children, and it was noted that this was how the goddess Isis would sedate her son Horus'. Wikipedia, 'Opium': 'In Egypt, the use of opium was generally restricted to priests, magicians, and warriors, its invention is credited to Thoth, and it was said to have been given by Isis to Ra as treatment for a headache' (accessed March 2022).

45 In addition to less psychoactive cannabinoids (100+), Russo 2007, 1615; Warf 2014, 416; Brunner 1973, 345.

46 Earliest evidence of *C. sativa* is textile imprints on ceramic, first half of fourth millennium BC, from Pan-P'o in central China, Merlin 2003, 304. The earliest undisputed ritual evidence from Eurasia appears to be funerary deposits dating from the first millennium in China, Ren et al. 2019, 4, and Bronze to Iron Age Pazyryk (Scythian) burial mounds, Merlin 2003, 313, Samorini 2019, 67–68, see also Clarke/Merlin 2016, 84–86.

47 Herodotus *Histories* IV.75, 'The Scythians then take the seed of this hemp and, crawling in under the mats, throw it on the red-hot stones, where it smoulders and sends forth such fumes that no Greek vapor-bath could surpass it.' Godley 1920, Perseus Digital Library, via http://www.perseus.tufts.edu/hopper/text?doc=Perseus%3Atext%3A1999.01.0126%3Abook%3D4%3Achapter%3D75%3Asection%3D1 (accessed: March 2021).

an eighth-century altar in the Levant.[48] There is, however, no evidence from Egypt before the Roman period[49] beyond a disputed finding of cannabis pollen from the mummy of Rameses II,[50] and the common ethnocentric confusion of the term 'hemp' with fibres made from reeds and rushes, such as papyrus.[51]

Shemshemet/šmšm.t

The process of lexical identification of this substance, like that of opium, begins in the nineteenth century—this time with Franz Unger's proposal that the Egyptians had knowledge of cannabis, based on the same lines from Homer that are cited for opium.[52] To support this attribution, he also repeated Diodorus' statements on *nepenthes* and the women of Thebes producing a powerful drug. In addition, Unger argued that the feather headdress of the Egyptian goddess Anukis was a cannabis leaf. This constitutes his entire argument, as he proposed no lexical identification. Thirty years later Victor Loret justifiably rejected Unger's claims as speculation and stated there was no evidence from Egypt for hemp.[53] Subsequently, Franz Wönig also argued that the Egyptians were unaware of hemp.[54]

The identification of cannabis does not take place until 1934 with a proposal by Dawson that the plant *shemshemet* from medical papyri was hemp.[55] Previous to that time this had been identified as sesame, on the basis that it could be a loanword from Semitic *smsm/shamshamu*.[56] Therefore, Joachim chose 'sesame' in his translation of

---

48 Arie et al. 2020. Cannabis resin has also been detected in a fourth-century AD grave at Beth Shemesh in the Levant, Merlin 2003, 314; Clarke/Merlin 2016, 103.

49 Abel 1980, 26; Ebeid 1999, 311; Germer 2008, 133; Harer 2015, 357; Sanchez/Harer 2019, 80.

50 Leroi-Gourhan 1985, 162–65. The pollen was detected in tissue of the mummy, which is problematic due to the fragile nature of cannabinoids; see Buckland/Panagiotakapolu 2001, 554, who argue this is due to contamination from a pesticide used by the museum in the late nineteenth or early twentieth century. Two further studies contribute little more to the identification of cannabis before the Roman period. The first, of nine mummies where cannabis was found in tissue, hair and bone, is found in Balabanova/Parsche/Pirsig 1992. The academic rigour of this study has been questioned with some validity, as the very brief paper did not provide the scientific methodologies (Councell 2008, 213–14 and Buckland/Panagiotakapolu 2001, 553–54). For a Roman-period mummy with pollen in the mummification resin, see Girard 1987. Both studies were of unprovenienced mummies from small museum or private collections established in the 1800s, therefore modern contamination cannot be excluded.

51 Citations of hemp from Egypt are Ptolemaic or Roman, see de Varvatan et al. 2010, 64-5; Germer 2008, 133; Abel 1980, 26. The common reference for hemp fibre is from the Brunton excavations of Roman- and Coptic-period burials at Mostagedda, as identified by Midgely (Brunton 1937, 145), it is cited in Lucas/Harris 1999, 149, and disputed by Vogelsang-Eastwood 2000, 269. *C. sativa* is also unconfirmed for a 'mat tied with hemp cords' from a house at Tell el-Amarna, Peet/Woolley 1923, 81; Lucas/Harris 1999, 149. Finally, the hemp fibre from the Amarna Royal Tomb is dated to the Roman period, Martin 1989, 62. In Egypt papyrus appears to have been the most common material for making ropes, Borojevic/Mountain 2013, *passim*; 2011, 139–40; Veldmeijer 2009, 2.

52 'Homer spricht nämlich in der Odyssee von einem νηπενθής φάρμακον, das den Kummer aus dem Herzen entfernt und aus Aegypten kommt' ... 'Wenn Mann aber bedenkt, wie allgemein jetzt im Oriente aus Cannabis bereitete Narkotica als Kurus und Hashisch sind, so drängt sich unwillkürlich der Gedanke auf, das dieses Mittel kein Opiat, sondern ein Präparat von Cannabis war,' Reichardt 1859, 149.

53 'Que la boisson de Polydamna ait été le Hashish, c'est là une pure hypothèse impossible à discuter scientifiquement,' Loret 1888, 22–23.

54 'Den Hanf kannten die alten Aegypter nicht,' Wönig 1897, 189.

55 Dawson 1934, 44.

56 'sesamum, von den Arabern simsim genannt', Brugsch 1868, 1392; *'Šemšemt; sesamum'*, Ebers 1875 II, 45; 'Le nom Arabe du Sésame est Semsem; or, une plante dont les grains se mangeaient se nomme en hiéroglyphs est Shemshem' Loret 1888, 26–27; 'Sesame', Budge 1920, II, 740.

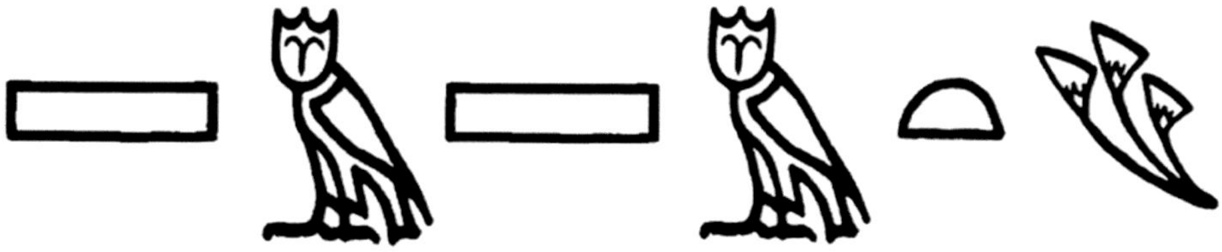

Figure 3. *Shemshemet*. Image A. Sinclair.

the Ebers Papyrus for the two recipes containing *shemshemet*.[57] In the early twentieth century the identification with sesame was rejected by Ludwig Keimer[58] and later by Dawson, whose proposal was immediately adopted and went on to be cited in most, but not all literature.[59] Dawson's identification however, while now an embedded 'fact', remains disputed because it was based on a single phrase from Pyramid Text 514 where *shemshemet* is mentioned for a rope that king Unas uses as a boat tie.[60] And it is worth noting here that authoritative translations of the Pyramid Texts over the past seventy years cite the original term for PT 514,[61] or translate it as a variety of cress on the basis of a possible connection with the herb *smt*.[62]

Notwithstanding the process of fine-tuning translation within Egyptology, this connection to cannabis was then applied to any Egyptian medical text that mentions *shemshemet*, with most citing remedies from the Ebers[63] or the Ramesseum Papyrus.[64] Yet there is no indication from these that hemp fibre, or cannabis proper, would be more efficacious than any other plant. Furthermore citations of these papyri to support these claims are tenuous when the identity of *shemshemet* is not confirmed. Because of this, the lexical identification has never been unanimously accepted within Egyptology and the term is often qualified by a cautionary note.[65] Yet regardless of the inherent weakness of the argument, this identification has now become embedded in contemporary publications both Egyptological[66] and pharmaceutical,[67] and subsequently is misrepresented in

57 Ebers Papyrus Spells 618 and 821, Joachim 1890, 134 and 176.

58 Keimer 1924, 135.

59 Émile Chassinat, for example, retained 'sesame' when translating two Coptic recipes, Chassinat 1950, 14, and it is still possible to find papers citing *shemshemet* for sesame today, see Hepper 2009, 27, for a discussion, also see *Economic Botany* articles on sesame by Bedigian 2004, 334, and Nayar/Mehra 1970, 27.

60 Pyramid of Unas, Corridor East, Utterance 319, PT 514.

61 '*šmšm.t'*, Faulkner 1969, 101; Piankoff 1968, 19, Mercer 1952, 171.

62 'Peppergrass cords/ties', Allen/Der Manuelien 2005, 61; Shmakov 2012, 171. For *smt* as cress – *Lepidium sativum*, Manniche 2006, 115; but 'eine Deutung ist zur Zeit nicht möglich', Germer 2008, 115.

63 Ebers Spells 618 and 821, an ointment for a toenail and a vaginal infusion for contracting the uterus.

64 For an eye ailment, Ramesseum Papyrus 3, Fragment A.23 (BM EA10756.8). There are also two remedies involving enemas and containing *shemshemet* or *shemshemet* water from the Chester Beatty Papyrus, and two from the Berlin Papyrus; one an ointment for a skin inflammation and the other for removing a poison from a god or dead person, Germer 2008, 132.

65 See Harer 2015, 356–57; Sanchez/Harer 2019, 80; Popko 2021, 271 'Eine falsche Deutung', who reject it outright. Also, Faulkner 1981, 267 'hemp (?)'; Hannig/Vomberg 1998 'unsicher'; Germer 2008, 133 'bisher für das pharaonische Ägypten noch nicht durch Funde belegt.' Ghalioungui 1987, 274, cites both hemp and sesame as proposals.

66 Manniche 2006, 82–83; Nunn 2006, 156.

67 Russo 2007, 1622; Kabelik 1955, 4; Hanuš 2008, 215–16; Escohotado 2010, 106; Clarke/Merlin 2016, 126–27, 245–46.

alternative Egyptology, where the existence of cannabis as an intoxicant is considered to be an established fact.[68]

In addition, highly questionable identifications are also made with Egyptian goddesses such as Seshat and Bastet, based on subjective interpretations of the iconography yet often citing the medical papyri and Pyramid Text given here as confirmation.[69] From this, elaborate false narratives are created to support a cannabis culture in pharaonic Egypt, from temple to private use.

Mushrooms

The final psychoactive plants discussed here are the most unsubstantial in terms of evidence, and they are in fact not plants, but fungi.

Amanita muscaria is a large neurotoxic mushroom with a wide red-orange cap that is often adorned with white flecks. The gills and stem are white with a distinctive frill on the stem. They grow in moist soil under oak, fir or birch trees in cool temperate and boreal forests, from late summer to autumn.[70] *Psilocybe cubensis* is a small brown mushroom with a lighter-coloured stem that grows in moist animal dung in temperate to tropical climates. Both species were first identified in Cuba[71] and stain blue when touched due to the psychoactive chemical psilocybin.[72]

Together, these mushrooms are the main protagonists in alternative narratives regarding ancient ritual use of psychedelic mushrooms. Neither, however, is native to Egypt—in fact no psychoactive mushroom is attested as native to Egypt—[73]and therefore this leads us to how these narratives have developed.

Plant of life

Predictably, Homer and *nepenthes* are again cited for mushrooms, but this time only in alternative publications, where a thriving narrative of ritual use in ancient Egypt has developed.[74] Much of this narrative may be attributed to a paper by Stephen Berlant,[75] and further back to a book by Andrija Puharich.[76] Berlant however is the most problematic, as his paper was published in an academic journal, and argues that certain Egyptian royal symbolism represents *P. cubensis*. Puharich's work, on the other hand, may be considered the foundation text for this topic, as he claimed a connection to ancient Egypt for the ritual use of *A. muscaria*. This was obtained from the past-life regressions of a

---

68 See Wikipedia, 'History of Medical Cannabis'; Bennett 2021, 2013, 56–7; 2010; Ledger 2021; Hartman 2019; Attia 2017, 6; Hilliard 2018; Brusco 2017; Wrona 2019; Tchakarov 2021; CBS Drug News 2002; Rawlinson 1996, 111.

69 See Bennett 2021; Attia 2017, 6; Hilliard 2018; Brusco 2017; Ledger 2021; Tully 2020; Wiki Talk: Seshat - https://en.wikipedia.org/?title=Talk:Seshat (accessed: April 2021); Lupoi 2020; Green entrepreneur/ Dispensaries.com 2021 (accessed: March 2021); Teenwitch.com (accessed: March 2021); Celestial Musings blog 2019 (accessed: March 2022). The source of the identification with Seshat appears to be Aleff 2015, originally published in 1982, http://www.recoveredscience.com/const201seshathempmath.htm (accessed: March 2021).

70 Arora 1986, 264–65 and 282–83; Guzman et al 1998, 203–4; Hall et al. 2003, 128; Laessoe/Petersen 2019, 363.

71 Hence '*cubensis*'.

72 Arora 1986, 373-4; Stamets 1999, 108–10; Guzman et al. 1998, 205 and 207.

73 Guzman et al. 1998, *passim*; Stamets 1999, 64.

74 Allegro 1973, 98–99.

75 Berlant 2005.

76 Puharich 1959.

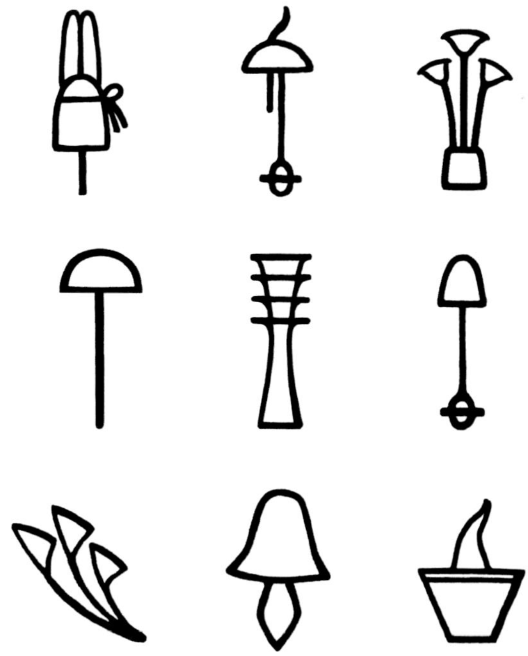

Figure 4. Hieroglyphic signs commonly identified as mushrooms on the basis of appearance. Image A. Sinclair.

sculptor who claimed to have been an Egyptian priest.[77] Unlike opium and cannabis, however, this topic has never had any traction within Egyptology, due to the unfortunate absence of evidence. Basically, no lexical term for any mushroom has been identified for pharaonic Egypt[78], always bearing in mind that fungi might reside among the words that remain unidentified. Therefore, this absence provides a singular handicap to citing texts or lexical proposals.

Nonetheless we begin with a legend of Egyptology, Ernest A. T. W. Budge, whose influence on fringe Egyptology is gigantic, not least because his books have been repeatedly published. As a result, he is the source of many claims about psychoactives in Egypt. In the early twentieth century narratives regarding the consumption of a Golden Bough or plant of immortality have been a mainstay of alternative publications, and in Budge's *Gods of the Egyptians* a plant of life is mentioned as eaten by the gods.[79] Because of the unclear reading, the assumed Classical and biblical undertones, and the connection to divinity it is a staple for this topic in alternative narratives.[80]

---

77 Jacobsen 2017, Ch. 2: 'The Puharich Theory', see also Sinclair 2018 and Sinclair 2022 for reviews of Berlant 2005 and Puharich 1959.

78 The exception being proposals for yeast (*srm.t*) and the grain parasite ergot (*ṯḥf*), see Hannig/Vomberg 1999, and *TLÄ Lemmata*. There is no reason to assume, however, that the ancient Egyptians were able to perceive a biological relation between mushrooms proper, fungal parasites and the microbe yeast.

79 'According to one myth the gods themselves lived upon a "wood, or plant of life" ... (Pepi I, line 430)', Budge 1904, I, 164, citing PT 51. See Allen/Der Manuelian 2005, Utterance 467, 'plant of life', or Mercer 1952, line 1216d, 'tree of life', Klotz 2006, 30, 'wood of life'.

80 Plant of Life/Immortality: Puharich 1959, 29 and 32; Arthur 2000, 19 and 28; Berlant 2005, 286; Dubay 2013, 265; Lloyd 2016; for mycological/medical publications see e.g. Kotowski 2019, 4; McHugh 2015; Shamtsyan 2011, 76; Smith et al. 2005, 328.

Budge's translation of the Book of the Dead is also cited as evidence that mushrooms were this 'Food of the Gods'.[81] Similarly, reference may be made to the Pyramid Texts and a spell from Chapter 17 of the Book of the Dead to argue that the Eye of Horus was a magic mushroom.[82] In alternative Egyptology the latter translation, now redundant, has been seamlessly reinterpreted through the assumption that any divine food must be a mushroom, because Budge translated faience as 'saffron' and later in the verse this 'food' is described as the Eye of Horus.[83] The Cannibal Spell from the Pyramid Texts is also used to argue that the red crown was a *P. cubensis*, because the deceased king purportedly consumes this.[84]

The story of Rededjet from the Westcar Papyrus[85] is also proposed, in which gods officiate at the birth of three kings and afterwards hide crowns in a pot of barley.[86] Berlant has argued that because *P. cubensis* can be sprouted in moist grain[87], the crowns must be mushrooms.[88] This deft identification by association is also applied to the scarab beetle, where it is rationalised that because dung beetles and *P. cubensis* are both associated with dung they are related.[89] These approaches are then extended to embrace cattle and wheat symbolism almost in their entirety.[90] But it does not stop there: alternative culture has leant heavily on Egyptian symbolism to argue for psychoactive mushrooms' value. But the attempt to identify a hieroglyph is, again, an elaborate exercise in subjectivity, where any sign that may resemble a stereotypical mushroom is proposed[91] and Egyptologists are derided for not recognising the obvious (fig. 4).[92] In the same vein, in monumental art any mushroom-like object is identified as such, with a wide range of results.[93] This is done in defiance of the known meanings of these symbols, presumably as a solution to the fact that there is no evidence for mushrooms from Egypt.

---

81 For Food of the Gods see Budge 1904, II, 62, who names *'tchefaut' (ḏfꜣw)*, which is now translated as 'provisions' or 'sustenance' and will have constituted the foodstuffs that were daily offered on behalf of the king to the gods in temples, see *TLÄ Lemmata*, Faulkner 1981; Hannig/Vomberg 1998.

82 'The gods nourished themselves with celestial food which was supplied to them by the Eye of Horus,' Budge 1904, I, 164. 'Now the cakes of saffron the eye of Horus are, now Tanenet the burial place is of Osiris,' Budge 1895, 53 plate X.

83 Eye of Horus: Berlant 2005, 286, Mabry 2000, 29; Food of Gods: Coppens 2002, Rush 2007, 87.

84 *A. muscaria*: Mabry 2000, *passim*; Klapp 2014, *passim* (citing Mabry). *P. cubensis*: Berlant 2005, 276, citing Faulkner 1998 (1969).

85 Papyrus Berlin 3033, dated to the late Middle Kingdom or 2nd Intermediate Period.

86 Berlant 2005, citing Lichtheim 1975, 220–22.

87 This is incidentally a modern growing technique.

88 Berlant 2005, 280.

89 *Kheper*, see Berlant 2005, the scarab associated with spiritual rebirth rites by Arthur 2000, 42; Puharich 1959, 130.

90 Berlant 2005, 278–79; Failla 2014, *passim*.

91 For example: the *ankh*, *djed*, *waz* sceptre, a fan, chisel, papyrus clump, drill, Abydos and Amentet standards.

92 Berlant 2005, 287; Berlant 2019a, 11; Failla 2014, 8; Arthur 2000, 42.

93 For example: the solar and Aten disks, lotus leaves, lotus flowers, incense burners, cult vessels, and capitals of temple pillars are interpreted as mushrooms.

Conclusion

While our current knowledge is not comprehensive, we are in possession of a large volume of evidence for herbs and medicine from Egypt. The plants under discussion here, however, only become securely traceable there from the Graeco-Roman period. I would add that often little attention is paid to the extensive literature on the use of known psychoactive plants, or indeed the popularity of alcohol as a ritual intoxicant in Egypt.[94] Instead, these are often mentioned to prop up claims of cannabis, mushroom or opium use.[95] Yet, there is in fact no unambiguous evidence from pharaonic Egypt for the psychotropic use of these. In addition, there are no confirmed lexical terms, only proposals for two. Until the names are identified these remain conjecture, and citing spells from medical papyri as confirmation is misrepresentation.

Equally, ethnocentric bias has played a significant role in past misidentification of psychoactives, like assuming that rope fibre must be hemp, or that opium will calm a colicky baby, both identifications based on culturally subjective assumptions.[96] Yet once an early misidentification or linguistic proposal such as *shepen*, *khasyt* or *shemshemet* is perpetuated in publications it becomes an embedded fact in media beyond Egyptology.

Nonetheless, I am aware that many of the claims described in this paper may appear flawed to Egyptologists and are easily dismissed as ridiculous. They are no laughing matter though, as academic publications have provided the foundation for these discussions, and the false narratives are widely distributed in popular culture. Furthermore, it is not uncommon to find these claims cited in otherwise legitimate publications, and this will continue as long as we do not address these topics in public fora.

Bibliography

Abel, E. L., 1980, *Marihuana: The First Twelve Thousand Years*, New York.

Aleff, H. P., 2015, 'Maat Soul-mate Seshat Convicted for Possessing Pot and Undeclared Math', in *Recovered Science*, http://www.recoveredscience.com/const289seshatemblem.htm (accessed: April 2022).

Allegro, J. M., 1973, *The Sacred Mushroom and the Cross*, rev. ed., London.

Allen, J. P., Der Manuelian, P., 2005, *The Ancient Egyptian Pyramid Texts*, Atlanta.

Allen, J. P., 2014, *Middle Egyptian: An Introduction to the Language and Culture of Hieroglyphs*, Cambridge.

Arata, L., 2004, 'Nepenthes and Cannabis in Ancient Greece', in *Janus Head*, 7(1), 34–49.

Arie, E., Rosen, B., Namdar, D., 2020, 'Cannabis and Frankincense at the Judahite Shrine of Arad', in *Journal of the Institute of Archaeology of Tel Aviv University*, 47(1), 5-28.

Arora, D., 1986, *Mushrooms Demystified: A Comprehensive Guide to the Fleshy Fungi*, Berkeley.

Arthur, J., 2000, *Mushrooms and Mankind: A Brief Introduction to Ethnomycology*, California.

Attia, V. I., 2017, 'Cannabis (Marijuana-hemp) in Ancient Egypt', unpublished paper via @ ResearchGate, https://www.researchgate.net/publication/321420351_Cannabis_marijuana-_hemp_in_Ancient_Egypt (accessed: May 2021).

94 Szpakowska 2003, 228; Samorini 2019, 68; Sanchez/Harer 2019, 80.

95 See Berlant 2005, 275; Brown/Brown 2016, 35, citing Emboden 1979, 12.

96 Ryan 1985.

Balabanova, S., Parsche, F., Pirsig, W., 1992, 'First Identification of Drugs in Egyptian Mummies', in *Naturwissenschaften* 79, 358.

Bedigian, D., 1985, 'Is se-gis-i sesame or flax?', in *Bulletin on Sumerian Agriculture*, 2, 159–78.

Bedigian, D., 2004, 'History and Lore of Sesame in Southwest Asia', in *Economic Botany*, 58(3), 329–53.

Bennett, C., 2010, *Cannabis and the Soma Solution*, Walterville, OR.

Bennett, C., 2021, 'Shemshemet: Cannabis in Ancient Egypt', published on https://www.cannabisculture.com/content/2021/02/18/shemshemet-cannabis-in-ancient-egypt/ (accessed: April 2022).

Bennett, C., McQueen, N., 2013, 'Cannabis and the Hebrew Bible', in Rush, J. A. (ed.), 2013, *Entheogens and the Development of Culture*, California, 51–84.

Berlant, S., 2005, 'The Entheomycological Origin of Egyptian Crowns', in *Journal of Ethnopharmacology*, 102, 275–88.

Bisset, N. G., Bruhn, J. G., Zenke, M. H., 1996, 'The Presence of Opium in a 3,500 Year Old Base-Ring Juglet', in *Ägypten und Levante*, 6, 203–4.

Borojevic, K., Mountain, R., 2011, 'The Ropes of Pharaohs: The Source of Cordage from "Rope Cave" at Mersa/Wadi Gawasis Revisited', in *JARCE*, 47, 131–41.

Borojevic, K., Mountain, R., 2013, 'Microscopic Identification and Sourcing of Ancient Egyptian Plant Fibres Using Longitudinal Thin Sectioning', in *Archaeometry*, 55(1), 1–32.

Breasted, J. H., 1980, *The Edwin Smith Surgical Papyrus* I, *Oriental Institute Publications* III, reprint, Chicago.

Brotteaux, P., 1967, 'The Ancient Greeks', in Andrews, G. (ed.), 1967, *The Book of Grass: An Anthology on Indian Hemp*, New York, 12–13.

Brown, J. B., Brown, J. M., 2016, *The Psychedelic Gospels: The Secret History of Hallucinogens in Christianity*, New York.

Brownstein, M. J., 1993, 'A Brief History of Opiates, Opioid Peptides and Opioid Receptors', in *Proceedings of the National Academy of Sciences*, 90(12), 5391–3.

Brugsch, H., 1868, *Hieroglyphisch-Demotisches Wörterbuch IV*, Leipzig.

Brugsch, H., 1880, *Hieroglyphisch-Demotisches Wörterbuch V*, Leipzig.

Brunner, T. F., 1973, 'Marijuana in Ancient Greece and Rome? The Literary Evidence', in *Bulletin of the History of Medicine*, 47(4), 344–55.

Brunton, G., 1937, *Mostagedda and the Tasian Culture*, London.

Brusco, R., 2017, 'A Versatile Plant: What Were the Many Uses of Cannabis in Egypt?' Published on https://www.ancient-origins.net/history-ancient-traditions/versatile-plant-what-were-many-uses-cannabis-ancient-egypt-007733 (accessed: March 2021).

Bryan, C. P., 1930, *The Papyrus Ebers: Translated from the German Version*, London.

Buckland, P. C., Panagiotakapolu, E., 2001, 'Ramses II and the Tobacco Beetle', in *Antiquity*, 75, 549–56.

Budge, E. A. T. W., 1895, *The Book of the Dead: The Papyrus of Ani in the British Museum*, London.

Budge, E. A. T. W., 1904, *The Gods of the Egyptians: Or Studies in Egyptian Mythology*, London.

Budge, E. A. T. W., 1920, *An Egyptian Hieroglyphic Dictionary*, London.

Bunimovitz, S., Lederman, Z., 2016, 'Opium or Oil? Late Bronze Age Cypriot Base Ring Juglets and International Trade Revisited', in *Antiquity*, 90(354), 1552-61.

Carlin, M. G., Dean, J. R., Ames, J. M., 2020, 'Opium Alkaloids in Harvested and Thermally Processed Poppy Seeds', in *Frontiers in Chemistry*, 8(737), 1–9.

Carod-Artal, F. J., 2013, 'Psychoactive Plants in Ancient Greece', in *Neurosciences and History,* 1(1), 28–38.

Chassinat, É., 1950, 'Deux formules pharmaceutiques coptes', in *Bulletin de l'Institut français d'archéologie orientale* 49, 9–22.

Chovanec, Z., Bunimovitz, S., Lederman, Z., 2015, 'Is there Opium Here? An Analysis of Cypriot Base Ring Ware Juglets from Tel Beth-Shemesh, Israel', in *Mediterranean Archaeology and Archaeometry,* 15(2), 175–89.

Chovanec, Z., 2019, 'Examining the History of the Opium Poppy in the Eastern Mediterranean and Central Europe', in *Open Archem,* published on https://openarchem.com/2019/04/07/examining-the-history-of-the-opium-poppy-in-the-eastern-mediterranean-and-central-europe/ (accessed: April 2022).

Clarke, R. C., Merlin, M. D., 2013, *Cannabis: Evolution and Ethnobotany*, Berkeley, Los Angeles & London.

Coppens, P., 2002, 'Are Mushrooms the Real Food of the Gods? Does it Contain a Hallucinogenic Substance that was Known and Used by Ancient Cultures and its Priests to Gain Access to the World of the Gods?' Published on https://www.eyeofthepsychic.com/mushrooms/ (accessed: March 2022).

Counsell, D. J., 2008, 'Intoxicants in Ancient Egypt? Opium, Nymphaea, Coca, and Tobacco', in David, R. (ed.), 2008, *Egyptian Mummies and Modern Science,* Cambridge, 211–5.

Dawson, W., 1934, 'Studies in Egyptian Medical Texts III', in *Journal of Egyptian Archaeology*, 19, 41–46.

Deines, H. von, Grapow, H., Westendorf, W., 1958, *Grundriss der Medizin der alten* Ägypter IV. Übersetzung *der medizinischen Texte*, Berlin.

Deines, H. von, Grapow, H., 1959, *Grundriss der Medizin der alten* Ägypter VI. *Wörterbuch der ägyptischen Drogennamen*, Berlin.

Diggle, J. (ed.), 2021, *The Cambridge Greek Lexicon*, Cambridge.

Dormandy, T., 2012, *Opium: Reality's Dark Dream*, New Haven and London.

Duarte, D. F., 2005, 'Opium and Opioids: A Brief History', in *Revista Braziliera de Anastesiologia,* 55(1), 135–46.

Dubay, E., 2013, *The Atlantean Conspiracy: Exposing the Global Conspiracy from Atlantis to Zion*, Lulu.

Ebbell, B., 1937, *The Papyrus Ebers: The Greatest Egyptian Medical Document*, London.

Ebers, G., 1885, *Papyros Ebers. Das Hermetische Buch über die Arzeneimittel der alten Ägypter*, Leipzig.

Ebeid, N., 1999, *Egyptian Medicine in the Days of the Pharaohs*, Cairo.

Emboden, W.A., 1979, *Narcotic Plants*, Michigan.

Erman, A., 1894, *Life in Ancient Egypt*, London.

Erman, A., Grapow, H., 1921, *Ägyptisches Handwörterbuch*, Berlin.

Escohodato, A., 2010, *The General History of Drugs* I, Chile.

Failla, N., 2014, 'A Contemporary View on Ancient Egyptian Royal Motifs as Referencing *P. cubensis'*, unpublished anthropology paper, Colorado State University (via https://www.academia.edu/10089593/Ancient_Egyptian_Royal_Motifs_as_referencing_P_Cubensis, accessed: January 2021).

Faulkner, R. O., 1969, *The Ancient Egyptian Pyramid Texts*, Oxford.

Faulkner, R. O., 1981, *A Concise Dictionary of Middle Egyptian*, Oxford.

Flascha, C., 2011, 'On Opium: Its History, Legacy, and Cultural Benefits', in *Prospect Journal*, University of California, via https://prospect-journal.org/2011/05/25/on-opium-its-history-legacy-and-cultural-benefits/ (accessed: March 2022).

Feagans, C., 2018, 'New World Drugs on Old World Mummies', Archaeology Review blog, published on https://ahotcupofjoe.net/2018/05/new-world-drugs-and-old-world-mummies/ (accessed: April 2022).

Gabra, S., 1956, 'Papaver Species and Opium through the Ages', *Bulletin de l'Institut d'Égypte*, 37, 39–56.

Germer, R., 1979, *Untersuchung über Arzneimittelpflanzen im alten Ägypten*, Hamburg.

Germer, R., 2008, *Handbuch der altägyptischen Heilpflanzen*, Wiesbaden.

Ghalioungui, P., 1987, *The Ebers Papyrus*, Cairo.

Girard, M., 1987, 'Étude palynologique', in *Nouvelles archives du Muséum d'histoire naturelle de Lyon* 25, 103–10.

Guerra-Doce, E., 2015, 'The Origins of Inebriation: Archaeological Evidence of the Consumption of Fermented Beverages and Drugs in Prehistoric Eurasia', in *Journal of Archaeological Method and Theory*, 22(3), 751-82.

Guzman, G., Allen, J. W., Gartz, J., 1998, 'A Worldwide Geographical Distribution of the Neurotropic Fungi, an Analysis and Discussion', in *Annali del Museo Civico di Rovereto* 14, 189-280.

Hall, I. R., Stephenson, S. L., Buchanan, P. K., Yun, W., Cole, A. L. J., 2003, *Edible and Poisonous Mushrooms of the World*, Portland & Cambridge.

Halpern, J.H., Blistein, D., 2019, *Opium: How an Ancient Flower Shaped and Poisoned Our World*, Boston & New York.

Hannig, R., Vomberg, P., 1999, *Wortschatz der Pharaonen in Sachgruppen*, Mainz.

Hanuš, L., 2009, 'Pharmacological and Therapeutic Secrets of Plant and Brain (Endo) Cannabinoids', in *Medical and Research Reviews*, 29(2), 212–72.

Harer, W. B., 2015, 'The Marijuana Myth in Ancient Egypt', in *JARCE*, 51, 356–7.

Hartman, B., 2019, 'Marijuana in Ancient Times: A History of Cannabis', published on https://cannigma.com/history/from-ma-to-cbd-history-of-medical-cannabis/ (accessed: April 2022).

Hilliard, B., 2018, 'Legalized Marijuana: Canada Comes Round to the Wisdom of Ages', published on https://www.ancient-origins.net/history/cannabis-journey-through-ages-003084 (accessed: March 2021).

Jacobsen, A., 2017. *Phenomena: The Secret History of the U.S. Government's Investigations into Extrasensory Perception*, New York and London.

Joachim, H., 1890, *Papyros Ebers. Das älteste Buch über Heilkunde*, Berlin.

Jouanna, J., 2012, *Greek Medicine from Hippocrates to Galen: Selected Papers*, Leiden.

Kabelik, J., 1955, *Hemp as a Medicant, Acta Universtatis Palackianae Olomucensis*, 4, Olomouc.

Kapoor, L. D., 1995, *Opium Poppy: Botany, Chemistry, and Pharmacology*, New York and London.

Kearney, M. V., 2019, 'Cocaine Mummies and the Search for Narcotics in Historic Collections', published on https://blogs.ucl.ac.uk/researchers-in-museums/2019/04/20/cocaine-mummies-the-search-for-narcotics-in-historic-collections/ (accessed: April 2022).

Keimer, L., 1924, *Die Gartenpflanzen im alten Ägypten I*, Munich.

Klapp, E., 2014, 'Der rituelle Gebrauch von psychoaktiven Pilzen bei den alten Ägyptern', in Bauer, W. (ed.), 2014, *Der Fliegenpilz. Geheimnisvoll, giftig und heilsam*, Aarau and München, 104.

Klotz, D., 2006, *Adoration of the Ram: Five Hymns to Amun-Re from Hibis Temple*, New Haven.

Kotowski, M. A., 2019, 'History of Mushroom Consumption and its Impact on Traditional View on Mycobiota: An Example from Poland', in *Microbial Biosystems Journal*, 4(3), 1–13.

Laessoe, T., Petersen, J.H., 2019, *Fungi of Temperate Europe*, Princeton and Oxford.

Ledger, E., 2021, 'Cannabis Use in the Ancient World: Ancient Egypt', published on https://canex.co.uk/cannabis-use-in-ancient-world-ancient-egypt/ (accessed: April 2022).

Lefebvre, G., 1956, *Essai sur la médecine Égyptienne de l'époque pharaonique*, Paris.

Leroi-Gourhan, A., 1985, 'Les pollens et l'embaumement', in Balout, L., Roubet, C. (eds.), 1985, *La momie de Ramsès II: recherches sur les civilisations*, Paris, 162–65.

Lewin, L., 1998, *Phantastica: A Classic Survey on the Use and Abuse of Mind-Altering Plants*, English reprint, Vermont.

Liddell, H. G., Scott, R., 2000, *An Intermediate Greek Lexicon*, 7th edition, Oxford.

Lichtheim, M., 1975, *Ancient Egyptian Literature I: The Old and Middle Kingdoms*, Berkeley, Los Angeles, London.

Lloyd, E. 2016, 'Mysterious Ancient Mushrooms in Myths and Legends: Sacred, Feared and Worshiped among Ancient Civilizations', published on https://www.ancientpages.com/2016/09/14/mysterious-ancient-mushrooms-in-myths-and-legends-sacred-feared-and-worshiped-among-ancient-civilizations-2/ (accessed: May 2021).

Loeben, C. E., Kappel, S., 2009, *Die Pflanzen im altägyptischen Garten: Ein Bestandskatalog der ägyptischen Sammlung im Museum August Kestner*, Rahden, Westfalen.

Loret, V., 1888, 'La flore pharaonique d'après les documents hiéroglyphiques et les spécimens découverts dans les tombes', in *Annales de la Société botanique de Lyon*, 15, *Notes et Memoires*, 1–64.

Lucas, A., Harris, J.R., 1999, *Ancient Egyptian Materials and Industries*, New York.

Lupoi, J. S., 2020, 'Cannabis in Ancient Egypt', in *Terpenes and Testing Magazine*, published on https://terpenesandtesting.com/cannabis-in-ancient-egypt/ (accessed: March 2021).

Lüring, H. L. E., 1888, *Die über die medizinischen Kenntnisse der alten Ägypter berichtenden Papyri verglichen mit den medizinischen Schriften griechischer und römischer Autoren*, Leipzig.

Mabry, M., 2000, 'Osiris: Eine Reidentifikation', in Bauer, W. (ed.)., 2000, *Der Fliegenpilz: Traumkult, Märchenzauber, Mythenrausch*, Aarau and München, 23–30.

Manniche, L., 2006, *An Ancient Egyptian Herbal*, London.

Martin, G. T., 1989, *The Royal Tomb at El-'Amarna I: Objects*, London.

McHugh, A. M., 2015, 'Mushrooms in History: Ancient Greece and Egypt', published on https://www.crazyaboutmushrooms.com/2015/05/27/mushrooms-history-greeks-egyptians/ (accessed: March 2022).

Mercer, S. A. B., 1952, *The Pyramid Texts*, Toronto.

Merlin, M. D., 2003, 'Archaeological Evidence for the Tradition of Psychoactive Plant Use in the Old World', in *Economic Botany*, 57(3), 295–323.

Nayar, N. M., Mehra, K. L., 1970, 'Sesame: Its Uses, Botany, Cytogenics, and Origin', in *Economic Botany* 24(1), 20-31.

Nicholson, P. T., Shaw, I., 2000, *Ancient Egyptian Materials and Technology*, Cambridge.

Nunn, J. F., 2006, *Ancient Egyptian Medicine*, London.

Peet, T. E., Woolley, L., 1923, *The City of Akhenaten I: Excavations of 1921 and 1922 at El-'Amarneh*, London.

Piankoff, A., 1968, *Egyptian Religious Texts and Representations 5: The Pyramid of Unas*, Princeton.

Pomeroy, L., 2012, 'The Addictive History of Medicine: Opium, The Poor Child's Nurse', published on https://blog.sciencemuseum.org.uk/the-addictive-history-of-medicine-opium-the-poor-childs-nurse/ (accessed: March 2022).

Popko, L., 2021, 'Der Inhalt des Papyrus Ebers. Eine Lesehilfe', in Popko, L., Schneider, U. J., Scholl, R. (eds.), 2021, *Papyrus Ebers. Die Größte Schriftrolle zur altägyptischen Heilkunst*, Darmstadt, 34–53.

Popko, L., 2022, 'Papyrus Ebers', published on https://sae.saw-leipzig.de/de/dokumente/papyrus-ebers (accessed: March 2022).

Puharich, A., 1959, *The Sacred Mushroom: Key to the Door to Eternity*, New York.

Rawlinson, R., 1996, *The Great Book of Hemp: The Complete Guide to the Environmental, Commercial, and Medicinal Uses of the World's Most Extraordinary Plant*, Vermont.

Reichardt, H. W., 1859, 'Übersicht der Pflanzen des alten Ägypten. Nach Vorträgen des Herrn Professor Dr. Franz Unger', in Österreichische Botanische Zeitschrift, 9(5), 145–53.

Ren, M., Tang, Z., Wu, X., Spengler, R., Jiang, H., Yang, Y., Boivin, N., 2019, 'The Origins of Cannabis Smoking: Chemical Residue Evidence from the First Millennium BCE in the Pamirs', in *Science Advances*, 5(6), 1–8.

Rosso, A. M., 2010, 'Poppy and Opium in Ancient Times: Remedy or Narcotic?', in *Biomedicine International*, 1, 81–7.

Ruck, C. A. P., Bigwood, J., Staples, D., Ott, J., Wasson, R. G., 1979, 'Entheogens', in *Journal of Psychedelic Drugs*, 11, 145–6.

Rush, J. A., 2007, *The Twelve Gates: A Spiritual Passage through the Egyptian Books of the Dead*, California.

Russo, E. B., 2007, 'History of Cannabis and Its Preparations in Saga, Science, and Sobriquet', in *Chemistry and Biodiversity*, 4, 1614–48.

Ryan, D. P., 1985, 'Misidentification of Ancient Egyptian Plant Fibres', in *Varia Aegyptiaca*, 1, 143–9.

Samorini, G., 2019, 'The Oldest Archaeological Data Evidencing the Relationship of *Homo Sapiens* with Psychoactive Plants: A Worldwide Overview', in *Journal of Psychedelic Studies*, 3(2), 63–68.

Sanchez, G., Harer Jr., W. B., 2019, 'Toxicology in Ancient Egypt', in Wexler, I. P. (ed.), 2019, *Toxicology in Antiquity*, London, 73–82.

Saunders, N. J., 2013, *The Poppy: A Cultural History from Ancient Egypt to Flanders Fields to Afghanistan*, London.

Schiff, P. L., 2002, 'Opium and its Alkaloids', in *American Journal of Pharmaceutical Education*, 66, 186–94.

Scholl, R., 2021, 'Georg Ebers. Forschungsreisender, Hochschullehrer, Promotor', in Popko, L., Schneider, U. L., Scholl, R. (eds.), 2021, *Papyrus Ebers. Die Größte Schriftrolle zur altägyptischen Heilkunst*, Darmstadt, 14–33.

Shamtsyan, M., 2011, 'Bioactive Compounds in Mushrooms', in *Encyclopedia of Biotechnology in Agriculture and Food*, 1(1), 76–81.

Sherratt, A., 2007, 'Alcohol and its Alternatives', in Goodman, J., Lovejoy, P. E., Sherratt, A. (eds.), 2007, *Consuming Habits: Global and Historical Perspectives on How Cultures Define Drugs*, 2nd edition, New York, 11–45.

Shmakov, T. T., 2012, *Critical Analysis of J. P. Allen's «The Ancient Egyptian Pyramid Texts»*, Omsk-Tricht.

Sinclair, A., 2018, review of Berlant 2005, 'The Entheomycological Origin of Egyptian Crowns', published on https://artisticlicenseorwhyitrustnoone.blogspot.com/2018/09/high-times-egyptian-princesses-picking.html.

Sinclair, A., 2022, 'Psychoactives in Ancient Egypt: The Mushroom Myths', published on https://artisticlicenseorwhyitrustnoone.blogspot.com/2022/03/psychoactives-in-ancient-egypt-mushroom.html.

Smith, J. E., Sullivan, R., Rowan, N., 2005, 'Mushrooms and Cancer Therapy', in *Biologist*, 52(6), 328-36.

Smith, R. K., Stacey, R. J., Bergström, E., Thomas-Oates, J., 2018, 'Detection of Opium Alkaloids in a Cypriot Base-Ring Juglet', in *Analyst*, 143, 5127–36.

Stamets, P., 1999, *Psilocybinpilze der Welt. Ein praktischer Führer zur sicheren Bestimmung*, Aarau.

Stefano, G. B., Pilonis, N., Ptacek, R., Kream, R. M., 2017, 'Reciprocal Evolution of Opiate Science from Medical and Cultural Perspectives', in *Medical Science Monitor*, 23, 2890–6.

Szpakowska, K., 2003, 'Altered States: An Inquiry into the Possible Use of Narcotics or Alcohol to Induce Dreams in Pharaonic Egypt', in Ayma, A. K., Bennett, C. J. (eds.), 2003, *A Delta-Man in Yebu, Occasional Volume of the Egyptologists' Electronic Forum* 1, USA, 225–37.

Tchakarov, V., 2021, 'Here's How the Ancient Egyptians Used Hemp and Cannabis 3500 Years Ago', published on https://curiosmos.com/heres-how-the-ancient-egyptians-used-hemp-and-cannabis-3500-years-ago/ (accessed: March 2022).

Tully, C. F., 2020, 'Did Women Use Cannabis as Medicine in Ancient Egypt?', published on https://www.leafly.com/news/lifestyle/did-women-use-cannabis-medicine-ancient-egypt (accessed: March 2021).

Varvatan, C. de, Arakelyan, A., Asensi Amorós, V., 2010, *Codex of Ancient Egyptian Plant Remains*, 2nd edition, London.

Veldmeijer, A. J., 2009, 'Cordage Production', in Wendrich, W., 2009, *UCLA Encyclopedia of Egyptology*, published on http//digital2.library.ucla/viewitem.do?ark=21198/zz001ndr4n (accessed: February 2021).

Vogelsang-Eastwood, G., 2000, 'Textiles', in Nicholson, P. T., Shaw, I. (eds.)., 2000, *Ancient Egyptian Materials and Technology*, Cambridge, 268–98.

Warf, B., 2014, 'High Points: An Historical Geography of Cannabis', in *Geographical Review*, 104(4), 414–38.

Wink, M., 1998, 'A Short History of the Alkaloids', in Roberts, M. F., Wink, M. (eds.), *Alkaloids: Biochemistry, Ecology, and Medicinal Applications*, New York, 11–44.

Wönig, F., 1897, *Die Pflanzen im alten Aegypten. Ihre Heimat, Geschichte, Kultur und ihre mannigfache Verwendung im sozialen Leben in Kultus, Sitten, Gebräuchen, Medizin, Kunst*, Leipzig.

Wrona, T., 2019, 'Ancient Egypt's Rich History of Medical Cannabis', published on https://cannigma.com/history/egypt-has-a-rich-medical-cannabis-history-discover-why/ (accessed: March 2021).

Digital resources

CBS Drug News, 2002, 'Ancient Drug Trade Unearthed', https://www.cbsnews.com/news/ancient-drug-trade-unearthed/ (accessed: March 2022).

Celestial Musings blog, 2018, 'Ancient Alien Goddesses: The Egyptian Hemp Goddess', https://ancientaliengoddesses.com/2018/01/18/the-egyptian-hemp-goddess/ (accessed: March 2022).

Diodorus Siculus, *Bibliotheca Historica*, trans. C. H. Oldfather, 1933, *Loeb Classical Library* I @ University of Chicago, Penelope, https://penelope.uchicago.edu/Thayer/E/Roman/Texts/Diodorus_Siculus/1D*.html (accessed: April 2022).

History.com, 2017, 'Heroin, Morphine and Opiates', https://www.history.com/topics/crime/history-of-heroin-morphine-and-opiates (accessed: March 2022).

Green entrepreneur/Dispensaries.com, 2021, 'This Is How Scholars Think Ancient Egyptians Used Cannabis 3,500 Years Ago', https://www.greenentrepreneur.com/article/364054?fbclid=IwAR2u9sn96SgIXv59cCO94Qf4Bl_3nHBzWkESVwhQ41xOKe5S_MjVbb9kXxI (accessed: March 2022).

Herodotus, *The Histories*, trans. A. D. Godley, 1920, Perseus Digital Library, http://www.perseus.tufts.edu/hopper/text?doc=Perseus%3Atext%3A1999.01.0126%3Abook%3D4%3Achapter%3D75%3Asection%3D1 (accessed: April 2022).

Homer, *Odyssey*, trans. A. T. Murray, 1919, Perseus Digital Library, http://www.perseus.tufts.edu/hopper/text?doc=Perseus%3Atext%3A1999.01.0135%3Abook%3D4%3Acard%3D219 (accessed: April 2022).

Milo @ Teen Witch website: 'Cannabis', http://www.teenwitch.com/plants/cannabaceae/cannabis.html (accessed: March 2022).

Papyrus Ebers – Albertina Library, University of Leipzig https://papyrusebers.de/en/.

SAE.SAW – Science in Ancient Egypt, Papyrus Ebers, trans. L. Popko (Eng. A. Sinclair) https://sae.saw-leipzig.de/de/dokumente/papyrus-ebers.

TLÄ (Thesaurus Linguae Ägyptiae*). Lemmata* https://aaew.bbaw.de/tla/servlet/BwlSearch?u=guest&f=0&l=0&db=0.

About the author

Andrea Sinclair obtained a BA in classics and archaeology at the University of Melbourne in 2008, subsequently completing an MA in eastern Mediterranean archaeology there. In 2012 she began a PhD in Egyptology at the University of Leipzig. The dissertation focused on New Kingdom Egyptian visual hybridity and was successfully defended in early 2018. Since 2019 she has been collaborating with the *Science in Ancient Egypt* website and the *Thesaurus Linguae Aegyptiae* on English translation projects for digital German editions of the Ebers Papyrus and the *TLÄ* hieroglyphic lexicon. This work has resulted in an interest in the misrepresentation of Egyptian drugs in contemporary media.

Figure 1. Detail of fig. 4a.

Batman and the Book of the Dead

Alternative Egyptology or 'Just for Fun'?

Arnaud Quertinmont

Introduction

This contribution aims to give a general overview of the presence of Egyptian gods in comic books. What different ways are there to integrate them into the plot of a story? It turns out that several mechanisms exist, but it is the use of the 'ancient astronauts' that seems to have the preference of the authors and the cartoonists.

Egyptian gods in comic books

Comic books appeared in the United States at the beginning of the 1930s.[1] These periodicals were generally around thirty pages long and focused either on a particular theme or on a hero. Some superheroes who have become world-famous, such as Superman (1938) and Batman (1939), were created at this time. From the outset, ancient Egypt became the backdrop for certain plots, including the origins of Hawkman (*Flash Comics* vol. 1 #1, January 1940) and Dynaman (*Daring Mystery Comics* vol. 1 #6, September 1940). We would have to wait until the 1960s and the revival of the genre, however, before the realms of Egyptian gods and the myths associated with them would be fully exploited, for example in *The Eye of Horus* (*Blue Beetle* vol. 3 #54, March 1966). Most of the time, it was the divinity's iconography that was of interest to authors and illustrators and not realistic contextualisation. Let us take, for instance, the mutant X-Factor team who have to confront Ammit, the Great Devourer (*All New X-Factor* vol. 1 #19, March 2015). The emphasis is on the animal's monstrous character. Sometimes, the tale borders on slapstick, as in the episode where Superman fights with the frog goddess Heqet, who has come to destroy the world in reprisal for the thousands of amphibians that are dissected in American highschools every year (*Action Comics* #768, August 2000). The depiction of hybrid divinities provides a fertile ground for the illustrator's imagination.

Travelling through time and the universe are also good excuses to incorporate Egyptian divinities into the story. Sometimes, the myth itself does not play a role in the story, as with the battle pitting Batman and Robin against Anubis (*Batman Odyssey* #4, January 2012),

1 For the history of comic books: Gabilliet 2005.

in Van den Bercken, B. J. L. (ed.), *Alternative Egyptology: Critical Essays on the Relation between Academic and Alternative Interpretations of Ancient Egypt*, Leiden, pp. 96–105.

Figure 2. Cat-headed Hathor purring with love (*Heroic Age: Prince of Power* #3, July 2010).

and sometimes it is revisited whilst retaining its fundamental lore. Thus we have Thor and Amadeus Cho clashing with Sekhmet, the fearsome lion goddess (*Heroic Age: Prince of Power* #3, July 2010). The story in the comic refers to Ra's shrewdness and the use of beer.[2] As the heroes do not have the time to brew beer, though, they use chloral hydrate as a sedative. This substance is also known as a Mickey Finn, taken from the name of the barman who used to drug his customers so that he could rob them. In any case, the use of this substance succeeds in transforming Sekhmet into... Hathor, goddess of love, as it is written in the comic. In all likelihood for graphic and humorous purposes, it was the feline form of Bastet that was chosen instead. The goddess is purring now—literally—with love for Thor, that proud, valiant, divine warrior (fig. 2).

If one puts aside the purely entertaining aspect of putting ancient Egypt into comics, what status is accorded to alternative tales and, more importantly, how can one gauge their impact on society?

Ancient astronauts

Egyptian divinities are incorporated into comic-book story lines that are consistent with the ancient-astronaut theory. *The Gods of Heliopolis* is an example (*Thor* #240, October 1975). When humans seize power in Egypt, the gods leave Earth and move into a parallel dimension where they establish the heavenly city of Heliopolis. Like the gods of Asgard (Thor, Odin, Loki), they keep in contact with Earth by visiting it, using a golden bridge called The Way of the Gods.

The ancient-astronaut theory, like using Egypt as a story line in science fiction, is not new. A quick mention should be made of the novel by American astronomer and writer Garrett Serviss titled *Edison's Conquest of Mars*, which was published in 1898. The story portrays Edison leading a group of scientists in the development of space ships and weapons—including a disintegration ray—for defending Earth against

2 Preys 2016, 292.

extraterrestrials whom they fight in space and on Mars. When the heroes land on the red planet, they discover human slaves and find out that Martians visited Earth thousands of years ago and built colossal structures here, including the pyramids and Sphinx. Nonetheless, this work is one of pure fiction and there is no doubt that Garrett Serviss saw no basis for this in reality.[3]

It is also important to mention that from the 1920s onwards, a number of authors wrote about entities coming from other worlds that could have influenced humankind's technological development. Fundamental to these beliefs is the Cthulhu myth, dreamed up by the American Howard Phillips Lovecraft (1890–1937). Indeed, the books that established the myth, such as *The Call of the Cthulhu* (1926), conjure up these entities from another place. Invisible, buried in the depths of the Earth, oceans, space, or our reality, they remain unknown to everyone apart from some rare initiated individuals who have devoted their lives and risked their mental stability to seek out the truth.

The ancient-astronaut theory originated from the combination of two hypotheses. Firstly, following the crash of what was presented as an Unidentified Flying Object in 1947 in the Roswell Desert, New Mexico, many people became convinced that extraterrestrials visit the Earth regularly and have been doing so for ages. Secondly, some authors have relayed and reinforced the notion that ancient (and therefore non-European) civilisations could not have constructed their emblematic monuments alone (e.g. the Egyptian and Mayan pyramids), because they were far too primitive. They would have needed the help and technology of a more advanced civilisation, traditionally presented as white. The people of this advanced civilisation, identified by some as coming from Atlantis or Mu, were worshipped as gods at the time. Hence this theory, known as 'the theory of the white gods',[4] joined with the extraterrestrial hypothesis and led to the absolute conclusion that these too-primitive civilisations of Antiquity either received the help of extraterrestrials or claimed ownership of the extraterrestrials' creations. At this point, we are at the beginning of the 1960s. This line of reasoning also frequently refers back to biblical sources.[5]

The hypothesis for an extraterrestrial influence, known by the name of neo-euhemerism or the 'ancient-astronaut theory', is based on ancient depictions, archaeological features perceived as mysterious, and the literal reading of religious texts. Some esoteric societies also refer to such an extraterrestrial presence. It has become particularly popular in the West, including in the French-speaking world with such journals as *Planète* (1961–1971) by Louis Pauwels and Jacques Bergier; books by Robert Charroux, *Le Livre des maîtres du monde* and *Le Livre des secrets trahis* (*The Book of the Masters of the World* and *The Book of Betrayed Secrets*); and more broadly, the book collections *L'Aventure mystérieuse* and *Les Énigmes de l'univers* (*The Mysterious Adventure* and *The Enigmas of the Universe*). Published in the 1960s and 1970s, these works were about the mysteries of history, vanished civilisations, occult sciences, paranormal phenomena and witness accounts of life on other planets. Of course we have Swiss writer Erich von Däniken to thank for the greatest written output of the last forty years in relation to the ancient-astronaut theory[6] (fig. 3).

---

3 See the contribution of Eleanor Dobson in this volume.

4 Highly widespread with regard to South American civilisations. For a review see Solsvik/Stokke 2020.

5 Mosleth King 2022; Kolosimo 1971.

6 See especially Von Däniken 1969 and 2013. For a critical review Story 1976.

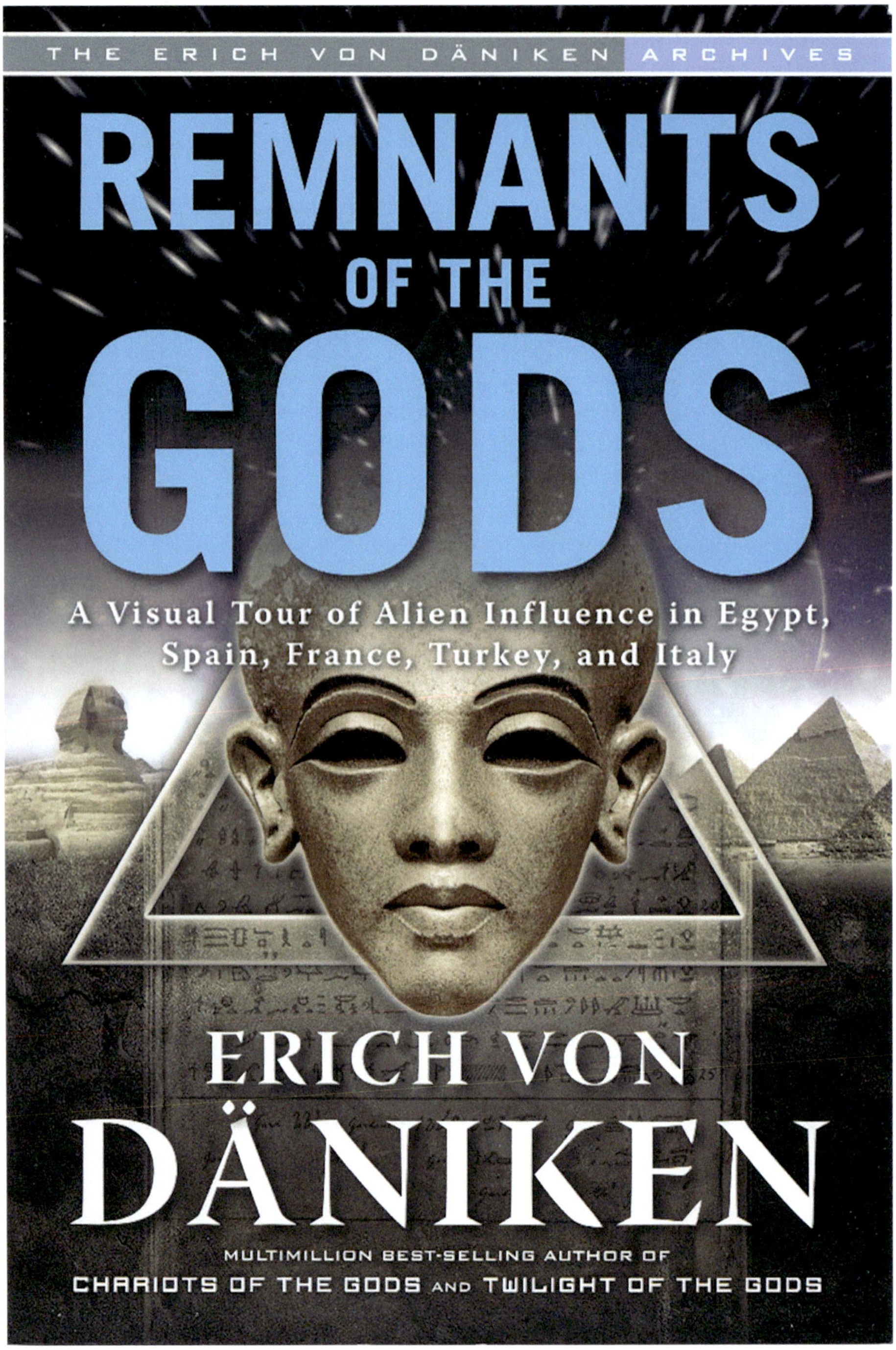

Figure 3. Cover of Erich von Däniken, *Remnants of the Gods: A Virtual Tour of Alien Influence in Egypt, Spain, France, Turkey, and Italy*, 2013.

Batman: The Book of the Dead

An excellent example of the crossroads between Egyptian mythology and the ancient-astronaut theory appears in the two volumes of *Batman: The Book of the Dead* (June-July 1999).

The Egyptian mood of the cover is provided by means of hieroglyphs and the crossed-arm position of the two characters shown (fig. 4a and b). The story contains all the essential clichés of the genre: ancient astronauts, hidden knowledge, the construction of the Great Pyramid… with all this being incorporated into the mythology of the hero of Gotham City. These various themes are common in alternative archaeology. For whatever reason, ancient civilisations possessed technological know-how that sometimes surpassed our present knowledge; consequently the theory arises that the know-how might be of extraterrestrial origin, as we have seen previously.[7] The notion of hidden knowledge and the question 'Who built the pyramids?' are equally important in alternative Egyptology, and the surpassing of our current knowledge by that of people in Antiquity can in alternative interpretation only be a sign of extraterrestrial involvement.[8]

But let us return to *Batman and the Book of the Dead*. It includes two parallel stories. The first transports us to a remote past 14,000 years ago, and tells of the dissent within a group of extraterrestrial humanoids living in Egypt. They possess technology far superior to the primitive humans, they hide behind masks—some with animal heads—and are worshipped like gods. Sensing that the end of the world is coming, they decide to leave Earth but before this, begin construction of the pyramids with the aim of hiding some of their technological expertise within. When the time comes, humans who will have evolved will discover this knowledge and be able to escape the next great cataclysm (fig. 5). One of the aliens, Seth, rebels, killing and dismembering the king, Osiris. Here, we return once again to a revamped presentation of the Egyptian myth of Isis and Osiris.

Nekhrun, who is loyal to his king, attempts to avenge him but is mortally wounded, so he shuts himself inside the Great Pyramid to watch over the knowledge hidden by Osiris. The second story takes place in our current era. It reveals to us that the parents of Bruce Wayne (Batman) had carried out excavations in Egypt and discovered a golden object there. This was the symbol of the Egyptian bat-god Nekhrun. Curiously, this god seemed absent from all known mythological reference material. Years later, Bruce Wayne understands that the murder of his parents is linked with this artefact whose appearance is exactly the same as the one he adopted to right wrongdoing. He then sets off to find the murderer of his parents, assisted by a young Egyptologist. She picks up on the ancient-astronaut theory thanks to an exposition of various items from different cultures, including Mayan civilisation (fig. 6). From then on, they both are convinced that a mysterious secret chamber lies at the heart of the Great Pyramid of Giza…

Is alternative Egyptology 'just for fun'?

Can we conclude that using the ancient-astronaut theory in a widely distributed comic-book helps the propagation of alternative theories to Egyptology and has a real impact on society and science?

---

7 Moshenska 2017, 126–28.
8 Moshenska 2017, 124–25.

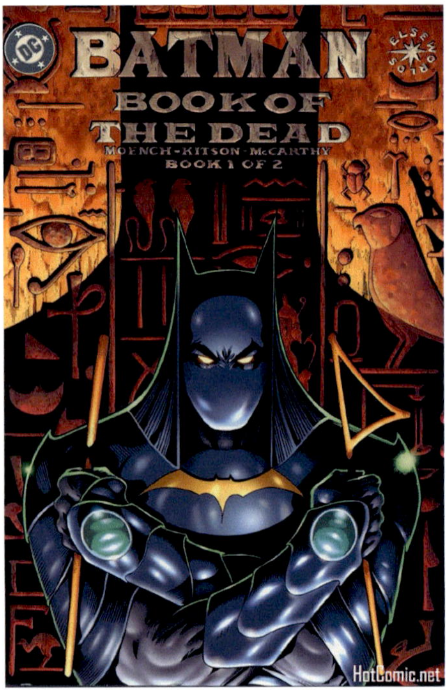

a.

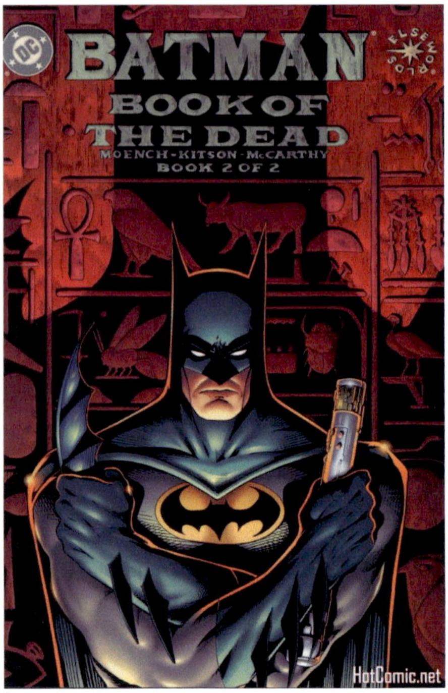

b.

Figure 4a. Cover of *Batman and the Book of the Dead*, vol. 1. Figure 4b. Cover of *Batman and the Book of the Dead*, vol. 2.

Figure 5. Humanoid in disguise in *Batman and the Book of the Dead*.

Figure 6. The proof of aliens existing on earth (from *Batman and the Book of the Dead*).

In 2016, the Musée Royal de Mariemont (Royal Museum of Mariemont) in Belgium organised an exhibition titled *Dieux, génies et démons en l'Égypte ancienne* (*Gods, Genies and Demons in Ancient Egypt*). During the preparations for the exhibition it quickly became clear that talking about Egyptian gods in popular culture, and 'geek' culture in particular, might be of interest. Therefore, we created a little exhibition called *De Stargate™ aux Comics. Les Dieux égyptiens dans la culture geek (1975–2015)*. (From *Stargate™ to Comics. Egyptian Gods in Geek Culture (1975–2015)*).[9] This exhibition also aimed to attract new visitors who do not, or only rarely, visit museums. This exhibition took the form of a short chronology in which one could drift from the atmosphere of a cabinet of curiosities to the Egyptomania of the nineteenth century and the 1960s. The first part was a small cabinet or room with items associated with the mysteries of history and vanished civilisations, such as the journal *Planète* (1961–1971) by Louis Pauwels and Jacques Bergier and the book collections *L'Aventure mystérieuse* and *Les Énigmes de l'univers* (*The Mysterious Adventure* and *The Enigmas of the Universe*).

Next to the cabinet, we played the conspiracy game by pinning some supposedly 'mysterious' discoveries on an old map (the so-called Abydos Helicopter, the Nazca Lines) and linking them up with a central point in the Atlantic Ocean, symbolising Atlantis. The next part of the exhibition focused on the comparison between Egyptian gods in certain film productions (for example, *Stargate* and *Stargate SG-1*), comics (including *Batman: The Book of the Dead*), and video games.

Some visitors who were between 50 and 70 years old recalled having read or leafed through publications associated with the journal *Planète* or *Les Énigmes de l'univers* and asked the open-ended question as to what could be true and what could remain a mystery. One felt a genuine desire to retain a certain mystery in the field of archaeology, and Egyptology in particular. Visitors aged between 35 and 50 were fascinated to explore the conspiracy map because it referred to several television series they knew, including the *X-Files*.

Once the moment of nostalgia had passed, all the visitors we asked told us that these various things only represented fiction to them and that it was limited to mere entertainment. That 'element of mystery' was reduced little by little in the face of scientific explanations intending to remove the mystique surrounding some artefacts linked to aliens (such as the Nazca lines and the Giza pyramids). Some visitors from all age groups, however, expressed their satisfaction at finally seeing a museum acknowledge some of the mystery *and* extraterrestrial/antediluvian influence in the construction of certain monuments (which was not the purpose of the exhibition at all). Even so, it was not fictional worlds such as *Stargate* or comics that inspired these thoughts but rather a selection of books, and documentaries accessible on YouTube.

From the example of *Batman: The Book of the Dead* and the museum experiment conducted in 2016, it would appear that the occurrence of the ancient-astronaut theory in works of fiction, whether films or comics, does not really contribute to the development of alternative Egyptology. Provided that these works of fiction are presented as fiction and not as a report or as being inspired by real events,[10] the theory is merely used for producing new Egyptophile works. After all, these creations are only sources of entertainment and not historical tools.

9 Federinov/Quertinmont 2016.

10 Mosleth King 2022.

Bibliography

Däniken, E. von, 1969, *Chariots of the Gods? Unsolved Mysteries of the Past*, London.

Däniken, E. von, 2013, *Remnants of the Gods: A Visual Tour of Alien Influence in Egypt, Spain, France, Turkey, and Italy*, New Jersey.

Federinov, B., Quertinmont, A., 2016, *De Stargate™ aux comics. Les dieux égyptiens dans la culture geek (1975–2015)*, Morlanwelz.

Gabilliet, J.-P., 2005, *Des comics et des hommes : histoire culturelle des comic books aux États-Unis*, Nantes.

Kolosimo, P., 1971, *Not of This World*, New York.

Moshenska, G., 2017, 'Alternative Archaeologies', in Moshenska, G. (ed.), 2017, *Key Concepts in Public Archaeology*, London, 122–37.

Mosleth King, M., 2022 (in prep.), 'Ancient Astronauts and Sumerian Aliens: The Fourth Kind as a Pseudo-Archaeological Narrative', in *Rosetta Journal*.

Preys, R., 2016, 'De l'ambivalence des dieux : l'œil de Rê et Seth', in Quertinmont, A. (ed.), 2016, *Dieux, génies et démons en Égypte ancienne. À la rencontre d'Osiris, Anubis, Isis, Hathor, Rê et les autres*, Paris, 291–5.

Solsvik, R., Stokke, E., 2020 (originally published in Norwegian in 2019), *White Gods, White Researchers, White Lies. Review of Thor Heyerdahl og jakten på Atlantis*, online via https://www.kon-tiki.no/wp-content/uploads/2020/04/White-gods-edits-ryan-stokke-solsvik-20042020.pdf (accessed: 02/03/2022).

Story, R., 1976, *The Space-Gods Revealed: A Close Look at the Theories of Erich Von Däniken*, New York.

About the author

Arnaud Quertinmont received his PhD in Egyptology in 2012 and is currently curator of the Egyptian and Near Eastern collections in the Musée Royal de Mariemont (Belgium). His research interests focus on hybrid divinities—with special attention for Anubis—and on the modern reception of ancient Egypt in popular culture. He realised several exhibitions on ancient Egypt; especially relevant here are *De Stargate™ aux comics. Les dieux égyptiens dans la culture geek (1975–2015)* in 2016 and *Egypt. Everlasting Passion* in 2022.

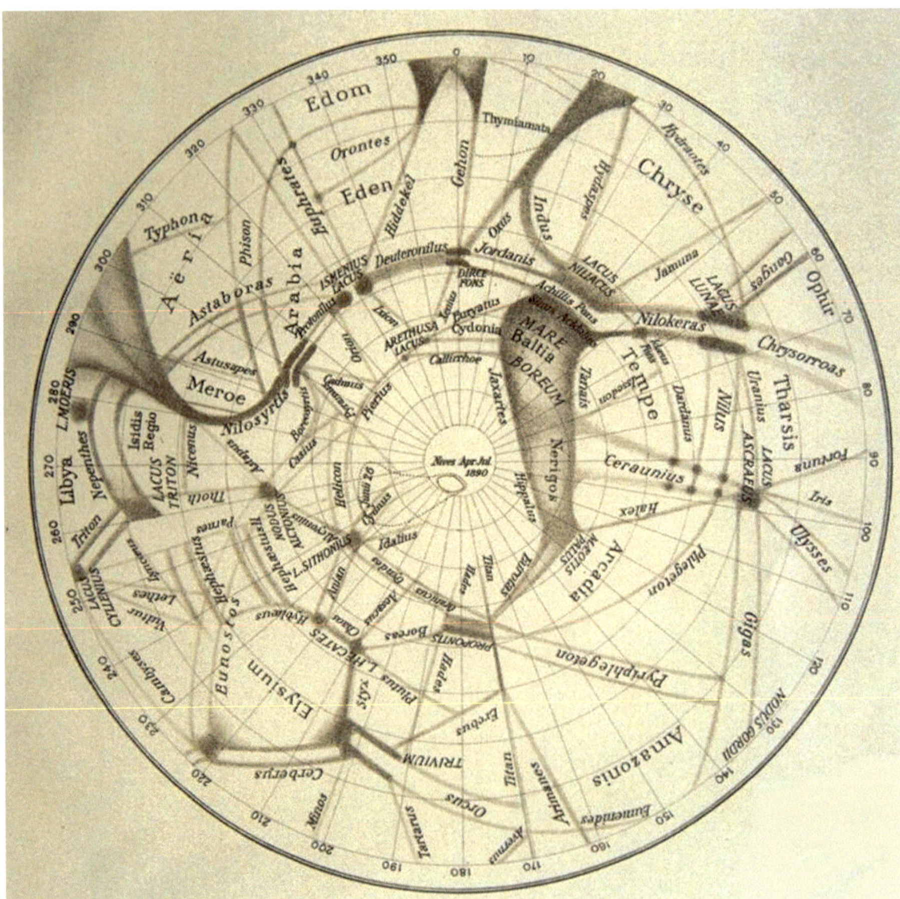

Figure 1. Giovanni Schiaparelli (1835–1910), map of the northern hemisphere of Mars, 1877–1888. Image Scala/SPL History.

Sphinxes of Mars

Science, Fiction, and Nineteenth-century Ancient Aliens

Eleanor Dobson

Introduction

Astronomy—specifically, astronomical interest in the planet Mars—and Egyptian archaeology may seem unlikely bedfellows, but their convergence as combined interests in the nineteenth century for several key figures in the history of science was integral to the development of the discipline now known as archaeoastronomy. In this contribution, I suggest that some of the earliest science-fiction novels that imagine ancient Egyptians as space travellers—written by Fred T. Jane (1865–1916) and Garrett P. Serviss (1851–1929), who have thus far attracted little scholarly attention—sprang from this context, and that speculative fiction in which ancient Egypt is not merely emblematic of the past but also of future civilisations and technologies was born of the space devoted in popular scientific works to imaginative speculations about the future of the Egyptian monuments. The controversial legacies of the popular science of the 1870s onwards and the popular fiction of the 1890s—namely, theories that ancient peoples were in contact with extraterrestrials—are ever more palpable in our own culture. It is in some of this work that we can detect the foundations of alternative Egyptological theories regarding the very nature of ancient Egyptian civilisation itself.

Mapping Mars

Central to an understanding of combined interests in astronomy and the ancient Egyptian monuments in the second half of the nineteenth century is the British astronomer Richard Proctor (1837–1888). Proctor is best-known for his maps of Mars, in which he understood dark patches to be oceans, and lighter patches to be land masses (fig. 2, for example). This work built on images and observations made by earlier astronomers, but Proctor's work proved enormously impactful in naming some of these areas. He also published, in the 1880s, on subjects including the Great Pyramid, which he hypothesised had originally

in Van den Bercken, B. J. L. (ed.), *Alternative Egyptology: Critical Essays on the Relation between Academic and Alternative Interpretations of Ancient Egypt*, Leiden, pp. 106–115.

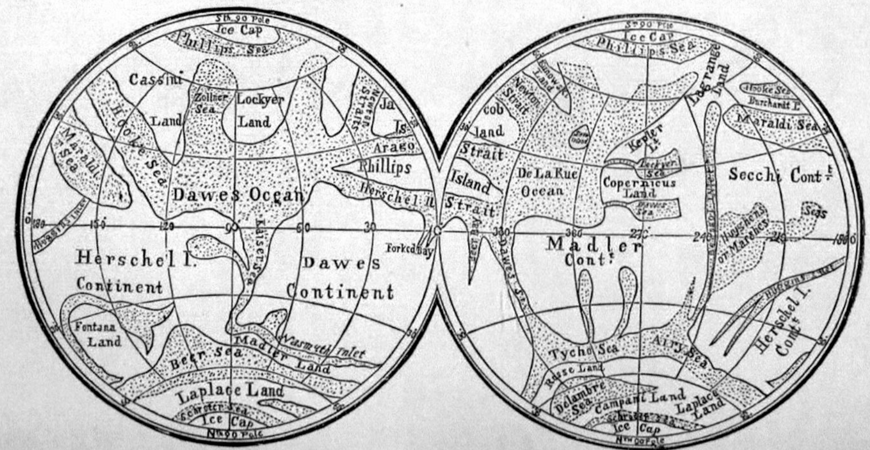

Fig. 22.—Chart of Mars, from 27 drawings by Mr. Dawes.

Figure 2. Richard A. Proctor, 'Chart of Mars, from 27 drawings by Mr. Dawes', *Flowers of the Sky* (New York: A. C. Armstrong & Son, 1879), 167.

been constructed as an astronomical observatory, again using technical drawings and measurements to support his hypothesis.[1]

Building on Proctor's mapping of Mars was the Italian astronomer Giovanni Schiaparelli (1835–1910). Schiaparelli's maps illustrate more surface detail than Proctor's, and between the 1870s and 1880s an interesting change is detectable in Schiaparelli's images: some of the dark lines Schiaparelli saw on the planet's surface were represented in much straighter, more regular ways. Schiaparelli continued Proctor's work in designating some of these features, deriving names from rivers on Earth and mythological figures, including Egyptian gods—Anubis, Isis, Thoth—as well as a Martian Nile: Nilus. It was Schiaparelli's terming of these lines as *canali* (Italian for 'channels') that famously led to the mistranslation of these patterns as 'canals' by the American astronomer Percival Lowell (1855–1916). This error implied that there was some kind of agency behind the creation of these features, rather than them simply being natural formations.[2] If they were artificially created, there had to be intelligent life on Mars.

While Lowell was by no means the first astronomer to propose the existence of an advanced Martian culture, his understanding of these dark lines as canals is hugely significant in its impact on science fiction of the 1890s and beyond. The implications of Lowell's theory were enormous for science, religion, politics, and culture, and the fierce debates (and resistance) they provoked in the scientific community ensured that the hypothetical canals of Mars were repeatedly conjured up in scientific fora, and through popularising works reached the mainstream press. Lowell's drawings of Mars from

1 Before Proctor, the astronomer Charles Piazzi Smyth (1819–1900) took measurements of the Great Pyramid in an effort to ascertain that divine units of measurement were the basis for the British inch. The archaeologist Flinders Petrie's (1853–1942) Egyptological career began with a survey of the Great Pyramid undertaken to verify Smyth's results (instead, Petrie's findings contradicted those of his predecessor). See also the contribution by Daniel Potter in this volume.

2 Fayter 1997, 268.

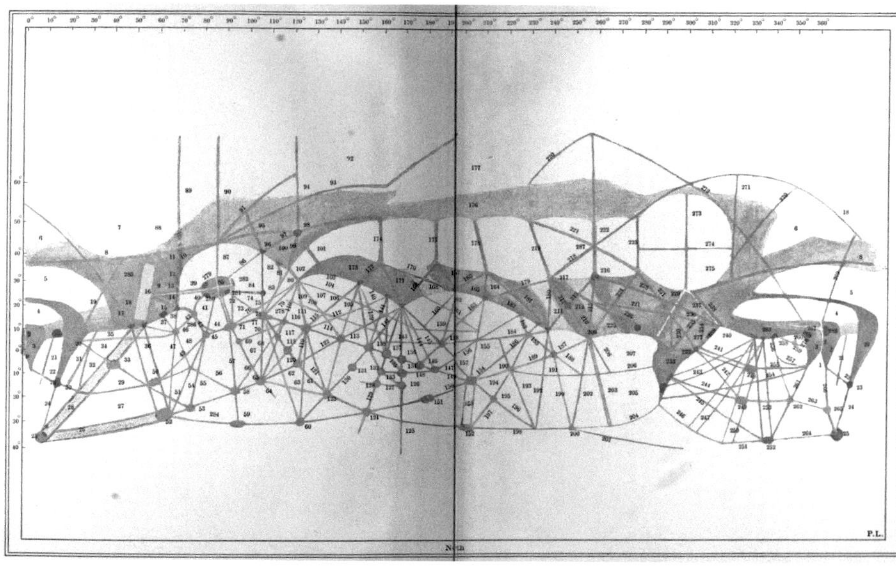

Figure 3. Percival Lowell, 'Mars, on Mercator's Projection', in *Mars* (Boston: Houghton, Mifflin, 1896), 290–91.

the 1890s onward suggest even more geometric shapes than Schiaparelli's, and picture a planet covered—supposedly—in a complex web of waterways far more sophisticated than had been achieved on Earth (fig. 3).[3] The completion of the Suez Canal in Egypt 1869 and the attempts to construct the Panama Canal across the 1880s and 1890s (not to be successful until the early twentieth century) were proving, and would prove, world-changing in terms of international trade.[4] The imperialistic fanfare with which the opening of the French-controlled Suez Canal was celebrated on the cusp of the 1870s—coinciding with Lowell's work—may well have encouraged parallels in the minds of those who were interested in the supposedly superior efforts of Martian engineers; such subjects certainly dominated scholarly and popular discussion about the planet in the 1890s. It was perhaps only a small leap to see the pinnacle of canal engineering in Suez as if it were replicated and superseded in the 288 canals Lowell documented on the surface of Mars.

Edison's Conquest of Mars

Emerging from this context, Garrett P. Serviss's 1898 novel *Edison's Conquest of Mars* features a textual and visual representation of the Great Sphinx of Giza constructed by Martians, depicted in an image by an illustrator by the name of P. Gray (fig. 4). Serviss himself was an astronomer, although his eclectic career also encompassed a period working for the *New York Sun* from 1876 to 1892. A sense of popular, journalistic writing is evident in his scientific works as well as his fiction. *Edison's Conquest of Mars* was Serviss's first novel, commissioned by the *Boston Post* as a sequel to an unauthorised and heavily edited version of H. G. Wells's (1866–1946) 1897 *The War of the Worlds* (titled *Fighters from Mars or the War of the Worlds*), which had been serialised in the *New York Evening Journal.*

3 Lowell 1906.

4 Weintraub 2020, 97.

Figure 4. P. Gray, 'The Martians Built the Sphinx', in Garrett P. Serviss, 'Marvellous Discoveries', *New York Evening Journal*, 3 February 1898. Courtesy of Greg Weeks.

In Serviss's text, a group of men venture to Mars, led by the American inventor Thomas Edison (1847–1931). Their aim is to destroy the Martians who had previously made a devastating attack on Earth, and they travel into space and to Mars itself to remove any future threat. There, they encounter a beautiful woman called Aina, whose ancestors hail from a utopian civilisation in Kashmir, and who tells the story of an ancient Martian invasion of Earth, which led to the construction of pyramids and the Sphinx. The Martians 'suddenly dropped down out of the sky [...] and began to slay and burn and make desolate.'[5] 'Some of the wise men', Aina relates, 'said that this thing had come upon our people because [...] the gods in Heaven were angry,' this reference being the first of several that understands the arrival of the Martians in terms of the Old Testament plagues in Egypt. Indeed, what follows is a blend of biblical narrative and pseudoarchaeology:

> ... they carried off from [...] our native land [...] a large number of our people, taking them first into a strange country, where there were oceans of sand, but where a great river [...] created a narrow land of fertility. Here [...] they remained for many years, keeping our people, whom they had carried into captivity, as slaves. [...] And in this Land [...], it is said, they did many wonderful works.[6]

Aina's language and syntax take on a biblical, archaic quality as she recounts this story. Uprooted from their original home, the former inhabitants of this utopian civilisation are taken to Egypt, where the Martians assume the role of the ruling class, while they themselves—like the biblical Israelites—are enslaved. Aina communicates that the Martians, who had been so impressed with the mountains in Kashmir, erected 'with huge blocks of stone mountains in imitation of what they had seen', the blocks making up these pyramids 'swung into their lofty elevation' not by 'puny man, as many an engineer had declared that it could not be, but [...] these giants of Mars.'[7] In keeping with biblical understandings of Egypt as emblematic of despotism and absolute power, the Sphinx is revealed to be 'a gigantic image of the great chief who led them in their conquest of our world' and who still lives as the Martians' reigning monarch, having sustained himself with water from a fountain of youth.[8] What follows in Aina's account is an allusion to *The War of the Worlds*: the invading Martians are revealed to have been overcome by a pathogen couched in biblical terms. It is only when 'a great pestilence broke out', interpreted as the 'scourge of the gods', that the Martians 'returned to their own world', taking with them the Kashmiri people. In turn, in the present, the band of human men destroys Martian civilisation with another disaster of Old Testament proportions: a devastating flood.

While the direct influence of one on the other cannot be determined, it is striking that a similar scenario is suggested in Richard Proctor's article *The Pyramid of Cheops*, which appeared in the *North American Review* in March 1883. Proctor states:

> Compared with the vast periods of time thus brought before our thoughts as among the demonstrated yet inconceivable truths of science, the life-time of [...] the great pyramid seems but as the duration of a breath. Yet, viewed as men must view the works of man, the pyramids of Egypt derive a profound interest from their antiquity. Young, compared with the works of nature, they are, of all men's works, the most

5 Serviss 1947, 143.
6 Serviss 1947, 143.
7 Serviss 1947, 143 and 146.
8 Serviss 1947, 143.

ancient. They were ancient when temples and abbeys whose ruins now alone remain, were erected, and it seems as though they would endure till long after the last traces of any building now existing, or likely to be built by modern men, has disappeared [...]. Nothing, it should seem, but some vast natural catastrophe ingulfing them beneath a new ocean [...], can destroy them utterly, unless the same race of beings which undertook to rear these vast masses should take in hand the task of destroying them.[9]

Returning to Proctor is useful in understanding how astronomers and scientific popularisers were themselves devoting part of their writing to the kinds of speculation more familiar to us from genre fiction—imagining here a scenario similar to Serviss's, in which the civilisation that produced the Egyptian monuments is destroyed by flood waters. Moreover, it offers up for examination intriguing linguistic nuances. Proctor credits the ancient Egyptians alone as having the power to remove their structures, referring to them as a 'race of beings'. In Proctor's use of the term 'beings' we are invited to imagine the ancient Egyptians as something other than human, chiming with their depictions in science fiction. Even if in some of these fictions the Egyptians are still human, they are nonetheless imagined as living an extra-terrestrial existence.

To Venus in Five Seconds

The other fictional work of especial interest to us deals not with Mars but with Venus, although the planets are essentially interchangeable. Both written and illustrated by Fred T. Jane, his novel *To Venus in Five Seconds* imagines pyramids as landing and take-off sites for vehicles that travel so fast that the effect is akin to teleportation, and ancient Egyptians (originally from Mexico) as effectively migrating to form a community of humans on Venus. There, they live alongside an indigenous species to which they refer as 'the Thotheen', presumably named after Thoth, the ancient Egyptian god of wisdom.[10] The Egyptians are inferior to the Thotheen in all sciences except medicine, and so they are permitted to remain on the planet in their capacity as superior physicians.

Jane's protagonist, a medical student called Plummer, encounters a fellow student named Zumeena, about whom Plummer reveals his initial and, crucially, misplaced prejudice in his relation that he 'had noticed [her ...] owing to her uncivilised sort of name'.[11] Zumeena, who is marked out as 'other' by her brick-red skin tone and 'foreign accent', takes Plummer into what appears to be a summer house but, once Plummer is inside, is evidently some kind of contraption.[12] Indeed, within five seconds of the door's closing Plummer has been transported to Venus. It is while there that Zumeena—as Aina does in Serviss's novel—provides the historical background detailing how ancient Egyptians came to be on another planet:

> The origins of the pyramids, which a later and more utilitarian age made into tombs, was really nothing more nor less than a convenient form for the system of transit we perfected some eight thousand years ago. You will find identical

9 Proctor 1883, 258.
10 Jane 1897, 63.
11 Jane 1897, 12.
12 Jane 1897, 18.

Figure 5. Fred T. Jane, 'Have You Married Him, Female?', in Fred T. Jane, *To Venus in Five Seconds: An Account of the Strange Disappearance of Thomas Plummer, Pillmaker* (London: A. D. Innes, 1897), facing page 111.

pyramids in Mexico and Egypt, and between these two points we carried on continual intercourse by means of argon-coated cars. By pure chance and accident a party of my ancestors, being in one of these cars upon a sandy plain, were suddenly transferred to this planet.[13]

The reference to argon, which had been first isolated from air just a few years before in 1894, underlines how the most up-to-date chemical knowledge (by nineteenth-century standards) had been integrated into Egyptian technologies eight thousand years prior.

While such details serve to underscore the ancient Egyptians' vastly greater scientific advancement, being 'far ahead of [nineteenth-century] Earth science', ultimately, the superiority of the humans on Venus—people who all sport 'an expression of passionate thirst for knowledge'—is called into question in one regard: while they are more scientifically and technologically developed, they have more problematic ethical systems.[14] Once Plummer ultimately rejects Zumeena's amorous advances (he returns her attention at the beginning of the novel not out of attraction but simply for the novelty of romancing a 'lady-doctor'), she resolves to vivisect him, along with other abductees. Zumeena, who wears a pharaonic-style headdress and is accompanied by attendants in similar garb, takes her captives through a utilitarian building whose pylon-shaped doors are another decorative nod to Egypt (fig. 5); the intended vivisection of their captives underscores their ruthless pursuit of medical advancement at the expense of human life. Plummer falls in love with and marries another British abductee and they escape to Earth, landing on the summit of the Great Pyramid. In a joking reference to H. Rider Haggard's *She* (1886–7), Jane reveals that Zumeena, who followed the fleeing couple, goes on to become the ruler of an African tribe, where he hints she assumes the role of Haggard's famed *femme fatale*, Ayesha.

Conclusions

Despite their differences, both Serviss's and Jane's texts relocate Egyptian presences to other planets, 'revealing' that ancient Egyptian civilisation is not confined to ruins, but lives on elsewhere. Both texts are noteworthy, too, for their imagination of Egyptian monuments as having an extraterrestrial origin or else a connection to extraterrestrial cultures: the Great Sphinx and pyramids' Martian construction, as in Serviss's case and, in Jane's, in the reimagination of the pyramids as transport devices between Earth and Venus. These sites, of archaeological and astronomical interest across the nineteenth century, cannot be comprehended by the practitioners of these disciplines, however, resisting conventional understanding. Instead, they highlight the work to be done in filling in the blanks left by advanced ancient peoples—if not blank spaces yet to be filled in Imperialist atlases, then in the scholarly tomes of archaeologists and astronomers.

These narratives seem at once familiar and unfamiliar to us. These are pulp, popular fictions, which are not often read today. And yet their tropes chime with modern readerships. While missions to send detailed images back from the surface of Mars later in the twentieth century showed that there were no canals, Mars remained a staple of science fiction until after the 1970s, with a face-like shape on the planet's surface photographed by NASA (fig. 6)

---

13 Jane 1897, 63.

14 Jane 1897, 51 and 98.

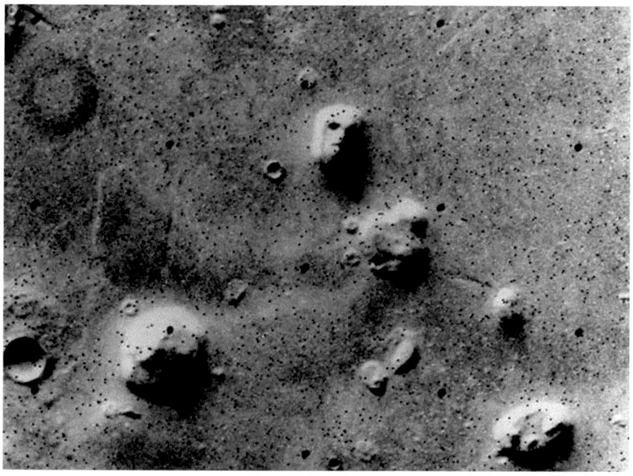

Figure 6. NASA, Viking 1 Orbiter, image F035A72 (Viking CD-ROM Volume 10), 25 July 1976.

even promising—to some—the real-life existence of a Martian sphinx.[15] As this has since been shown to be a mere optical illusion, fiction, television, and film writers have repeatedly imagined alien-ancient Egyptian interactions to involve extraterrestrial civilisations from beyond our solar system, rather than from Earth's nearest planetary neighbours.

Yet although extraterrestrials are imagined as coming from much further afield, we still feel the cultural ripples of this collision, and several features of Serviss's and Jane's narratives are recognisable. We still witness this combination of an antique and ultra-modern or futuristic aesthetic suffusing television, film, literature and the media, with its roots in a longstanding paradox by which Egyptological and other scientific discoveries are simultaneously understood as ancient and cutting-edge. Science fiction of the 1890s, buoyed by a popular astronomical culture that had whipped up Mars-mania, is still familiar to us in the alternative or fringe archaeological narratives of today.

Bibliography

Fayter, P., 1997, 'Strange New Worlds of Space and Time: Late Victorian Science and Science Fiction', 256–80, in Lightman, B. (ed.), *Victorian Science in Context*, Chicago.

Jane, F. T., 1897, *To Venus in Five Seconds: Being an Account of the Strange Disappearance of Thomas Plummer, Pill-Maker*, London.

Lowell, P., 1906, *Mars and Its Canals*, New York.

Morrison, D., 1998, 'Mars Global Surveyor Photographs "Face on Mars"', in *Skeptical Inquirer*, 22.4 23–24.

Proctor, R. A., 1883, 'The Pyramid of Cheops', *The North American Review*, 136.113 257–69.

Serviss, G. P., 1947, *Edison's Conquest of Mars*, Los Angeles.

Weintraub, D. A., 2020, *Life on Mars: What to Know Before We Go*, Princeton.

About the author

Eleanor Dobson is Associate Professor of Nineteenth-Century Literature at the University of Birmingham. She is the author of *Writing the Sphinx: Literature, Culture and Egyptology* (Edinburgh University Press, 2020), and editor of *Victorian Literary Culture and Ancient Egypt* (Manchester University Press, 2020).

15 Morrison 1998, 23–24.

Figure 1. The ruins of Saïs, from Edmund Ollier, *Cassell's Illustrated Universal History,* vol. I: *Early and Greek History*, 1890. Image The Print Collector/Alamy Stockphoto.

Dr Paul Schliemann: Reality or Fake News?

Jean-Pierre Pätznick

Introduction

Have you ever heard of Dr Paul Schliemann? Of his revelations on the relation between the lost continent of Atlantis and ancient Egypt, on which he worked in the name of his illustrious grandfather Heinrich Schliemann?[1] The quest of the enigmatic Paul Schliemann could begin with 'Once upon a time' on 20 October 1912, when the *New York American* published his famous article 'How I Found the Lost Atlantis, the Source of All Civilization' and made him famous overnight.[2]

Mainly centred on his article, this contribution will attempt to retrace part of Paul Schliemann's life. He has been accused of being an impostor, a notorious storyteller afflicted with mythomania who used the name of Schliemann to get his theories published. But is this really the case? Or was Schliemann a passionate scientist with all the shortcomings this can involve?

A family quest

According to Paul Schliemann's article the story began in Naples on 26 December 1890, one hour before Heinrich Schliemann died. Feeling that his time had come, he wrote these few words: 'Break the owl-headed vase. Pay attention to the contents. It concerns Atlantis. Investigate the east of the ruins of the temple of Sais and the cemetery in Chacuna Valley. Important. Night approaches—farewell.' Then he sealed the letter and wrote: 'This can be opened only by a member of my family who solemnly vows to devote his life to the researches outlined therein.'[3]

---

1 See http://www.smb.museum/ausstellungen/detail/schliemanns-welten (accessed: 28/05/2022) with an exposition commemorating Heinrich Schliemann's 200th birthday at the James-Simon-Galerie, 13/05–6/11/2022, Neues Museum Berlin.

2 Schliemann 1912. About Paul Schliemann, see Nesselrath 2021, 111–17, Ebon 1978, Sykes 1952, O'Connell 2010 (with further sources), Beier 2003.

3 Hare 2004, col. 1.

in Van den Bercken, B. J. L. (ed.), *Alternative Egyptology: Critical Essays on the Relation between Academic and Alternative Interpretations of Ancient Egypt*, Leiden, pp. 116–131.

Figure 2. Vase with owl head engraved with an inscription. Illustration from Schliemann 1912.

It was sent to a relative who was already in possession of all the handwritten information to be given to a family member only. Sixteen years later Paul Schliemann wrote: 'Although everyone was curious as to what the mysterious packets contained, not one of the children or friends dared to break the seals. No one desired to devote his life to something he could know nothing about until too late to recede.'[4]

After having studied in Germany, Russia and the Near East, he came in contact with the entrusted relative. He hesitated for days to open the envelope, thinking the last letter of his grandfather might have been the result of a mind weakened by the approach of death. But he finally broke the seal.

Besides a number of documents, photographs and some collected notes, there was a letter from his famous grandfather in which it was expressly said:

> Whoever opens this must solemnly swear to carry out the work which I have left unfinished. I have come to the conclusion that Atlantis was not only a great territory between America and the west coast of Africa and Europe, but the cradle of all our civilization as well. [...] In the included material records, notes and explanations are to be found, the proofs that exist in my mind of the matter. [...] Whoever takes charge of this mission is solemnly obligated to continue my researches and crediting me with my just dues in the discovery. [...] A special fund is deposited in the Bank of France to be paid to the bearer of the enclosed receipt, and this should pay the expenses of the research.[5]

4 Hare 2004, col. 1. This mention is so interesting because its impersonal character would imply that Paul Schliemann did not consider himself or was not considered a full member of the Heinrich Schliemann family, thus highlighting a problem of legitimacy in this family, revealing de facto his deep feeling of illegitimacy. This would also explain why Paul Schliemann so often emphasises that he was a grandson of Heinrich Schliemann.

5 Hare 2004, col. 1. An inquiry I made personally at the Department of the Archives of the Banque de France in Paris about the existence of a Schliemann bank account unfortunately was unsuccessful. I was told that after a long keeping period private documents were systematically destroyed.

Figure 3. Sphinx statuette with a human face. Phoenician art? Illustration from Schliemann 1912.

Errors and inaccuracies in Paul Schliemann's claims

The statements by Paul Schliemann discussed in the above paragraph are riddled with errors and inaccuracies.[6] In his contribution to the *New York American*[7] several other inconsistencies can be identified that provide insight into alternative ideas at the end of the nineteenth century.

According to Paul Schliemann, his grandfather's documents also referred to a bronze vase with a Phoenician text in hieroglyphic script mentioning a 'King Chronos of Atlantis' (fig. 2). This vase was apparently found in 1873 in the Second City of Troy at Hissarlik,[8] that is to say in the archaeological layer of the so-called 'Treasure of Priam' (*Schatz* A) which is now on display in the Pushkin Museum in Moscow.

In this early layer of the city of Troy, now dated to about 2500 BC,[9] a bronze vase might have been a logical find. An engraved Phoenician-hieroglyphic inscription for that period, however, is completely anachronistic, since the Phoenician alphabet is not written with hieroglyphic signs and appeared during the eleventh century BC.[10]

Concerning the mention of a 'King Chronos', little is known, but there is an interesting mention by Eusebius of Caesarea (AD 265–340), in his *Praeparatio evangelica*, where Chronos is said to have given Egypt to Taaut (Thot) and Greece to Athena.[11]

Comparing some artefacts found in Hissarlik (Troy) and objects from what he calls Tiahuanaco, Paul Schliemann writes that Hissarlik lies in Crete and Tiahuanaco in Central

6 Nesselrath 2021, 115, with further publications on this topic.

7 Hare 2004, col. 2.

8 One can see the remains of an inscription on the vase. See Sayce 1880, 691–705 with an early syllabary writing system antedating the Phoenician script.

9 Korfmann 2001, 373-83.

10 We must note however that Heinrich Schliemann would have been able to read this inscription, because he was registered as a student of Oriental antiquities and languages at the Sorbonne in 1866.

11 Eusebius of Caesarea wrote a history of the Phoenicians that was an echo of the one written by Philo of Byblos, who himself referred to a Phoenician author named Sanchuniathon who had written a history in three volumes in Phoenician for King Abibaal of Berytus at the time of Queen Semiramis of Assyria; see Kirby/Pearse 2003, ch. IX and X, and https://tertullian.org/fathers/eusebius_pe_01_book1.htm (accessed: 28/05/2022).

America.[12] Misplacing Hissarlik is a strange mistake for Heinrich Schliemann's grandson. Moreover Tiahuanaco is located in Bolivia and not in Central America. Did Schliemann actually confuse it with Teotihuacan, near Mexico City?[13]

Then we learn that in the museum in Saint Petersburg Heinrich Schliemann found a papyrus dated to a Pharaoh Senet of the 2nd Dynasty (dated to 4571 BC by Schliemann) that contained a description of how this pharaoh sent out an expedition 'to the West in search of traces of the Land of Atlantis, whence 3,350 years ago the ancestors of the Egyptians arrived carrying with themselves all the wisdoms of their native lands.' The expedition returned after five years and reported that 'they had found neither people nor objects which could give them a clue as to the vanished land.'[14]

A Pharaoh Senet is unknown, but perhaps Pharaoh Sened—who reigned in the second half of the 2nd Dynasty—is meant, dated *c.*2750 BC. Unfortunately, nothing is known about (the whereabouts of) this papyrus.[15] Additionally, no papyri dated to the Early Dynastic Period are known.[16] Schliemann also speaks of a papyrus written by Manetho, the Egyptian historian living in the third century BC, that referred to a period of 13,900 years as 'the reign of the Wise of Atlantis'.[17] This papyrus would place this at the very beginning of Egyptian history, approximately 16,000 years ago.

This would mean that the museum in Saint Petersburg would have in its collection the most complete version of Manetho's *Aegyptiaca*, of which we only have summaries by several Classical authors. If this were true, the Hermitage curator Vladimir Golenishchev would have published it, becoming famous overnight.

---

12 But as with Tiahuanaco and Teotihuacan, we can also ask whether the object discovered in Troy was not in fact discovered in Crete, which Heinrich Schliemann visited. Because we know that the Phoenicians had established some trading posts with sanctuaries on Crete, this would fit better with the vase engraved with a Phoenician inscription. See Ioannou 2019, 5, 9–10; Bourogiannis 2018, 60–67; Kourou 2000, 1067–1081.

13 Sykes 1952.

14 Hare 2004, col. 3. This voyage reminds us of the expedition sent by Pharaoh Necho II (seventh century BC) all the way around Africa (Herodotus, Book IV, § 42).

15 One can guess that if Heinrich Schliemann had really found this papyrus, he must have been in contact with Vladimir Golenishchev, who at that time was in charge of the Egyptian collection of the Hermitage Museum. The collection was previously exhibited in the Kunstkamera, and Golenishchev transferred it to the Hermitage Museum in 1881. As director of the museum (1870–1891), he made its first inventory in 1891 during which he discovered a number of papyri (Hermitage/Saint Petersburg 1116 A, The Teaching of Merikare; and 1116 B, Prophecy of Neferty). We know also that Golenishchev published in 1881 also the hieratic papyrus Hermitage 1115, The Tale of the Shipwrecked Sailor, whose origin is unknown. If Golenishchev had found this papyrus of King Senet, he would certainly have published it. The Golenishchev texts and collection were moved to the Pushkin Museum in Moscow in 1909. See also Claude 2020. If Heinrich Schliemann was able to read this document, it must have been written in Greek, or Golenishchev must have translated for him if it was written in hieratic or in demotic. Thus, if we were to discover such a document, it would certainly be written in Greek or in demotic, like the history of King Neferkare of the 2nd Dynasty. See Burkard 1990, 107–133 (P. Berlin 23071 vs) and Quack 1997, 299. One must also take into account that the collections of the Greek, Ptolemaic and demotic papyri preserved in Saint Petersburg in the Hermitage Museum as well as in the Oriental Faculty and in the Institute of the Oriental Manuscripts are unfortunately not fully published, so a surprise cannot be completely excluded.

16 We know only of an unwritten papyrus found in the Mastaba S 3038 of Hemaka in Saqqara North (middle of the 1st Dynasty (2950 BC)), Emery 1938, 41 Cat. Nr. 432, whereas the oldest known written papyri are dated back to King Khufu of the first half of the 4th Dynasty (2500 BC) and were found at Wadi el-Jarf on the Red Sea Coast, Tallet 2021; Tallet 2017.

17 On the period of 13,900 years: this concerns the 'period of the Gods in Egypt'. It is mentioned in the Armenian version of Eusebius' *Chronica*, which contains excerpts from the *Aegyptiaca* by Manetho. See Waddel 1964, 4–5.

Heinrich Schliemann subsequently writes about another piece of evidence, which he excavated himself:

> An inscription which I excavated at the Lion Gate at Mycenae in Crete recites that Misor, from whom, according to the inscription, the Egyptians were descended, was the child of Taaut or Thoth, the God of History, and that Taaut was the emigrated son of a 'priest of Atlantis, who having fallen in love with a daughter of King Chronos, escaped and landed after many wanderings in Egypt.' He built the first temple at Sais and there taught the wisdom of his native land. This full inscription is most important, and I have kept it secret. You will find it among the papers marked D.[18]

Here again, the Lion Gate is not in Crete, but in Mycenae in Greece. Heinrich Schliemann, who excavated there, would never have made such an error and had he really found such an inscription, he would surely have published it.

Once again, King Chronos of Atlantis is mentioned. What is interesting in this love story is that Misor and Taaut are both well known. They also appear in the work of Eusebius of Caesarea, *Praeparatio evangelica*, in which the relationship is reversed: it is Misor who was the father of Taaut.[19] On the other hand, Taaut was said to be the inventor of the first writing characters and of the first alphabet and was assimilated to the Egyptian Thoth, god of wisdom and writing.

Moreover, Paul Schliemann mentioned in his article another written source that he claims his grandfather discovered in Troy: 'One of the tables of my Trojan excavation gives also a medical treatise of the Egyptian priests for the removal of cataract from the eye and ulcer from the intestines by means of surgery.'[20]

The find of an Egyptian medical text in Troy would have been of such importance that Heinrich Schliemann would have published it immediately.[21] This was not the case, however, and Paul Schliemann added: 'There were other notes and allusions to the material proofs which were in the secret safe in Paris, and besides these was the strict injunction that I should keep the matter secret until I had followed up his instructions and had finished my research.'[22]

At the end of his contribution Paul Schliemann concluded, 'Yet it is absolute truth', but in the light of the above arguments, was it really?

Paul Schliemann

Beside the fact that these fantastic revelations are full of scientifically proven inaccuracies and errors, what do we really know about Dr Paul Schliemann? When we consider the person Paul Schliemann, we can observe some interesting clues to his character from his own words: 'I am an individualist and will do the work in my individual way.'[23] 'In my

---

18 Hare 2004, col. 3.

19 For the translation see Kirby/Pearse 2003, ch. X.

20 Hare 2004, col. 3.

21 Concerning the Egyptian medical surgical treatise, one of the most brilliant papyri dealing with surgery in ancient Egypt is the Pap. Edwin Smith preserved at the New York Academy of Medicine, but it was found in Egypt, not in Crete nor in Troy. NYAM Inv. Nr. 217. See Resche 2016.

22 Hare 2004, col. 4.

23 Ibid.

research I have made a principle to retire to such a seclusion that no periodical could reach me, and no curiosity of the public could disturb me in this serious and important work. I shall pursue the same course until my book is finished.'[24] 'However, I have been willing to follow the invitation of this newspaper and to reveal this secret of my illustrious grandfather and to give some of the facts which I have discovered and why I claim to be the discoverer of Atlantis. I proceed to what happened after I read Heinrich Schliemann's documents.'[25] 'For these reasons I have avoided up to this time all notoriety, through the press and every association with any scientific expeditions.'[26]

On his work he wrote in his article: 'My grandfather had written that I should first pay attention to the ruins of the Temple of Saïs and the Chucuna Valley in America.'[27] So he travelled to Egypt and to South America, on which he wrote: 'For six years (that is to say from 1906–1912) I have worked indefatigably in Egypt, in Central and South America and in all the archeological museums on the globe.'[28]

Excavations at Saïs in Egypt

We know that Paul Schliemann spent five months in the ruins of the city of Saïs (today Sa el-Hagar), where among other things he discovered a sarcophagus of a priest dating from the 1st Dynasty and a complex of catacombs.[29]

One of the graves contained a great sarcophagus dated from the 3rd Dynasty that belonged to one of the great musicians of the time. Paul Schliemann found inside the sarcophagus a collection of musical instruments made of wood, porcelain (!) and copper: trumpets, harps, and flutes. He claimed to have found a papyrus written in a musical language as well.[30]

Paul Schliemann claimed that the hieroglyphic inscription on this sarcophagus indicated that these musical instruments once belonged to the 'orchestra' of the temple at Saïs and that they would have been used for the coronation ceremonies of King Amenemhat I (1991–1962 BC, 12th Dynasty).[31]

Again there are several problems with Paul Schliemann's account of events. Even though Saïs, modern Sa el-Hagar in the Nile Delta (fig. 4 and 5), was one of the oldest cities of Egypt, no graves of the 1st Dynasty nor a sarcophagus of the early dynastic time have been discovered at the site.[32]

---

24 Ibid.

25 Ibid.

26 Ibid. In contrast with these claims the *Fränkischer Kurier* (Nürnberg) of 20 Oct. 1912 published the story as well, while *The Weekly Budget* and *The London Budget Sunday*'s magazine section had already printed it three days before. See Nesselrath 2021, 112 n. 28 and 116.

27 Hare 2004, col. 5.

28 Ibid.

29 Ibid. One will note that the *Rapport sur la marche du Service des Antiquités de 1899–1910*, Cairo 1912, 227 and 241 mentions for the year 1907 under the heading 'Touristes' an important (about 7000 LE) payment in Sa-el-Hagar (Saïs) and excavations at this site. This was the only year there were excavations; see the appendix.

30 See appendix, the *Sunday Times* (Sydney), 19 Apr. 1914, p. 3.

31 See appendix, the *Sunday Times* (Sydney), 19 Apr. 1914, p. 3. Was Paul Schliemann able to read a hieroglyphic inscription?

32 Penelope Wilson, project director of the Joint Archaeological Mission of the EES and the University of Durham in Sa el-Hagar since 1997, told me that she never heard of an excavation by Paul Schliemann at this site. See also https://sais.webspace.durham.ac.uk (accessed: 28/05/2022).

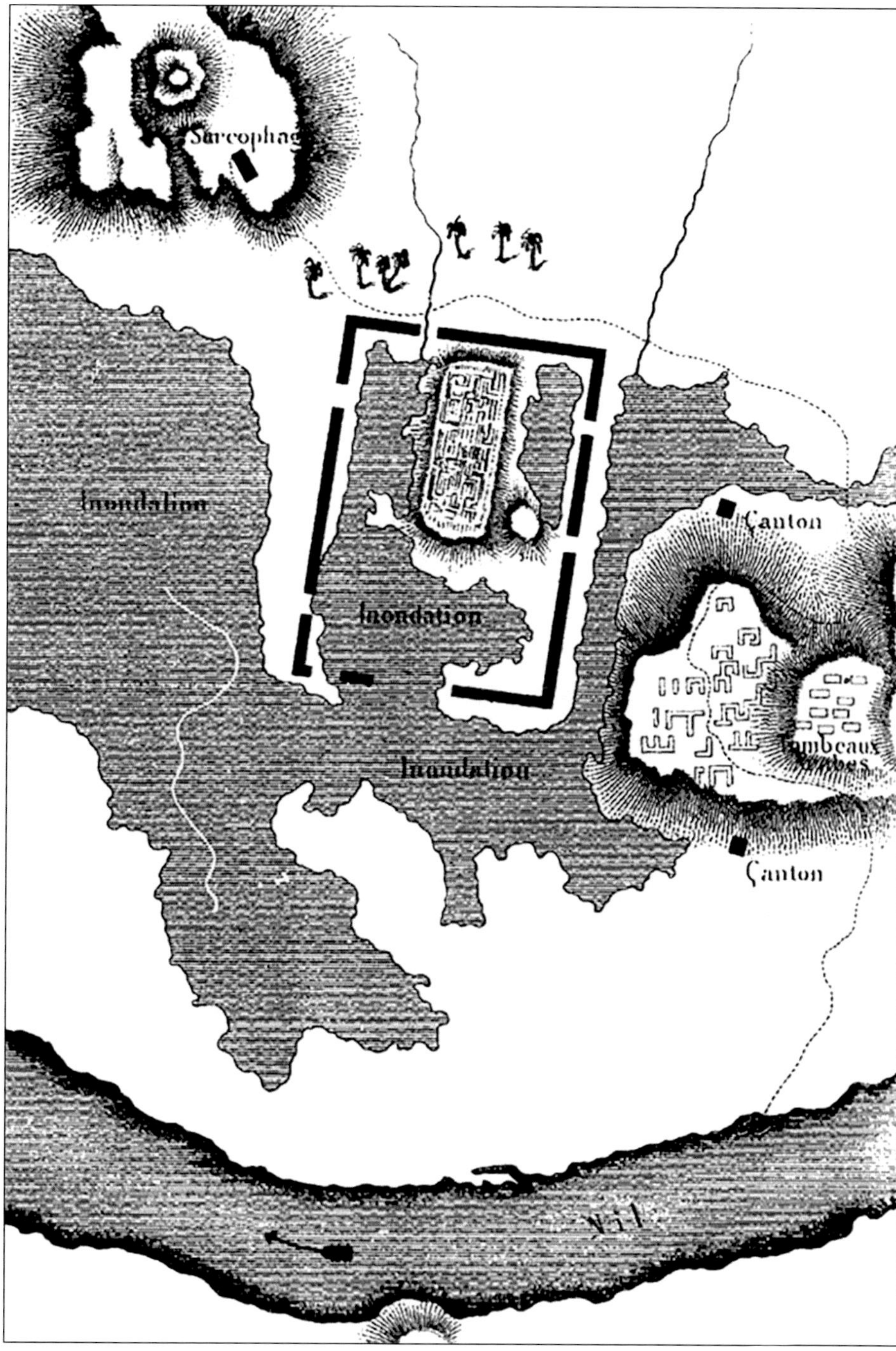

Figure 4. Map of the ruins of Saïs. J. F. Champollion, *Lettres écrites d'Égypte et de Nubie en 1828 et 1829*, Paris 1868 (http://gallica.bnf.fr/ark:/12148/.image.f45).

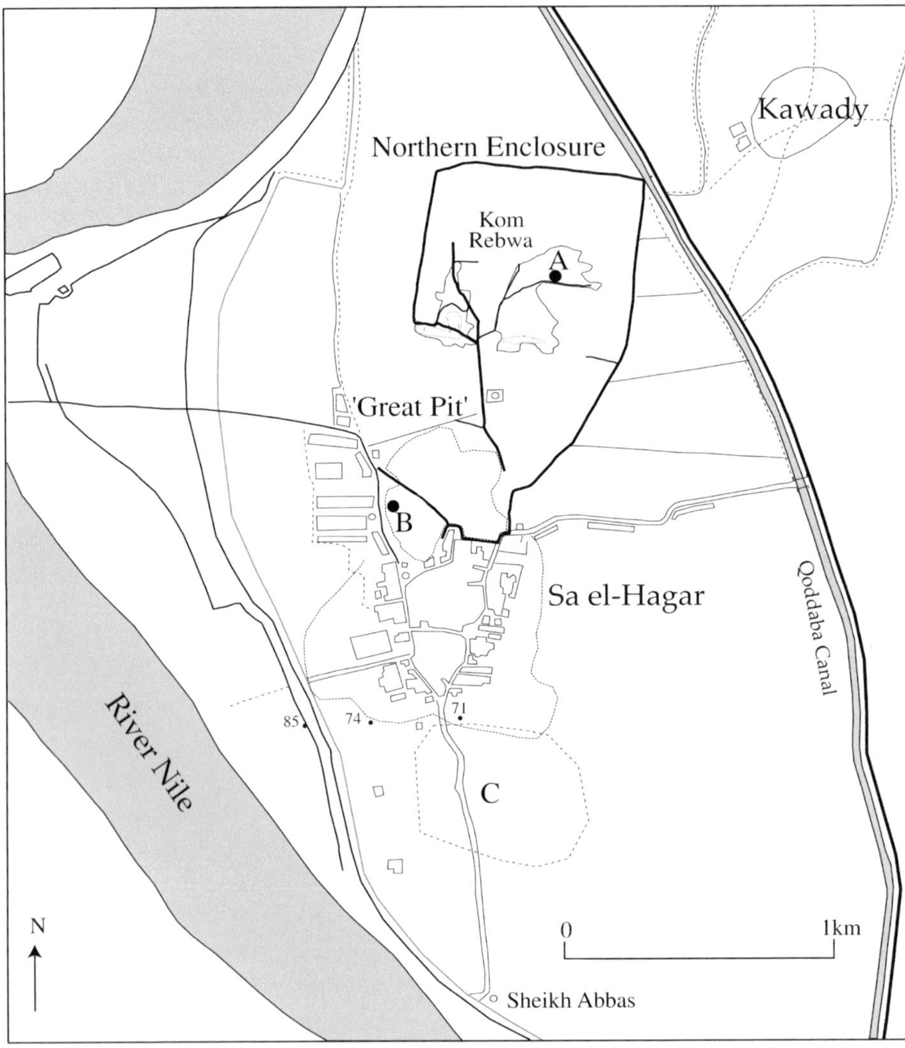

Map of the Saïs Area

A Excavation 1: New Kingdom-Third Intermediate Period
Old Kingdom

B Excavation 4 : Late Saïte, Neolithic-Predynastic

C 2004 Drill Augurs: Old Kingdom, Late Period

Figure 5. Saïs Report, spring 2004, by Dr P. Wilson (https://sais.webspace.durham.ac.uk).

We must also point out that the discovery of a sarcophagus of the 3rd Dynasty (the end of the Early Dynastic Period/beginning of the Old Kingdom, *c.*2600 BC) that records the coronation of King Amenemhat I (Middle Kingdom, 1995 BC) would of course completely upset ancient Egyptian chronology.

Moreover, as far as these wonderful musical instruments mentioned by Paul Schliemann are concerned, no one knows where they are now or what happened to the records of their discovery. We only know that Paul Schliemann 'had a serious talk' with Giacomo Puccini and Eduard Strauss about the musical papyrus he had found,[33] and that he contacted two famous French geologists who examined with him the west coast of Africa at the points 'where my grandfather had indicated.'[34]

South and Central America

Paul Schliemann described his visit to Mexico and Peru, where he excavated graveyards and sites in cities. Especially the cemetery of the Chucuna/Chacuna Valley, where the ancient Chimú are buried,[35] seems to have been an important source of clues.

Again several problems and inaccuracies can be identified. If the Chucuna/Chacuna Valley is to be identified with the Valley Mochica, Paul Schliemann could have dug up remains of the Chimú pre-Columbian civilisation settled on the coast of Peru. The kingdom was called Chimor and its capital Chan Chan (AD 900–1470). One cannot exclude that he also found remains of an early period of this culture dated AD 100–500 and named Early Chimu or Mochica. Great pyramids were built during this period. Paul Schliemann might also have confused it with the old city of Caral.[36]

Schliemann further claimed: 'I pass on to the translation of a Maya manuscript which is part of the famous collection of Le Plongeon, the Troano manuscript. It can be seen in the British Museum.'[37] Even though we know that a copy of the Codex Troano is on display for the public and that the original has belonged to the Museum of Archaeology in Madrid since 1888, the possibility that it was at the British Museum at that time cannot be completely excluded.[38]

After this episode we have no information on Paul Schliemann for eight years. It is in the period 1924–1925 that by now Prof. Paul Schliemann reappears to give several interviews on his fantastic submarine discoveries near Cuba (fig. 6), especially near Punta del Este on

33 See appendix, the *Sunday Times* (Sydney), 19 Apr. 1914, p. 3, and *Maryborough Chronicle*, 20 Feb. 1914, p. 8. It would also be very interesting to verify this in the correspondence or the archives of the two composers.

34 Hare 2004, col. 5. When attempting to identify these two French specialists of geology I came across two names: Pierre Termier (1859–1930) and Louis Gentil (1868–1925). Both were well-known French geographers who have published some studies on the topic of Atlantis and its evidence in the Atlantic not far from the west coast of Morocco and Mauretania. Termier 1922, 117–46 and Termier 1913; Gentil 1912. See also Medioni 2011, 11–12. It would also be appropriate to consider the scientific correspondence of these geologists to verify their cooperation with Paul Schliemann.

35 Hare 2004, col. 7.

36 See Shady Solís 2006. For the pre-Columbian ancient culture Mochica and Chimu, see https://warbletoncouncil.org/cultura-chimu (accessed: 06/02/2022) with further references.

37 Hare 2004, col. 8.

38 See Lindow 1936 : 'The article makes mention of the *Troano Codex* being stored in the British Museum. This is true. The original *is* technically stored in the House of Coins' vault *under* the British Museum. It has never been available for public viewing (for obvious reasons).'

BAS-RELIEF FOUND IN A CAVE TEMPLE WHERE PROFESSOR SCHLIEMANN BELIEVES THE PEOPLE OF ATLANTIS WORSHIPPED—NOW A PART OF THE OCEAN'S BED.

Figure 6. Frieze of five hybrid anthropomorphic figures with crocodile tails discovered by Prof. Paul Schliemann off the Isla de Pinies near Punta del Este (Cuba). In *The Mail Adelaide*, 28 Febr. 1925, p. 17.

the Isla de Pinies (today Isla de la Juventud).[39] In December 1925, more convinced of his quest than ever, Paul Schliemann was on the West-African coast, pursuing his research on the continent he believed to have sunk beneath the waters of the Atlantic Ocean. This is the last we know of his quest.[40]

Many questions arise about his claimed fantastic discoveries and no less numerous errors and inaccuracies, but a fundamental question actually is whether Paul Schliemann really was a grandson of Heinrich Schliemann.[41]

We know that Heinrich Schliemann married twice.[42] In Russia he married Katherina Lyschin in 1852, with whom he had three children (Sergei, Natalia, and Nedeshda). Some years later, as an American citizen, he divorced Katherina in Indianapolis and remarried a bit later with Sophia Engastromenos. She was 17 years old when he was 47 and the couple had two children: Agamemnon and Andromache. Agamemnon married Nadine

---

39 See appendix, *The Mail Adelaïde*, 28 Febr. 1925, p. 17. 'Now, however, as a result of a long series of submarine explorations, I am able to support it with many important pieces of evidence which have been brought up from the ocean's depths—from the lost continent itself.' 'I have discovered and photographed on the tops of undersea mountains the walls of certain caves that show every evidence of having once been inhabited by men. On the top of one rocky mountain, about 40 feet under water, I discovered fragments of a remarkably well preserved cave temple.' 'My first discovery in the deep sea research was a huge square rocktablet. After cleaning it I found a bas-relief of five stunning figures, a remarkably harmonious and well designed composition.' 'The most astounding discovery of my deep-sea explorations was a mountain peak, on the side of which I came upon the remnants of a rocktemple.'
My request to the Fondation Fernando Ortiz concerning Schliemann's submarine investigations at Punta del Este between 1920 and 1925 and his relation to Mr Ortiz have remained unanswered until now. See González Herrera 2008 on Fernando Ortiz's discoveries at Punta del Este as well as O'Connell 2010 with further literature.

40 We know that a book should have been published in Germany in which the results of his work would have been presented for the first time.

41 Paul Schliemann is a well-attested name since the sixteenth century up until the recent death of the German poet Paul Schliemann in 2020; it was also the name of a brother of Heinrich Schliemann.

42 American School of Classical Studies at Athens: http://www.ascsa.edu.gr/index.php/archives/heinrich-schliemann-finding-aid#Series_B:_Correspondence_" (accessed: 28/05/2022).

Figure 7. Map showing the supposed extent of the Atlantean Empire, from Ignatius L. Donnelly, *Atlantis: The Antediluvian World*, 1882. Image Allard Pierson, UBM: F 89-333.

Bornemann and they had no children, whereas Andromache had three children with Leno Melas. None of these was called Paul though.[43]

For Martin Ebon, referring to Edgerton Sykes, Agamemnon and Paul Schliemann were in fact one and the same person[44] whereas for Lilian Melas, Paul Schliemann was a 'personnage imaginaire' of the family history.[45] Another possibility could be that Paul Schliemann descended from Heinrich via an affair his grandfather had during his time in California from 1849 to 1851.[46]

Paul Schliemann's life work, supposedly following the will of Heinrich Schliemann, is full of topographical, historical, and scientific inaccuracies and errors. His research and results, which are fixated on proving the existence of Atlantis which connected the European, African and American continents, correspond to the trend of an Atlantean intellectual movement at this time, as advocated by I. Donnelly, James Churchward, Auguste Le Plongeon, Leo Frobenius, Pierre Termier, Louis Gentil, Paul Le Cour, Edgerton Sykes, Edgar Cayce, and Pierre Benoît.

---

43 Even the German Institute of Archaeology in Athens knows no Paul Schliemann in the archives of the Schliemann family. Prof. George Korres, the leading Schliemann authority in modern Greece, had heard the name Paul Schliemann *en passant*, but the lack of birth or death dates and of letters by him made Korres doubt he ever existed. See Beier 2003.

44 See Beier 2003. The only question that remains is why Agamemnon would have named himself 'grandson' rather than the son of Heinrich Schliemann he really was. Concerning the localisation of Mycenae on Crete, we can guess that Agamemnon was educated enough to avoid this error which Paul Schliemann made twice, so I therefore doubt that Agamemnon Schliemann was Paul Schliemann.

45 Beier 2003.

46 See Hare 2004, col. 1. If one suggests that Paul Schliemann was about 25 in 1912, so he would have been born around 1887, that is to say three to four years before Heinrich Schliemann's death in Naples. Therefore, his mother or father who might have been a daughter or a son of Heinrich Schliemann would have been the fruit of an affair of the young Heinrich Schliemann. Moreover, one knows that, like Heinrich and Agamemnon Schliemann, Paul Schliemann had the American citizenship, see *The Bathurst Times* 1913, p. 3.

Conclusion

Paul Schliemann was an independent researcher, he was not a ghost.[47] His relationship to the illustrious Heinrich Schliemann is not entirely clear and he may even have been an unofficial, illegitimate grandson of Heinrich.

In 1912 he left New York shortly after the publication of his controversial article. If we take in account his articles and the interviews he gave, we can tentatively reconstruct the path of his journey leading him from the east coast of the USA to the West-African coast, and his trips from America to Australia where he spent some years. From the beginning of 1916, nothing is heard from Paul Schliemann until some eight years later (1924/1925), when he reappears in the USA. He then holds the title of professor and reports about his fantastic underwater discoveries near Cuba.

Ever passionate about his research, he once more sounds the west coast of Morocco, where he definitely disappears by the end of 1925. Was he carried away by the same tropical disease that took Louis Gentil in Morocco in June 1925? Did he die violently?

Whoever he might have been, Paul Schliemann left us with the memory of a passionate man, determined to follow his path against all odds. Having fulfilled and even exceeded the wish of Heinrich Schliemann, he was absolutely convinced of the existence of the lost continent of Atlantis and its civilisation, mother of the ancient Egyptian civilisation, even if his desire to reveal it cost him his life.[48]

47 Beier 2003, where Martin Ebon concludes: 'It is difficult to understand why, in the intervening years (meanwhile), we have received neither confirmation nor denial from lawyers, bankers, and others involved with the execution of Heinrich Schliemann's will. Any absence of negative evidence seems to confirm the accuracy of the story.'

48 See also Lindow 1936, a very interesting statement on Paul Schliemann by an archivist in Gothenburg.

Appendix

Due to the list of papers concerning Paul Schliemann's discoveries and the interviews with him published in America as well as in Australia, it is possible to trace a part of his short life, from 1912 to 1925.

Date	Place	Publication	Title and remarks
20 Oct. 1912	East coast, USA	*The New York American*	'How I Found the Lost Atlantis, the Source of All Civilization'
27 Oct. 1912	West coast, USA	*San Francisco Examiner*	
17 Nov. 1912	London	*The Weekly Budget*	'The Lost Atlantis': Dr Paul Schliemann was last seen in 1912 in New York harbour, where he lived on his small yacht. Then, according to Egerton Sykes, he is said to have sailed for Germany, from where he joined the German troops in France and fell at Fromelles in the north of France on June 19/20, 1916. But the distribution of his papers and interviews suggest that he did leave the harbour of New York shortly after the publication of his famous article, but did not sail to Germany nor fell in France. He stayed on the east coast of the States for about two months and decided to sail to New Zealand and Australia. A perfectly thought-out destination in view of some members of the Schliemann family who had settled in Queensland since 1871; he spent about one year with them. Then he travelled through America for a month and came back to Australia where he spent two years (1914–1916). He went to Nebraska in 1916 and then his trail is lost.

Date	Place	Publication	Title and remarks
25 Dec. 1912		*Newcastle Morning Herald & Miners' Advocate*, p. 11	'The Lost Atlantis'
28 Jan. 1913	Nelson, New Zealand	*The Colonist* (New Zealand) Vol. IV, p. 6	'The Lost Atlantis'
1 Febr. 1913	New South Wales, Australia	*The Bathurst Times*, p. 3	'The Lost Atlantis: American Archaeologist's Great Discoveries'
			This article states that Paul Schliemann was an American scientist.
22 Feb. 1913	New South Wales, Australia	*Newcastle Morning Herald & Miners' Advocate*, p. 5	'A Submerged Continent'
24 Feb. 1913	New South Wales, Australia	*Lithgow Mercury*, p. 1	'The Submerged Continent'
19 Apr. 1913	Adelaide, Australia	*The Journal*, p. 6	'A Submerged Continent. After the Pole, What?'
22 Nov. 1913	East coast, USA	*Atlanta Georgia Evening*, image 3	Paul Schliemann disappeared for about seven months and came back with astonishing discoveries he made in Saïs (Egypt) during his excavations.
23 Nov. 1913	East coast, USA	*The Times Dispatch* (Richmond. Va), image 55	'Astonishing Discoveries in Ancient Egypt'
23 Nov. 1913	USA	*Sunday American*	
31 Dec. 1913	West coast, USA	*San Francisco Examiner*	
14 Feb. 1914	Melbourne, Australia	*The Age Melbourne*, p. 4	'Music in Ancient Egypt'
20 Feb. 1914	Queensland, Australia	*Maryborough Chronicle, Wide Bay and Burnett Advertiser*, p. 8	'Music in Ancient Egypt'; this paper states that Paul Schliemann was in contact with Giacomo Puccini and Eduard Strauss, with whom he discussed the papyrus he had found in the temple ruins of Saïs.
25 Feb. 1914	Sydney, Australia	*Globe Sydney*, p. 6	'Music of the Pharaohs: Sweet and Weird'
25 Feb. 1914	New South Wales, Australia	*Newcastle Morning Herald and Miner's Advocate*, p. 13	'Music in Ancient Egypt'
19-25 Apr. 1914	Sydney, Australia	*Sydney Times*, p. 3	'Music of the Pharaohs: Sweet and Weird'
25 Apr. 1914	Perth, Australia	*Western Mail*, p. 49	'The Theosophical Path'; a previous communication by Paul Schliemann in the *Scientific American* is mentioned.
Jan. 1916			Paul Schliemann is back in the USA, in Nebraska.
16 Jan. 1916	Nebraska, USA	*The Omaha Bee Sunday Magazine*	'Does Europe Face the Fate of the Fabled Atlantis?'
17 Jan. 1916	Nebraska, USA	*The Omaha Daily Bee*	Schliemann disappeared for eight years and reappeared during 1924–1925 with the title of professor. On the American east coast and in Australia he gives some interviews about his new discoveries at Punta del Este on the Isla de Pinies, Cuba (today Isla de la Juventud).
16 Nov. 1924	East coast, USA	*The Philadelphia Inquirer*, p. 118	
16 Nov. 1924	East coast, USA	*The Atlanta Constitution*, Georgia, p. 62	
16 Nov. 1924	East coast, USA	*The Spokesman – Review*, Washington	
11 Jan. 1925	West coast, USA	*San Francisco Chronicle* Interview with Paul Schliemann	
28 Febr. 1925	Adelaide, Australia	*The Mail*, p. 17	Prof. Paul Schliemann *New Light on the World's Lost Continent.* Announcing a forthcoming publication of his book in Germany.
11 Aug. 1925	New South Wales, Tumut, Australia	*The Tumut Advocate and Farmers and Settler's Adviser*, p. 4	'Atlantis found at last by Prof. Paul Schliemann'
20 Aug. 1925	South East Australia, Werribee /Melbourne	*Werribee Shire Banner*, p. 3	'Atlantis found at last by Prof. Paul Schliemann'
21 Aug. 1925	New South Wales, Australia	*The Independent (Deniliquin) NSW*, p. 4	'Atlantis found at last by Prof. Paul Schliemann'
21 Sept. 1925	New South Wales, Australia	*Newcastle Morning Herald and Miner's Advocate*, p. 2	'Atlantis found at last by Prof. Paul Schliemann'
20 Nov. 1925	Western Australia, Beverley	*The Beverly Times*, p. 2	'Atlantis found at last by Prof. Paul Schliemann'
5 Dec. 1925	Western Australia, Growangerup	*Growangerup Star and Tambellup-Ongerup Gazette, vol. XI, no. 18*, p. 1	'Atlantis found at last by Prof. Paul Schliemann'

Bibliography

Beier, B., 2003, *Paul Schliemann. Das Phantom der Atlantisforschung*, published on forum.grenzwissen.de and https://www.atlantisforschung.de (both accessed: 31/01/2020).

Bourogiannis, G., 2018, 'The Phoenician Presence in the Aegean during the Early Iron Age: Trade, Settlement and Cultural Interaction', in *Rivista di Studi Fenici*, XLVI, 60–67.

Burkard, G., 1990, 'Frühgeschichte und Römerzeit', in *Studien zur Altägyptischen Kultur* 17, 107–133.

Ebon, M., 1977, *Atlantis: The New Evidence*, New York.

Emery, W. B., 1938, *The Tomb of Hemaka, Excavated at Saqqara*, Cairo.

Gentil, L., 1912, *L'Histoire physique du Maroc*, Nouvelle Collection Scientifique vol. 1, Paris.

Kirby, P., Pearse, R., 2003, transcribed and amended text of Gifford, T. E. N., 1903, *Eusebius of Caesarea, Preparatio Evangelica: Book I, Chap. IX and X*, Ipswich.

González Herrera, U. M., 2008, *La Cueva del Templo. Contribución de la historia regional de Punta del Este – Isla de la Juventud*, via https://www.academia.edu/37564500/La_Cueva_del_Templo (accessed: 13/02/2022).

Hare, J. B., 2004, online edition of Schliemann 1912 on https://www.sacred-texts.com/atl/hilf/index.htm (accessed: 31/05/2022).

Ioannou, C., 2019, 'La Présence phénicienne en Crète', in Ferjaoui, A. and Redissi, T. (eds.), *La Vie, la mort et la religion dans l'univers phénicien et punique: Actes du VIIe Congrès International des Etudes Phéniciennes et Puniques, Hammamet, 9–14 Nov. 2009*, Institut National du Patrimoine, Tunis, 89–100.

Korfmann, M., 2001, 'Neue Aspekte zum "Schatz des Priamos". Der Schatz A von Troia, sein Auffindungsort und seine Datierung', in Theune-Großkopf, B. (ed.), *TROIA Traum und Wirklichkeit, Ausstellung von 17. März–17. Juni 2001 Stuttgart Archäologisches Landesmuseum Baden-Württemberg*, Stuttgart, 373–83.

Kourou, N., 2000, 'Phoenician Presence in Early Iron Age Crete reconsidered', in Aubet Semmler, M. E., and Barthélemy, M. (eds.), *Actas del IV Congreso international de estudios fenicios y púnicos, Cádiz, 2–6 Oct. 1995, Vol. III*, Cádiz, 1067–81.

Lindow, E., 1936, Report Paul Schliemann, via http://www.wheelandvoid.com/arcane-archives/2018/6/18/report-paul-schliemann (accessed: 28/05/2022).

Marion, C., 2020, 'Le Fonds Wladimir Golenischeff', published on https://archivescwg.hypotheses.org/46 (accessed: 31/ 05/ 2022).

Medioni, R., 2011, 'L'oeuvre des géologues français au Maroc', in *Travaux du Comité français d'Histoire de la Géologie, Comité français d'Histoire de la Géologie*, 2011, 3ème série (tome 25, 1), 1–52.

Nesselrath, H. G., 2021, 'From Plato to Paul Schliemann: Dubious Documents on the "History" of Atlantis', in Lennartz, K., Martinez, J., 2021, *Tenue est mendacium. Rethinking Fakes and Authorship in Classical, Late Antique and Early Christian Works*, Groningen, 105–18.

O'Connell, T., 2010, 'Paul Schliemann', via https://www.atlantipedia (accessed: 28/05/2022).

Quack, J. F., 1997, 'Ein ägyptisches Handbuch des Tempels und seine griechische Übersetzung', in *Zeitschrift für Papyrologie und Epigraphik* 119, 297–300.

Resche, F., 2016, *Le Papyrus médical Edwin Smith: chirurgie et magie en Egypte ancienne*, Paris.

Schliemann, P., 1912, 'How I Found Atlantis, the Source of All Civilization', in *New York American* 20 October, via https://www.sacred-texts.com/atl/hif/hif00.htm (accessed: 28/05/2022).

Shady Solís, R., 2006, *Caral: Supe La Civilización más Antigua de América*, Lima.

Sykes, E., 1966, 'Caribbean', in *Atlantis* 105 July/August vol. 19 no. 4, via www.seachild.net/products (accessed: 28/05/2022).

Sykes, E., 1952, 'The Schliemann Mystery', in *Atlantis* 23, January vol. 4 no. 5, via www.seachild.net/products (accessed: 28/05/2022).

Tallet, P., 2021, *Les Papyri de la Mer Rouge II – « Le Journal de Dedi » et autres fragments de journaux de bord (Papyrus Jarf C, D, E, F, Aa), Mémoires de l'Institut Français d'Archéologie Orientale* 145, Cairo.

Tallet, P., 2017, *Les Papyri de la Mer Rouge I – « Le journal de Merer » (Papyrus Jarf A et B), Mémoires de l'Institut Français d'Archéologie Orientale* 136, Cairo.

Termier, P., 1922, 'L'Atlantide, À la gloire de la Terre – souvenirs d'un géologue.' *Bibliothèque française de Philosophie*, Paris, 117–46.

Termier, P., 1913, 'L'Atlantide', in *Revue Scientifique*, année 51, 37–45.

Zhirov, N. T., 1958, 'The Paul Schliemann Mystery', in *Atlantis* 59 January Vol. 11 Nr. 2, via www.seachild.net/products (accessed: 28/05/2022).

Online sources

https://www.sacred-texts.com/atl/hif/hif00.htm (accessed: 28/05/2022).

https://www.atlantipedia.ie (accessed: 28/05/2022).

https://archivescwg.hypotheses.org/46, 31 (accessed: 28/05/2022).

https://www.atlantisforschung.de (accessed: 31/01/2020).

https://www.wheelandvoid.com/arcane-archives/2018/6/18/report-paul-schliemann (accessed: 28/05/2022).

http://www.seachild.net/products/at.html (accessed: 01/06/2022).

http://www.smb.museum/ausstellungen/detail/schliemanns-welten (accessed: 28/05/2022)

https://archivescwg.hypotheses.org/46, (accessed: 31/ 05/ 2022).

http://www.ascsa.edu.gr/index.php/archives/heinrich-schliemann-finding aid#Series_B:_Correspondence_" (accessed: 28/05/2022).

https://warbletoncouncil.org/cultura-chimu (accessed: 06/02/2022).

https://sais.webspace.durham.ac.uk (accessed: 28/05/2022).

https://tertullian.org/fathers/eusebius_pe_01_book1.htm (accessed: 28/05/2022).

About the author

Jean-Pierre Pätznick is a researcher and associate scientific member at the research lab Mondes Pharaoniques, Joint Research Center 'Orient et Méditerranée', Sorbonne, Paris IV, France. As a specialist in the Early Dynastic period and in the sigillographic material of ancient Egypt, he is creator of the DICTHICOM (*Dictionnaire du Thinite Commenté/ Dictionary of Early Dynastic Egyptian: Texts and Comment*). He obtained his PhD at Heidelberg (Germany) with *Die Siegelabrollungen und Rollsiegel der Stadt Elephantine im III. Jahrtausend v. Chr.: Zur Spurensicherung eines archäologischen Artefaktes* (2005).

Pätznick worked on various projects in Elephantine, Tell ed-Dab'a, and Tell el-Amarna. He is currently charged with the publication of the seals of the Old Kingdom town at Buhen.

Figure 1. Recto side of the Narmer Palette, *c.*3200–3000 BC, Egyptian Museum, Cairo CG 14716. Image Wikimedia Commons.

Was Narmer a Chinese Emperor?

Alternative History of Ancient Egypt in China

Tian Tian

Introduction

Like the conventional studies of ancient Egypt, many alternative ideas about this civilisation discussed in this volume are European-American. From the Hermetic Order of the Golden Dawn to comic books, classical, medieval and modern traditions and colonialism have shaped alternative ancient Egypt. Outside Europe and North America, however, local politics, cultures and traditions have also given rise to alternative images of ancient Egypt that are rather different from their Western counterparts.

This contribution examines one of many alternative histories of ancient Egypt cultivated in China. In this particular one, ancient Egypt was ethnically and culturally Chinese, and pharaohs such as Narmer were mythical Chinese emperors. Although this alternative history is popular online today, similar ideas could be found in the late nineteenth century, when the Chinese encountered ancient Egypt for the very first time. This alternative history, ridiculed or ignored as a 'crackpot theory' by academia, is treated as a social phenomenon here.[1] Within the limitations of this publication, the author will focus on elements in Chinese society that have played a role in the creation of this theory: ancient dynasties interwoven with national myth, presumed similarities between Chinese and Egyptian writings, everlasting nationalistic sentiment, and disagreements with the European powers.

Narmer, a Chinese king

In 2011 Luo Lingjie (羅靈傑) started writing his blog on Sina.com, the most popular blog site in China, proposing that the Shang dynasty (商朝 *c.*1600–1046 BC) in China was founded by the Hyksos, after they were defeated by the kings of Thebes.[2] For Luo the histories of the Shang dynasty and the Hyksos people are the same: each had defeated a local dynasty that once ruled in China or Egypt respectively; both migrated later. According to traditional

---

1 For a recent similar study that put alternative archaeology in the ideological context, see Turner/Turner 2021.

2 Luo 2011b.

in Van den Bercken, B. J. L. (ed.), *Alternative Egyptology: Critical Essays on the Relation between Academic and Alternative Interpretations of Ancient Egypt*, Leiden, pp. 132–145.

Chinese accounts the Shang dynasty moved its capital five times;[3] and the Hyksos migrated from Egypt, Luo believed, because of frequent riots in Upper Egypt. At the same time as Luo, Liu Guangbao (劉光保) started his blog on Sina.com. Inspired by Luo, Liu created a more complex theory proposing that the history of ancient Egypt was the history of the Xia dynasty (夏朝 *c.*2070–1600 BC). He named it Ai Xia Yiti Lun (埃夏一體論), which literally means 'ancient Egypt and the Xia dynasty are one'. In other words, ancient China and ancient Egypt are two sides of the same coin. In Liu's theory the ancient Egyptians are the same as the Hua Xia people (華夏族).[4] The Hua Xia people/Egyptians founded the Xia dynasty in Egypt. Later they migrated to East Asia and founded the Shang dynasty.

Apart from their blogs with over two million views, Luo and Liu published their alternative history in 2012[5] and 2017 respectively.[6] Liu has also been uploading his papers with English titles and abstracts to *Social Science Research Network* (SSRN) since 2016.[7] It was an article by Sun Weidong (孫衛東) that introduced their ideas to the international community of Egyptologists and archaeologists in 2016.[8] Sun compared the results of existing isotopic studies of lead in bronze Yin-Shang (殷商) vessels from c.1400 BC with those of copper ore deposits from Tongkuangyu (铜矿峪), South Africa, and Zimbabwe. He concluded that there was no copper deposit in China that could contain the highly radiogenic lead found in Yin-Shang vessels, while those from copper sources from cratons along the Nile or in the Sahara desert contain highly radiogenic lead. Thus the copper for the Yin-Shang vessels probably originated from Africa. Although Sun mentioned that results from the study on lead isotopes from Late Bronze Age Egypt by Shortland[9] partially overlap with those on Yin-Shang vessels, he did not articulate a Chinese-Egyptian connection in this article. He did claim that ancient Chinese people single-handedly created ancient Egyptian and other civilisations in an online article.[10] Sun's ideas and supporting evidence are very similar to those of Liu, who accused Sun of plagiarism.

Both Liu and Luo went to great lengths to collect evidence to support their alternative histories. Sporadic empirical similarities between ancient Chinese and Egyptian art,[11] costume,[12] and rituals[13] were commonly used arguments. Liu also ventured into the field of, as he claimed, molecular anthropology in search of a connection between the ancient Chinese and Egyptian peoples.[14] Many of their arguments, however, are based on hieroglyphs, which brings them close to their precursors from the late nineteenth century. Liu and Luo often mention the 'oracle script' (甲骨文), the 'script on bronze vessels'

---

3 Sima 1972, vol.1, 102; Xu 1966, 345.

4 The Hua Xia are a people that is related to the ancestry of the Chinese people and culture. Today the word Huaxia broadly refers to Chinese people.

5 Luo 2012a.

6 Liu 2017a.

7 See Liu's page on SSRN https://papers.ssrn.com/sol3/cf_dev/AbsByAuth.cfm?per_id=2607588 (accessed: 21/03/2021).

8 Sun et al. 2016. Its impact can be seen in Lewis 2016, Behr 2018, 158 and Weststeijn 2019.

9 Shortland 2006.

10 Sun 2016.

11 Liu 2013.

12 Luo 2011d and Liu 2013.

13 Luo 2011a and Liu 2012.

14 Liu 2016a and Liu 2017c. Liu argued that Egyptians, Sumerians and the Chinese are descendants of different branches of the 'Yellow Race', who migrated from Central Asia to the Near East and America, which might be considered politically incorrect.

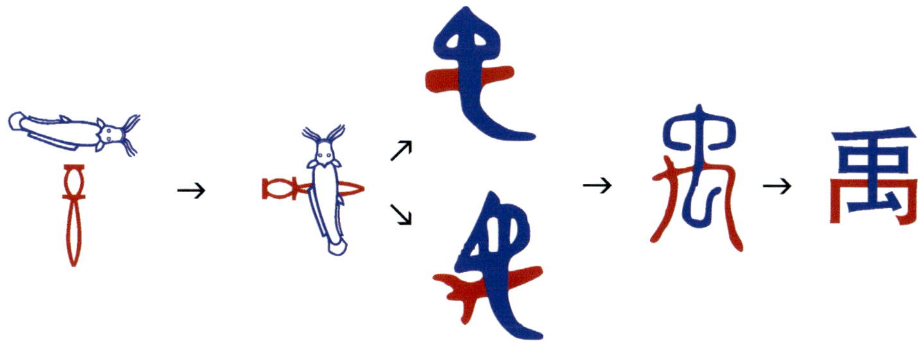

Figure 2. The king's name *Nr mr* read as Yu.

Figure 3. The toponym *Mn nfr* read as Bo.

(金文) and the 'seal script' (篆書)—these three scripts are some of the earliest forms of Chinese scripts from c.1300 to 220 BC. They believe that if the Chinese are Egyptians, then Egyptian hieroglyphs are the prototype for the later Chinese scripts. In many cases, they see a composition of hieroglyphs as one Chinese character. The name *Nr mr*, for example, depicts a catfish pierced by a chisel. The name is rotated and flipped to match the shape of the character 禹 Yu, the name of the first emperor of the Xia dynasty (fig. 2).[15] In other cases individual signs from hieroglyphic words were selected and regrouped into a new sign that resembled particular Chinese characters. Thus four out of seven signs forming the toponym *Mn nfr* (the name of the city of Memphis) happen to be the parts of the character 亳 Bo (fig. 3).[16] With this method, names of pharaohs from the 1st to 18th Dynasties were painstakingly identified with those of mythical rulers of the Xia dynasty mentioned in the traditional Chinese account *Records of the Grand Historian* or *Shi Ji* (史記).

The name of Narmer on the Narmer Palette is interpreted as a catfish pierced by a bronze chisel. Liu argued that the barbels of the catfish resemble the signs from the Bronze script in the box on the right, which are all characters of the name Yu, according to Liu 2018a.

15 Liu 2018a.

16 Liu 2017b, 3. Bo is a capital of the Shang dynasty, according to traditional accounts.

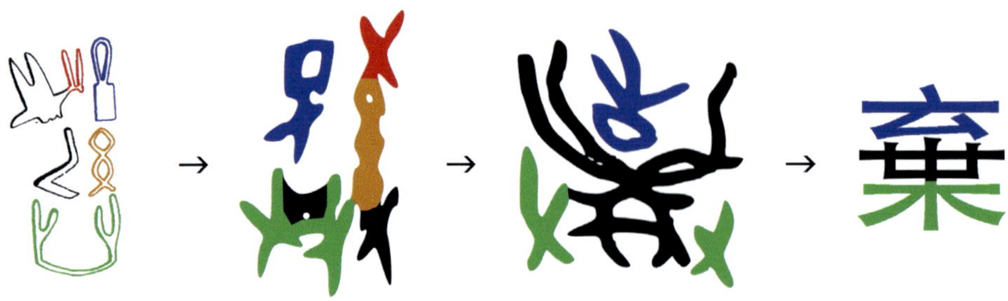

Figure 4. The title and the name *ḥtm.w bi͗t.y ḥ-mꜣ-kꜣ* is read as a whole, after Liu 2016b, 15, fig. 5.

Signs O24, D21, I19 and F35 in the toponym were selected and positioned in a specific order to form an image that resembles the character Bo, after Liu 2017b, 4.

The idea that the ancient Egyptians were somehow connected to the Chinese is not just an invention of twenty-first-century bloggers. Chinese intellectuals from the late nineteenth century already wove the history of ancient Egypt into that of China, and hieroglyphs were the main pillar of their evidence as well. One prominent figure is Guo Songtao (郭嵩燾), Chinese ambassador to the United Kingdom and France from 1876 to 1878. On his way to England, Guo commented that hieroglyphic signs on Cleopatra's Needle, the obelisk on the Victoria Embankment in London, are similar to signs used in ancient Chinese scripts, and recorded them in his journal.[17] One year later, when visiting the Bibliothèque Nationale de France, he concluded that ancient Egypt and China must once have been connected and Egyptians acquired their writing system from the Chinese.[18]

Guo's drawings of hieroglyphic inscriptions reached his friend Zhang Zimu (張自牧), who avidly proposed in 1877 that before the Great Flood,[19] the world was once ruled and civilised by ancient emperors and saints of China. And the striking similarities shared by Egyptian and Chinese scripts (based on Guo's drawing) proved that Chinese writing systems were once used globally.[20]

Chinese intellectuals from the nineteenth century and bloggers today have access to introductions to the hieroglyphic script and Egyptian language accepted by academia. This situation however does not make them embrace the 'canonical' reading of hieroglyphs. On the contrary, they believe their way of reading, a Chinese way, is superior to the decipherment of hieroglyphs by westerners, which will be proved wrong eventually. Guo had a discussion about hieroglyphs with Samuel Birch, but it did not stop Guo from developing the aforementioned ideas.[21] Chen Jitong (陳季同), a diplomat in France, read a book on hieroglyphs (he did not specify which) and argued against its treatment of most of the hieroglyphic signs on the Rosetta Stone as phonetic signs.[22] Similarly, Luo and Liu ridiculed western scholars for reading signs from Egyptian names

17 Guo 1891, 155.

18 Guo 1984, 652. Like Liu in the twenty-first century, Guo also mentioned that the ancient Egyptian ceramic vessels are similar in style to those of ancient China. See also Tian 2017, 176.

19 Again, the Great Flood here refers to that recorded by Chinese myth, and the person who successfully dispelled the water is no other than the Emperor Yu, identified by Liu as Narmer.

20 Zhang 1891, 504–05. See also Tian 2021, 72.

21 Guo 1984, 233–34.

22 Zhang 1896, vol. 8, 23.

(and sometimes titles as well) as phonetic signs. For them the correct way was treating an entire name as one Chinese character, without disassembling it into multiple phonetic signs and spelling out the name (fig. 4).[23]

Liu believes that the Egyptian hieroglyphic names can only be read when grouped in a specific way that resembles some Chinese characters. Here the hieroglyphic signs from the title and name *ḥtm.w bỉt.y ḥ-mꜣ-kꜣ* are correlated to various parts in the character *qi* (棄) in the oracle script.

Factors in the construction of an alternative history

The rise of this alternative ancient Egypt in China was influenced by several factors. The first is related to a long tradition of philology that shaped the idea that ancient Egyptian writing is a Chinese invention. From the mid-eighteenth century, the concern of Chinese scholarship shifted from morality and metaphysics (Neo-Confucianism, which emphasised introspection and self-cultivation) to empirical knowledge (philology, which promoted the study of ancient scripts).[24] The history of the Chinese script as described around AD 121 became the centre of attention by the early nineteenth century.[25] In the description from 121, the first Chinese scripts are pictures that show what they mean. For some literati well-versed in this history, Egyptian hieroglyphs are the earliest Chinese scripts because in their eyes, hieroglyphs are very faithful depictions of people, animals and objects. This connection can be perceived as proof for the idea that the ancient Egyptians and the Chinese once shared the same writing system, and that the ancient Egyptians either learnt writing from the Chinese, as intellectuals from the late nineteenth century imagined, or that the Egyptians and the Chinese were in fact identical, as the bloggers Liu and Luo propose. In both perspectives, hieroglyphs should be read like Chinese characters, which feature both sound-signs and sense-signs, while treating most hieroglyphic signs as phonetic signs and spelling them like alphabetic writing is neither Chinese nor correct.[26]

A second factor is related to mythological rulers and dynasties in historical Chinese accounts and the absence of archaeological evidence to underpin their existence. This creates a void that could be filled with the alternative history of ancient Egypt and China. Traditional Chinese history includes legendary emperors who ruled China until the Xia or first dynasty created by Yu, a hero who successfully saved China from the ravage of a great flood.[27] Later came the Shang and the Zhou dynasties. To many Chinese, these are historical facts. Moreover, since the late nineteenth century the Chinese have believed that the history of China covers five thousand years. This has been enshrined as a fact thanks to a popular and continuously reprinted history book with the title *Across Five Thousand Years*[28] as well as decades of repetition of this idea. Archaeology however tells a different story, as there is no direct or uncontroversial archaeological evidence related

23 Luo 2011c, Liu 2016b, Liu 2015.

24 Elman 2001.

25 This refers to *Shuowen Jiezi* (說文解字) or *Analysis of Characters as an Explanation of Writing* by Xu Shen (許慎) and the commentary on it by Duan Yucai (段玉裁) in 1807. See also Duan 1815. For the history of the Chinese script told by Xu Shen, the English version can be found in O'Neill 2016, 258–73.

26 Tian 2021, 62–67.

27 Sima 1972, 50, 82; Xu 1966, 149–50.

28 Lin/Cao 1979.

to the Xia dynasty or the period preceding it.[29] The earliest kings' names identified archaeologically are from the late Shang period, *c.*1300 to 1046 BC: thus the conventional history of China is about two thousand years shorter than the expected five thousand years. Nor does Chinese material culture from 2000 BC live up to the expectation of a glorious dynasty created by early historical accounts.[30] Therefore, the bloggers' solution is filling these lacunae in the early chronology and archaeology of China with Egyptian history and material culture.[31]

A third factor concerns nationalistic sentiments, which are also widely attested in this alternative history of ancient Egypt. These sentiments are hyperdiffusionistic because of their uncritical view of meagre evidence and the lack of consideration of a wider context.[32] Hyperdiffusionism believes that certain knowledge or skills, such as writing or metallurgy, must have a single origin and therefore ancient civilisations usually developed and spread from a single place. The proponents of hyperdiffusionism usually intend to glorify their favourite culture.[33] Thus by reducing ancient Egypt to a humble student and subject of Chinese culture, nineteenth-century intellectuals validated a long-lasting cultural notion that China is the sole origin of culture and civilisations. The history of dynastic Egypt from 3100 to 331 BC (incidentally also five thousand years) once dwarfed the dynastic history of China in length. But if one fills the supposed gap of three thousand years with the chronology of dynastic Egypt before the 19th Dynasty, Chinese history spans five thousand years and is no longer challenged by that of ancient Egypt.

Manifestations of nationalistic sentiments

These nationalistic sentiments are rooted in contemporary events.[34] After a series of defeats in wars against European powers since the First Opium War in 1840, European technology challenged the traditional idea of Chinese superiority.[35] To remedy this ideological crisis, some intellectuals, such as Wang Tao (王韜), formulated the idea that all Western knowledge originated in China.[36] Hence there would be no shame in procuring knowledge from Europeans or being defeated by their gunboats—they are just Chinese

29 Liu 2009, 831–33.

30 Such disappointments can be found in Sun 2016. He pointed out that the Xia dynasty is known for the luxury enjoyed by its ruling class in the historical account, but the capital of Xia, Erlitou site, yields no bronze vessels or inscribed objects and the urban settlement looks rather shabby.

31 Luo 2012b. Luo believes that there is much archaeological evidence from the ancient Near East in the third and second millennium BC, but no recorded history as precise and systematic as that of the Chinese traditional accounts was found; at the same time, China has systematic records of Xia and other kings during the third and second millennium BC. Thus the only 'logical' conclusion which can unite archaeological and textual evidence should be that the Xia and Shang Dynasties lived in the ancient Near East.

32 Moshenska 2017, 124, Schadla-Hall 2004, 257 and Williams 1991, 256. Moreover, Liu 2018b openly supports hyperdiffusionism and denounces those who reject it as 'racists' who cannot accept the truth that all cultures originated from a single, brilliant civilisation that outshines them all.

33 Moshenska 2017, 124.

34 Tang and Darr 2012, Zhang et al. 2008. For some recent examples see Boylan et al. 2020.

35 Townsend 1992, 98. Teng and Fairbank 1954, 18–19. But the degree, formation and xenology of the Chinese depend on the historical context and the view of sinocentrism found among Chinese during the late nineteenth century; it should not be taken for granted and is always under some debate, see for example Basu 2014.

36 Wang 1882, vol. 1, 3. Also Hao/Wang 1980, 201, Teng/Fairbank 1954, 137.

technology harnessed by the foreigners.[37] The long history of China is also an instrument for promoting national pride weaponised by the rising chauvinism of recent years. A year after Sun's controversial article, Xi Jinping met Donald Trump at the Forbidden Palace. Xi mentioned that China has a recorded history of three thousand years, but Trump replied that Egypt is the oldest culture, about eight thousand years old, and thus challenged the nationalist pride of the Chinese leader.[38] Later Xi announced the Four Confidence doctrine that has been promoting national self-confidence in propaganda, and five thousand years of history is the pillar of national confidence.[39] Currently, grassroots nationalism is also fanned by nationalistic action movies seeking to make a profit from zealous audiences. Sun's alternative history that identifies China as the source of the glorious Egyptian civilisation could be a good clickbait to win readership as well.[40] As China suffered from European colonialism during the late nineteenth century and Egyptology, a European discipline, had revealed a civilisation whose history could be longer than that of China, it is not surprising that some Chinese intellectuals and netizens show contempt for the West. Guo complained that Western scholars claimed a long history for ancient Egypt too easily; and if the history of ancient Egypt is contemporary to that of the Xia and Shang dynasties in China, then Chinese history must be longer than Egyptian history, because there were legendary emperors before the Xia dynasty.

Connecting Chinese and Egyptian scripts and ridiculing the European way of reading hieroglyphs also suggested the Chinese are better than Europeans in philology. This conflict strengthens as bloggers build a dichotomy between China and the West. In this dichotomy, Western Egyptologists and archaeologists conspire to hide the truth that ancient Egyptians are racially and culturally Chinese by changing noses of sculptures or mummies[41] as well as by reading hieroglyphic signs as a phonetic system instead of reading them as Chinese characters.[42] Thus Egyptologists and archaeologists help Western powers to suppress the achievements of the Chinese and to stop the rise of China. The Chinese, however, have been under the yoke of those Western powers and had no say in the interpretation of hieroglyphs. The Chinese have been blinded by Western Egyptologists. Hence, bloggers believe they are the ones who know the truth and battle this grand, colonial conspiracy.[43]

Certainly, we can argue that this resentment against Western academia is a symptom of the failure to distinguish *ad datum* (evidence) and *ad hominem* (the proponents) in academic critiques;[44] or that the bloggers have fallen into the omnipresent trap of creating battling categories of 'we' and 'they' in alternative archaeology.[45] But such resentment is

---

37 Although the Confucianists have shown a tendency to accept foreign technologies as Chinese ones long before this period, see Le 2002. For the idea that China is the origin of Western knowledge and its connections with Chinese intentions to procure military technologies from Europeans, see Huter 2005, 27–42.

38 Hernández/Zhao 2017.

39 Huang/Liu 2018, 1. For the full text of Xi Jinping's report in English see https://www.chinadaily.com.cn/china/19thcpcnationalcongress/2017-11/04/content_34115212.htm (accessed: 09/03/2022).

40 Huang 2021, 123.

41 Luo 2011e.

42 This point is related to the cultural nationalism based on Chinese characters and its competition with the alphabetic systems, see Guo 2004, 91–108.

43 Liu 2018b.

44 Williams 1991, 285.

45 Schadla-Hall 2004, 258–9.

Figure 5. Plate 11 from the *Description de l'Égypte, vol. V: Antiquités-Descriptions (Pyramides de Memphis)*, showing the pyramids of Giza and the Sphinx. Image Allard Pierson, OL 63-1000.

more than that, and deeply rooted in nationalism[46] and the narrative of 'national shame brought by Western colonial power' in the patriotic propaganda.[47]

Interestingly, the boundary between the 'canonical' history of ancient Egypt and the alternative one is not always clear in China. On the one hand, Chinese historians and Egyptologists always have a hunch that the comparative studies between hieroglyphs and Chinese scripts deserve to be done. They believe that the knowledge of Chinese scripts will contribute greatly to the understanding of the Egyptian writing system.[48] Some studies have compared the determinative signs with the Chinese *bushou* (部首), or radical system, while others have made a tentative comparison between Chinese, cuneiform and hieroglyphics based on the Chinese Six Writings system.[49] On the other hand, some academics in China also propose various alternative histories of ancient Egypt with a strong sense of conspiracy theory and zealous nationalism.

In 2019, at the peak of Chinese nationalism, the famous scholar He Xin (何新) published his blog articles in a book claiming that ancient Greek was fabricated by the West in order

46 Again, nationalism in China is othering the West such as the United States, by implementing a 'we' and 'they' mentality, see Boylan et al. 2020, 34. For the reappropriation of postcolonialism for cultural nationalism which opposes the West and its 'colonial culture', see Guo 2004, 108–23.

47 Callahan 2006 and 2004.

48 Zhou et al. 1985. See also Tian 2017, 183.

49 Chen 2016 and Wang 2015; Gong et al. 2005.

to break the confidence of the Chinese in their culture.[50] Later this idea expanded to ancient Egypt as well.[51] In the beginning of 2021, Huang Heqing (黄河清), a professor at the School of Humanities at Zhejiang University, proposed that the pyramids of Giza did not exist and were fabricated by the French after 1809. Huang argued that images of the Giza pyramids and Sphinx from the Renaissance are never similar, indicating that they were purely imaginary. After the Napoleonic expedition to Egypt, the French built the Giza pyramids from concrete or 'man-made stone', and Denon's plates in the *Description de l'Égypte* are nothing but construction plans (fig. 5).[52] Also in 2021, Chinese articles repeating Anatoly Fomenko's theory that pyramids are made of man-made stone circulated on Wechat, the most prominent Chinese social-media app, and gained many readers and much popularity.

And like their nineteenth-century counterparts, He and Huang are well-educated, familiar with generally accepted history of ancient Egypt and works of Egyptologists, and were trained as academics. Huang even obtained his PhD in art history at Université Paris I–Panthéon-Sorbonne. Bloggers like Luo and Liu are also well-educated and spend much time studying Egyptian languages. But wide-spread nationalism and grievances against the West led them to an alternative history of ancient Egypt.[53] To support their ideas, they cherry-pick their evidence, e.g. by selecting and disassembling hieroglyphic words arbitrarily. This suggests that the line between an academic argument and a 'crackpot theory' could be very thin. It is important that instead of ridiculing proponents of alternative Egyptology, readers from academic circles should also learn from them and that our knowledge on ancient Egypt is always created under the influence of certain ideologies. The problem does not lie in proposing an alternative history of ancient Egypt—everyone has the liberty to ask unconventional questions—but in the uncritical methods and thin evidence applied to support them.

Bibliography

Basu, D. K., 2014, 'Chinese Xenology and the Opium War: Reflections on Sinocentrism', in *The Journal of Asian Studies*, vol. 73, no. 4, 927–40.

Behr, W., 2018. '"Monosyllabism" and some other perennial clichés about the nature, origins and contacts of the Chinese language in Europe', in Malinar, A., Müller, S. (eds.), 2018, *Asia and Europe – Interconnected: Agents, Concepts, and Things.* Wiesbaden, 155–209.

Boylan, B. M., McBeath, J., Wang, B., 2020, 'US–China Relations: Nationalism, the Trade War, and COVID-19,' *Fudan Journal of the Humanities and Social Sciences*, 14.1, 23–40.

Callahan, W. A., 2006, 'History, Identity, and Security: Producing and Consuming Nationalism in China', in *Critical Asian studies*, 38.2, 179–208.

50 He 2013.

51 He 2019.

52 The argument was there long before it entered the headlines of online news, see Huang 2020.

53 The influence of propaganda could be detected in their blogs. For example, Liu states on the home page of his blog that he supports the 'rejuvenation of the nation of China', which is constantly featured in national propaganda. The website on which both He and Huang have their columns, ict88.com, clearly states in the banner on the home page: 'debunk the fake history fabricated by the West, establish cultural confidence, learn from the creditable history, rejuvenate China.' Both the 'cultural confidence' concept and the 'rejuvenation of China' were endorsed by, for example, Xi's report of the Four Confidences.

Callahan, W. A., 2004, 'National Insecurities: Humiliation, Salvation, and Chinese Nationalism', in *Alternatives: Global, Local, Political*, 29.2, 199–218.

Chen, Y., 2016, 'The Prototypical Determinatives in Egyptian and Chinese Writing', in *Scripta*, 8, 101–126.

Duan, Y., 1815, 說文解字註, [Jiangsu].

Elman, B. A., 2001, *From Philosophy to Philology: Intellectual and Social Aspects of Change in Late Imperial China*, Los Angeles.

Gong, Y., Yan, H., Ge, Y., 2009, 苏美尔、埃及及中国古文字比较研究, Beijing.

Guo, S., 1984, 伦敦与巴黎日记, Changsha.

Guo, S., 1891, 使西紀程, (小方壺齋輿地叢鈔; 11[2]). Shanghai.

Guo, Y., 2004, *Cultural Nationalism in Contemporary China: The Search for National Identity Under Reform*, London and New York.

Hao, Y, Wang, E., 1980, 'Changing Chinese Views of Western Relations, 1840–95', in Fairbank, J. K., Liu, K.-C. (eds.), *The Cambridge History of China*, Vol. 11, Cambridge, 142–201.

He, X., 2013, 希腊伪史考, Beijing.

Huter, T., 2005. *Bringing the World Home: Appropriating the West in Late Qing and Early Republican China*, Honolulu.

Huang, H., 2021, 'From "The Moon Is Rounder Abroad" to "Bravo, My Country": How China Misperceives the World', in *Studies in comparative international development*, 56.1, 112–30.

Huang, H., Liu, X., 2018, 'Historical Knowledge and National Identity: Evidence from China', in *Research & Politics*, 5.3, 1-8.

Le, A., 2002, 'View on the "Theory of Western Learning Being of Chinese Origin" from Confucian Culture', in *Studies in Dialectics of Nature*, vol. 18 (no.10), 53–56.

Lin, H., Cao, Y., 1979, 上下五千年, Shanghai.

Liu, G., 2017a, 发现夏朝：从文字演变和文献记载实证华夏文明起源, Beijing.

Liu, L., 2009, 'Academic Freedom, Political Correctness, and Early Civilisation in Chinese Archaeology: The Debate on Xia-Erlitou Relations', in *Antiquity*, 9.321, 831–43.

Luo, L., 2012a, 跨越三千年的因缘：揭示华夏文明起源的惊天秘密, Beijing.

Moshenska, G., 2017, 'Alternative Archaeologies', in Moshenska, G. (ed.), *Key Concepts in Public Archaeology*, London, 122–37.

O'Neill, T. M., 2016, *Ideography and Chinese Language Theory: A History*, Berlin and Boston.

Schadla-Hall, T., 2004. 'The Comforts of Unreason: The Importance and Relevance of Alternative Archaeology', in Merriman, N. (ed.), 2004, *Public Archaeology*, London, 255–71.

Shortland, A. J., 2006. 'Application of Lead Isotope Analysis to a Wide Range of Late Bronze Age Egyptian Materials', in *Archaeometry*, 48, 657–69 .

Sima, Q., 1972. 史記, Beijing.

Sun, W., Zhang, L., Guo, J., Li, C-Y., Jiang, Y-H., Zartman, R. E., Zhang, Z-F., 2016., 'Origin of the Mysterious Yin-Shang Bronzes in China Indicated by Lead Isotopes', in *Scientific Report*, 6, 1–9.

Tang, W., Darr, B., 2012, 'Chinese Nationalism and Its Political and Social Origins', in *The Journal of Contemporary China*, 21.77, 811–26.

Teng, S, Fairbank, J. K., 1954, *China's Response to the West: A Documentary Survey*, 1839–1923, Cambridge (MA).

Tian, T., 2021, 'Thoth with Four Eyes—Chinese Views of Egyptian Hieroglyph in Late Qing Period (1840–1912)', in *Journal of Ancient Egyptian Interconnections*, vol.31, 55-80.

Tian, T., 2017, 'Budding Lotus: Egyptology in China from the 1840s to Today', in Langer, C., (ed.), 2017, *Global Egyptology: Negotiations in the Production of Knowledges on Ancient Egypt in Global Contexts*, London, 173–89.

Townsend, J., 1992, 'Chinese Nationalism', in *The Australian Journal of Chinese Affairs*, 27, 97–130.

Turner, D. D., Turner, M. I., 2021, '"I'm Not Saying It Was Aliens": An Archaeological and Philosophical Analysis of a Conspiracy Theory', in Killin, A., Allen-Hermanson, S. (eds.), 2021, *Explorations in Archaeology and Philosophy*. Synthese Library (Studies in Epistemology, Logic, Methodology, and Philosophy of Science), vol. 433, 7–24, Cham.

Wang, H., 2015, 'Chinese Approaches to Egyptian Hieroglyphs: Liushu and Bushou', in *Zeitschrift der Deutschen Morgenländischen Gesellschaft*, 165,2, 279–302.

Wang, T., 1882, 弢園文錄外編, Hong Kong.

Weststeijn, T., 2019, 'The Chinese Isis, or the Sino-Egyptian Hypothesis', in Versluys, M. J. (ed.), *Temple – Monument – Lieu de mémoire. The Iseum Campense from the Roman Empire to the Modern Age, Rome*, 301–13.

Williams, S., 1991, *Fantastic Archaeology: The Wild Side of North American Prehistory*, Philadelphia.

Xu, W-J., 1966 [1877], 竹書紀年統箋, Taipei.

Zhang, X., Fish, S., Jameson, F., 2008, *Postsocialism and Cultural Politics: China in the Last Decade of the Twentieth Century*, North Carolina.

Zhang, Y., 1896, 三洲日記. Jingdu.

Zhang, Z., 1891, 蠡測巵言, (小方壺齋輿地叢鈔; 11 [8]). Shanghai.

Zhou, G., Wu, Y., Lin, Z., 1985, 古典文明研究在我国的空白必须填补, *World History*, 11, 1–3.

Online resources

He, X., 2019, 《职方外纪》暴露埃及伪史, via https://www.ict88.com/page/view-post?id=381 (accessed: 20/03/2022).

Hernández, J. A., Zhao, I., 2017, 'Trump's Visit to China Provides a Propaganda Bonanza', The New York Times, Nov. 10, via https://www.nytimes.com/2017/11/10/world/asia/china-trump-visit-propaganda.html (accessed: 20/03/2022).

Huang, H. Q., 2020, 以图证史：埃及金字塔是1809年之后新建伪造--希腊雅典、埃及金字塔和伊朗波斯波利斯"古迹"都是现代新建伪造, via https://www.ict88.com/page/view-post?id=527. (accessed: 20/03/2022).

Lewis, R., 2016. 'Does Chinese Civilization Come From Ancient Egypt?', in Foreign Policy, via https://foreignpolicy.com/2016/09/02/did-chinese-civilization-come-from-ancient-egypt-archeological-debate-at-heart-of-china-national-identity/ (accessed: 15/01/2021).

Liu, G., 2018a,《发现夏朝》是怎样把古埃及文字解读为汉字的？('How Did the Book Discovery of the Xia Dynasty Interpret Ancient Egyptian Hieroglyphs As Chinese Characters?'), SSRN, via https://ssrn.com/abstract=3306636 (accessed: 21/01/2021).

Liu, G., 2018b, 让种族主义者吐血的理论：考古学中的超扩散主义, via http://blog.sina.com.cn/s/blog_6a4e1c6f0102x65r.html (accessed: 18/03/2021).

Liu, G., 2017b, 夏朝地图 (The Map of the Chinese Xia Dynasty), SSRN, via https://ssrn.com/abstract=2913322 (accessed: 02/03/2021).

Liu, G., 2017c, 苏美尔-古埃及黄种人体质之谜来源猜想, via http://blog.sina.com.cn/s/blog_6a4e1c6f0102wmdz.html (accessed: 18/03/2021).

Liu, G., 2016a, 黄种人和人类文明起源, via http://blog.sina.com.cn/s/blog_6a4e1c6f0102whqo.html (accessed:18/03/2021).

Liu, G., 2016b, 'Study on the Formation of Chinese Characters Based on the Hieroglyphs of Ancient Egypt', SSRN, via https://ssrn.com/abstract=2871190 (accessed: 18/03/2021).

Liu, G., 2015, 西方人用拼音方法解读古埃及文字的根源, via http://blog.sina.com.cn/s/blog_6a4e1c6f0102vmqk.html (accessed: 18/03/2021).

Liu, G., 2013, 古埃及的水墨画和草书, via http://blog.sina.com.cn/s/blog_6a4e1c6f0101c104.html (accessed: 18/03/2021.

Liu, G., 2012, 丧葬习俗： 印第安人， 华北汉人， 古埃及人, via http://blog.sina.com.cn/s/blog_6a4e1c6f0100ws8h.html (accessed: 18/03/2021).

Luo, L., 2012b, 世界考古学和中国考古学的区别, via http://blog.sina.com.cn/s/blog_7c1d31150100zvvc.html (accessed:25/02/2021).

Luo, L., 2011a, 办丧事披麻戴孝及哭丧的由来 , via http://blog.sina.com.cn/s/blog_7c1d31150100wsi9.html (accessed: 25/02/2021).

Luo, L., 2011b, 商汤、伊尹----喜克索人的国王, via http://blog.sina.com.cn/s/blog_7c1d31150100xycp.html (accessed: 25/02/2021).

Luo, L., 2011c, 西方人解读古埃及象形文字的一大错误, via http://blog.sina.com.cn/s/blog_7c1d31150100vocq.html (accessed: 25/02/2021).

Luo, L., 2011d, 最古老的"汉服", via http://blog.sina.com.cn/s/blog_7c1d31150100zlzx.html (accessed: 25/02/2021).

Luo, L., 2011e, 故意把法老雕像的鼻子敲掉或改掉， 西方考古界的卑劣行径, via http://blog.sina.com.cn/s/blog_7c1d31150100uu0p.html (accessed: 25/02/2021).

Sun, W., 2016, 世界四大古文明是中华民族的祖先创立的？ via https://mp.weixin.qq.com/s?__biz=MzA5MDkyNDIzNw==&mid=207596700&idx=1&sn=26e47aa4864a44f3da4e3a92a089e147&scene=19#wechat_redirect. (accessed: 25/02/2021).

About the author

Tian Tian obtained his PhD in Egyptian archaeology at University College London in 2020 and is now a postdoc at the World Arthistory Institute (WAI), Shanghai International Studies University. His research interests are Egyptian grave goods and funerary practices, particularly changes in grave goods during the third millennium BC. Apart from his archaeological studies, Tian looks into Chinese perspectives on ancient Egypt from the eleventh century to the present, and has published two articles that would complement the present contribution.

Figure 1. Reconstruction of the door to the Lost Steps Room of Independência Lodge as it may have been in 1874. Artistic conception by Daniel Clabunde.

The Occult Egyptian Mural Discovered in a Brazilian Freemasons' Temple

Thomas Henrique de Toledo Stella

Introduction

In the Brazilian city of Campinas, a wall painting with ancient Egyptian iconography was discovered toward the end of 2012. This unexpected discovery was made in the temple of a Freemasonry lodge named Independência n. 131. The painting has scenes reproduced from the tombs of the 12th- and 18th-Dynasty officials Amenemhat, Djehutyhotep and Rekhmira, showing representations of manual labour and crafts with hieroglyphic texts. It dates back to the year 1874, when the temple was inaugurated with great pomp. The lodge was founded some years before, aiming to promote the republican and abolitionist causes—Brazil was still a monarchy based on a slave economy.

The members of this lodge were key figures in the process of abolition that culminated in 1888 and in the overthrow of the monarchy in 1889. Two members of Independência n. 131 were ministers in the new republican government, including Campos Salles, who became president in 1898.

The mural was covered over, probably in the 1930s, and remained hidden until 2012. I studied it in 2019 and concluded that the Egyptian iconography was reframed and oriented to represent a Freemason's point of view. The hieroglyphic text is a poem stressing the spiritual meaning of manual labour. Scenes and text together express the spirit of the 1870s. Half a century later, the reason for it existence was forgotten and it was removed from view.

Brazilian Freemasonry and Egyptomania in the nineteenth century

Brazil reached its independence from Portugal on 7 September 1822. At this time, the colonial system was in crisis and the Freemasonry lodges were instrumental in

in Van den Bercken, B. J. L. (ed.), *Alternative Egyptology: Critical Essays on the Relation between Academic and Alternative Interpretations of Ancient Egypt*, Leiden, pp. 146–155.

its downfall.[1] As secret societies, they found a way to safely share illuminist ideas and conspire against the colonial system. Freemasons were instrumental in the independence of the United States of America in 1776. Other movements on the American continent followed it.[2] By the end of the nineteenth century, almost all American countries were liberated from European colonial control.

The earliest record of Freemasonry's presence in Brazil dates from around 1800.[3] In 1822, the Grand Orient of Brazil was founded, uniting forces involved in the process of independence.[4] On 7 September 1822, the Portuguese prince-regent declared Brazil an independent monarchy; he was crowned emperor on 12 October. The chosen regime was an imperial monarchy, but the political leaders could not overcome the will of the agrarian elite, who decided to maintain the slave regime.

After a crisis over the country's path after independence, the Emperor Dom Pedro I prohibited Freemasonry in Brazil in October 1822. In 1831, he abdicated under political pressure. Regents governed the country and Freemasonry progressively returned to its activities, divided into a monarchist and a republican camp.[5] Both were mostly abolitionist, except the landed aristocracy.

In São Paulo, the Faculty of Law São Francisco became a centre where illuminist, liberal, republican and abolitionist ideas thrived. The students created a secret society called Burschenschaft Paulista; it was inspired by the ideas of a German immigrant, professor Johann Julius Gottfried Ludwig Frank.[6] Most of the Burschenschaft members were also Freemasons and they became politically important during the reign of Dom Pedro II, from 1840 onward.

The Freemasonry lodge Independência n. 131 was founded in the city of Campinas in the 1850s, but closed down soon.[7] In 1867, it was reinstalled. Its goal was to promote republican and abolitionist ideas, contributing to freeing enslaved people and ending the monarchist regime, in collaboration with other lodges. This lodge had many well-known members; foremost among them was Campos Salles, president of the country (1898–1902), but there were intellectuals, scientists, journalists and architects as well.

Like nineteenth-century Europe, Brazil was also influenced by the Egyptomania that resulted from Napoleon's expedition to Egypt.[8] During his reign, Dom Pedro I added many ancient Egyptian objects to the National Museum collection. His son, Dom Pedro II, visited

---

1 According to Hobsbawm, in the Age of Revolutions (1789–1848) Freemasonry was involved in political, social, economic, and scientific transformations. Revolutionary ideas connected to Enlightenment and classical liberalism were spread by Freemasonry lodges (Hobsbawm 2015, 66).

2 Haiti (1804), Paraguay (1811), Argentina (1816), Chile (1818), Venezuela and Colombia (1819), Mexico (1821), Brazil and Ecuador (1822), Peru (1824), Bolivia (1825), Uruguay (1828), Nicaragua, Costa Rica, El Salvador, Guatemala and Honduras (1838), Canada (1867) and Cuba (1898).

3 Castellani/Carvalho 2009.

4 The Grand Master was Dom Pedro I, who would be the first Brazilian emperor. The First Vigilant was José Bonifácio, a monarchist leader. The Second Vigilant was Gonçalves Ledo, a republican leader. This trinity was the union of three different forces committed to the process of independence: the heir to the Portuguese throne, a conservative, and a liberal. Bonifácio and Ledo were both supporters of the abolitionist cause (Stella 2022).

5 Carneiro 2016.

6 Bandecchi 1982.

7 Stella 2019.

8 Bakos 1998.

Egypt in 1871 and 1876, bringing back objects and mummies that were gifts from the Egyptian *khedive* (viceroy).

The discovery of an Egyptian mural in a Freemasons' lodge

The current temple of the Independência lodge is different from the original one inaugurated in 1874. It underwent many rearrangements until it reached its now monumental form.[9] Between 1900 and 1902, the Rituals Room was enlarged. In the 1930s, the biggest renovation was made, converting the front house and the temple into a single building.[10]

In the Rituals Room, there is an Egyptianising decoration (fig. 2), which according to the registers probably dates from 1874 or 1902.[11] The Egyptianising scenes located in the Lost Steps Room, the antechamber of the Rituals Room, were discovered during a rearrangement in 2012.

According to the members of the lodge the wall in the Lost Steps Room was always painted in a single colour and decorated with portraits of old members (fig. 3). The workmen who worked on the last rearrangement of the room and who found the mural confirmed this. They identified three layers of paint when they 'excavated' the wall.

The discovery of the Egyptian wall painting was photographed and filmed, showing the situation in which it was found. Unfortunately, the 'excavation' of the wall was not carried out by archaeologists but by masons, resulting in much information being lost. The current state of the mural can be seen in fig. 4.

In the photographs taken during the rearrangement, I was able to identify some pillars and a staircase below the floor of the Lost Steps Room.[12] The work plan made by the architect of the 1930s renovation was also found. These clues revealed that the current Lost Steps Room once was a vestibule and that the temple was erected on a higher level than the street floor. It means that the Egyptianising scenes were approached from a lower viewpoint, resulting in a monumental sight. The mural was probably created for the inauguration in 1874. It conforms to the measures of the original temple wall (5m x 8m). The expansion of the temple between 1900 and 1902 is clearly marked by the foundations. In this expansion, no paintings were found on the wall.

The newspaper *Gazeta de Campinas*—whose editor was the president of Independência n. 131, Francisco Quirino dos Santos (1841–1886)—ran a series of articles about the temple's inauguration in 1874. On 4 February 1874 the newspaper reported that the Catalan immigrant José Maria Villaronga y Panellas was honoured for his involvement in the building of the temple. He owned a company specialising in mural paintings, but his style was different from the one found in the temple.[13] He probably was the person responsible for coordinating the painting, but not the painter.

---

9 Stella 2019, 230.

10 The landscape that surrounds the temple of the Independência lodge changed drastically. The place was far from the main village that originated the city. Today, the building is in the heart of the city centre, surrounded by skyscrapers and commercial facilities in a metropolis with 1.2 million inhabitants.

11 The oldest record of this inner decoration is a picture taken during a public session on 7 September 1921, the 99th anniversary of Brazil's independence.

12 Stella 2019, 233.

13 Correio Popular 2013.

Figure 2. The Rituals Room of Independência Lodge with Egyptianising decoration.

Figure 3. The Lost Steps Room before the discovery of the Egyptian mural.

From 5 to 7 February 1874 the temple was open to the public. The newspaper describes the vestibule as 'exquisitely painted'. It does not mention an Egyptian theme, but accurately describes the door to the Rituals Room: 'On the door on the right, the Portuguese and Brazilian flags are faithfully imitated, together with the eagle with the starry band of the United States; on the door on the left, the Spanish and French flags and between them, a crest with the Swiss Phrygian cap.'[14]

It revealed clearly the ideology of the Independência lodge at that time (fig. 1). The Portuguese and Brazilian flags were there due to the common historical roots of these countries. The symbols related to the United States referred to the abolitionists who

14 *Gazeta de Campinas*, 5/2/1874.

Figure 4. The mural in its current state.

had won the American Civil War (1861–1865). The Spanish flag was shown because that country lived its ephemeral First Republic (1873–1874) exactly during the period of the inauguration of the temple. The reference to France concerned its revolutionary tradition of 1789, 1830 and 1848, which was highlighted by another image:

> '(...) in front of the door, there is a majestic allegorical image of Liberty on the wall with the natural proportions of a slender and tall woman, with fine contours, expressing in her features and gestures the virile characteristics of the idea of which she is the emblem and visible consubstantiation.'[15]

Everything together resulted in a very eclectic style: a wall with Egyptianising painted scenes, a door with flags representing the lodge's ideology, and a picture of the revolutionary icon Marianne, more famously depicted by Eugène Delacroix in *La Liberté guidant le Peuple*, which commemorates the French revolution of 1830. There are Egyptian references in the liberty painting as well (fig. 5).

The speech of the Independência lodge's orator was published in the *Gazeta de Campinas* in two parts on 5 and 9 February 1874. It underlines the importance of ancient Egypt in the beliefs of Independência n. 131, presenting a mythical narrative about the history of humanity and recognising ancient Egypt as source of the initiations to the Masonic mysteries. The orator also lists the figures from Greek culture Orpheus, Homer, Plato and Pythagoras, and the Hebrews Moses and Solomon as continuing this Egyptian tradition, which extends to medieval and modern Europe. He reveres ancient Egypt because of its sacred and initiatory works and mentions Thebes as the city of one hundred

15 *Gazeta de Campinas*, 5/2/1874.

Figure 5. Allegoric painting of Liberty (painter unknown).

gates, being the place where neophytes tore the veil of the sanctuary, saw the globe of fire and the Eye of Providence. The discourse is inaccurate about historical events. It was based on the knowledge of that time and was interwoven with mythical elements. All the evidence so far suggests that the Egyptian mural in the Lost Steps Room dates from the temple's inauguration in 1874.

Decoding the mural's iconography

The images in the painting were taken from a single book: *The Manners and Customs of the Ancient Egyptians* by John Gardner Wilkinson (1841). The wall is divided into (fig. 6):

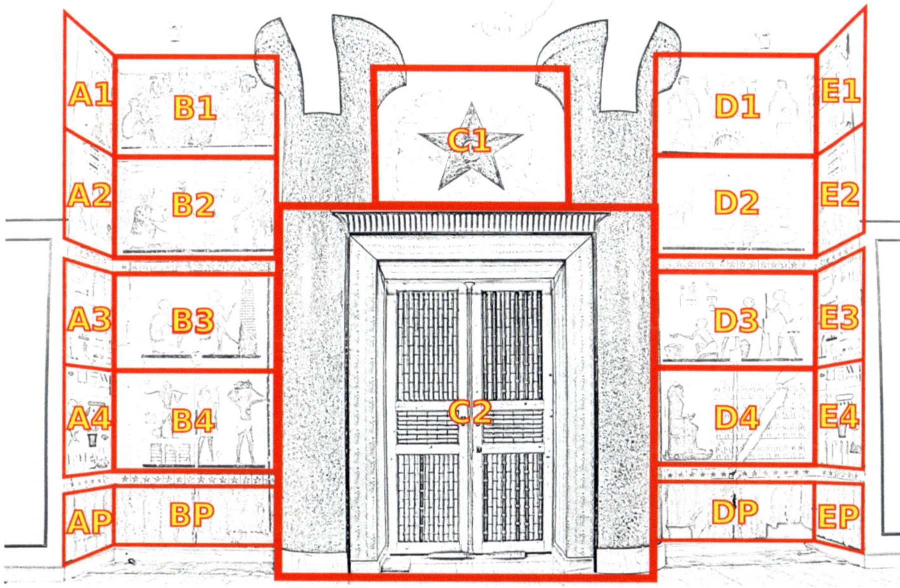

Figure 6. Schematic of the mural's registers (image by the author).

a. two vertical strips of texts with the same hieroglyphs on the north and south walls (A and E);
b. two vertical strips of images on the left and right sides of the door (B = centre-north wall and D = centre-south);
c. the part over the door and the door itself (C).

The scenes are reproduced from tombs at three different archaeological sites in Egypt:

a. Beni Hasan: tomb BH2 from the nomarch Amenemhat, 12th Dynasty (1985–1773 BC). B1, B2 and B3.
b. Deir el-Bersha: tomb DB2 of the nomarch Djehutyhotep, 12th Dynasty (1985–1773 BC). D4.
c. Sheikh Abd el-Qurna: tomb TT100 of the vizier Rekhmira, 18th Dynasty (1550–1295 BC). B4, C1, D1, D2, and D3.

The wall painting has nine registers with scenes showing various crafts, both in the production stage (top three registers) and in the transport stage (bottom register). Starting at the top and reading from left to right, we can see the following sequence:

a. Polishing a sphinx statue, symbol of wisdom (C1).
b. Glassblowing with a tube (B1) and stepping on bellows to melt metals (D1).
c. Shaping vases (B2) and decorating a column (D2).
d. Firing ceramics (B3) and grinding corn to make bread (D3).
e. Transporting bricks (B4) and moving a colossal statue (D4).
f. Sequence of papyrus/lotus flowers at the base (line F).
g. An Egyptian-style door (C2).

The text in hieroglyphs is almost the same in strips A and E. Analysing it, we can conclude that it is a translation into hieroglyphs of a Portuguese text, according to what was known about ancient Egyptian grammar by the last quarter of the nineteenth century. The text contains many grammatical errors.

A possible translation is an inverse sonnet with four stanzas, two triplets and two quartets:

A/E 1.1		*tr wꜣ ỉs*	At the time of the journey indeed
A/E 1.2	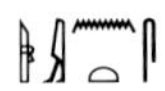	*ỉst ỉỉ nts*	The workers come to it
A/E 1.3		*rmṯw*	For all mankind

A/E 2.1	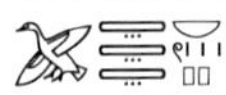	*pꜣ tꜣw nb.w p(p)*	All these lands of the meadow
A/E 2.2		*mryw*	Loved by us
A/E 2.3		*swr šww*	Charged by sunlight

A/E 3.1		*mꜣꜥw*	The truths
A/E 3.2		*rwỉ*	Revealed
A/E 3.3	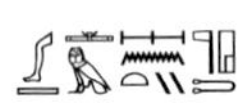	*sbḳ m spꜣt*	In the splendid province
A/E 3.4		*nty ḥwt nṯr=ṯ*	Which is our divine temple

A/E 4.1		*r kꜣ mꜣꜥ py n ỉst*	To the fair soul of these workers
A/E 4.2		*snṯ tꜣ*	Who measure the land
A/E 4.3		*pꜣ snṯr*	(With) this incense
A/E 4.4		*ỉỉ=s y nb*	To the return of the master

It refers to the spiritual meaning of work performed in the masonic ritual. The mention of meadows fits perfectly with the characteristics of the fields surrounding Campinas. Everything is also related to masonic vocabulary, especially when read in the Portuguese translation.

Conclusion

The Egyptianising mural was probably made in 1874 for the inauguration of the temple. The images were extracted from Wilkinson's book from 1841. Probably the paintings were made by Villaronga's company. In line with the republican spirit, the iconography does not show pharaohs, but common workmen and nomarchs. The text is a poem, an inverse sonnet that makes sense in the context of the temple. The painting also fits well with the Egyptianising decoration in the Rituals Room.

One question that remains is: why was the mural covered over? This probably happened during a reform in the 1930s when the members of the lodge decided to change the style of the temple building from an Egyptianising to a neoclassical theme, which still remains today.

Bibliography

Bandecchi, P. B., 1982, *A Bucha, a Maçonaria e o Espírito Liberal*, Parma, São Paulo.

Bakos, M. M., 1998, 'Three moments of Egyptology in Brazil', in *Proceedings of the Seventh International Congress of Egyptologists*, Cambridge, 3–9 September 1995, Leuven, 87–91.

Carneiro, L., 2016, *Maçonaria, política e liberdade*, Paco Editorial, Jundiaí.

Castellani, J., Carvalho, W., 2009, *História do Grande Oriente do Brasil: a Maçonaria na História do Brasil*, Madras, São Paulo.

Hobsbawm, E., 2015, *A Era das Revoluções (1789-1848)*, Paz e Terra, Rio de Janeiro.

Novais, F., 1989, *Portugal e Brasil na crise do Antigo Sistema Colonial (1777-1808)*, Hucitec, São Paulo.

Stella, T. (ed.), 2019, *A Descoberta Arqueológica na Loja Maçônica Independência: o templo egípcio e sua história abolicionista e republicana (1859-1889)*, Campinas.

Stella, T., 2022, 'As rupturas incompletas no processo civilizatório brasileiro: personagens, instituições e o papel da maçonaria na história do país', in *Revista Principios*, 164, May–August 2022.

Wilkinson, J. G., 1841, *The Manners and Customs of the Ancient Egyptians: Including Their Private Life, Government, Laws, Arts, Manufactures, Religion, Agriculture and Early History*, New York.

Online resources

Correio Popular, 19/05/2013, https://correio.rac.com.br/2013/05/capa/campinas_e_rmc/60812-artigo-da-pista-sobre-obra-em-templo.html (accessed: 10/8/2019).

Gazeta de Campinas, 1869–1875, http://bndigital.bn.br/acervo-digital/gazeta-campinas/091995 (accessed: 10/8/2019).

About the author

Thomas Henrique de Toledo Stella currently is a PhD candidate in archaeology at the Museum of Archaeology and Ethnology of the University of São Paulo. He was a visiting graduate researcher at the Department of Near Eastern Languages and Cultures of the University of California Los Angeles and completed a Master in economic development at the Institute of Economy of the State University of Campinas. He completed his postgraduate studies at the Institute for the Study of the Ancient Near East of the Autonomous University of Barcelona and graduated in history at the University of São Paulo. He currently is Professor of History in the Federal Institute of Education, Science and Technology - São Paulo (IFSP).

Figure 1. Akhenaten making an offering to the Aten, detail of a relief fragment from a boundary stele at Amarna, 18th Dynasty. Egyptian Museum, Cairo. Accession no. TR 30.10.26.12. Serial no. 12. Image DeAgostini Picture Library/Scala, Florence.

The Royal Son of the Sun

Christian Egyptosophy and Victorian Egyptology in the Egyptian Romances of H. Rider Haggard

Simon Magus

Introduction

Sir Henry Rider Haggard (1856–1925) was one of the most prolific and popular author-novelists of his age. Although now remembered principally as the author of *King Solomon's Mines* (1885) and *She* (1887), he penned fifty-six other novels and numerous works of non-fiction. The study of Haggard's oeuvre has tended to follow two main trajectories, both of them polemical: the postcolonialist perspective regarding Haggard as an éminence grise and propagandist of Empire, and the feminist perspective from which Haggard is viewed as a misogynist and opponent of the emerging New Woman.[1]

In the following paper, I shall endeavour to redress the balance by demonstrating that there are other equally important influences on Haggard's fiction, namely those of the ideas circulating in the nineteenth-century occult milieu, which continued to influence him throughout his working life into the first decades of the twentieth century. I shall argue that Haggard's stories portray an esoteric quest for a 'hidden God' or 'hidden Nature,' and are demonstrative of what I have termed an 'Imperial Occult.'[2] This Imperial Occult is to be considered more a historiographical category than the descriptor of a literary genre. It credits the imperial project with authorial responsibility for the syncretism and hybridity of the esoteric thought of the period and its particular qualities, contingent as they were upon British forays into Egypt, Southern Africa, India and Tibet—all of which impacted on the literature of Henry Rider Haggard. For the purposes of this paper and in keeping with the theme of this volume, my focus will be on Egypt.[3]

---

1 For Haggard as an imperialist, see Katz 1987. For Haggard from a feminist perspective, see in particular Gilbert/Gubar 1989.

2 To clarify, the collocation 'Imperial Occult' occurs as a stand-alone title and section divider in Brown, Burdett, and Thurschwell 2004, 195. Whilst not strictly my coinage, I have defined and conceptualised it as a term. See Magus 2022, XIV.

3 Rider Haggard visited Egypt on four occasions—in 1887, 1904, 1912 and 1924—and Egyptology was a life-long passion. See Addy 1998, 1–35, in which the trips to Egypt are described in some detail.

in Van den Bercken, B. J. L. (ed.), *Alternative Egyptology: Critical Essays on the Relation between Academic and Alternative Interpretations of Ancient Egypt*, Leiden, pp. 156–165.

Egyptosophy, mnemohistory, and metageography

Rather than the common perception of Haggard as a dyed-in-the-wool imperialist, his romances reveal a more complex individual who articulates a palimpsest of esoteric, Romantic and occult idioms to create parables of sin and redemption, and the pursuit of 'Truth.' In the following I shall focus on Haggard's Egyptian romances, and deploy three concepts to spatially and temporally locate Haggard's Egypt: Christian Egyptosophy, mnemohistory and metageography. I shall consider the influence of the occult milieu on Haggard's literature concentrating on Christian Egyptosophy, but also briefly consider some elements of Romanticism. 'Egyptosophy' is a term coined by Erik Hornung, who elucidates his concept as follows:

> Already in antiquity, there was an opinion that the land of the Nile was the fount of all wisdom and the stronghold of hermetic lore. Thus began a tradition that is still alive today, and which I venture to designate 'Egyptosophy.' It was only after the decipherment of the hieroglyphs by Jean-François Champollion in 1822 that its younger sister, the discipline of Egyptology, made its appearance.'[4]

Dovetailing with this concept of Egyptosophy is Jan Assmann's notion of 'mnemohistory.' Mnemohistory is concerned not with the past as such, but with the past as it is remembered. 'It surveys the story-lines of tradition, the webs of intertextuality, the diachronic continuities and discontinuities of reading the past.'[5] Mnemohistory is 'reception theory' applied to history—but reception is not to be understood here simply in the narrow sense of transmitting and receiving. The past is not simply 'received' by the present: 'The present is haunted by the past and the past is modelled, invented, reinvented, and reconstructed by the present.'[6] Thirdly, we consider the concept of metageography. Martin W. Lewis and Kären E. Wigen have defined this concept as follows: 'By metageography we mean the set of spatial structures through which people order their knowledge of the world: the often-unconscious frameworks that organize studies of history, sociology, anthropology, economics, political science, or even natural history.'[7]

The visions of Harmachis

In his imaginary reworking of the story of Cleopatra VII in *Cleopatra* (1889), Haggard tells the story of the priest Harmachis, who is initiated into the mysteries of Isis via a series of mystical and eventually anacalyptic visions.[8] Harmachis seeks to destroy Cleopatra, seen by the priestly hierarchy as a Greek usurper. He falls in love with the Egyptian queen, however, betraying his hieratic affiliation to Isis as a result. When Cleopatra shuns him, he poisons her, but is himself subsequently buried alive for his transgression against the goddess. The visions of Harmachis are particularly demonstrative of Haggard's reception of Victorian Egyptology. Describing one of his visions, Harmachis says:

4 Hornung 2001, 1.
5 Assmann 1997, 9.
6 Ibid.
7 Lewis/Wigen 1997, ix.
8 Haggard 1889.

> I saw that man was created vile, but Those who are above took pity on him, and came down to make him good [...]. But man returned to his wicked way, and then the bright Spirit of Good, who is of us called Osiris, but who has many names, offered himself up for the evil doing of the race that had dethroned him.[9]

Haggard goes on to tell the reader, through the voice of Harmachis, that 'the mummy cloths of symbol and of ceremony that wrap Osiris round fell from him, and I understood the secret of religion, which is Sacrifice.'[10] Here is a clear statement and assertion of the Christian doctrine of vicarious atonement, cast in the Egyptian idioms of the Isis-Osiris cycle. Haggard went on to reprise this Christian Egyptosophical refrain in *Smith and the Pharaohs*, where the protagonist muses: 'When one came to think of it, beneath a mass of unintelligible symbolism there was much in Egyptian faith which it was hard for a Christian to disbelieve. Salvation through a Redeemer, for instance, and the resurrection of the body.'[11]

These passages provide evidence for the influence of Rider Haggard's friend Sir Ernest Arthur Thompson Wallis Budge (1857–1934), the Keeper of the Department of Egyptian and Assyrian Antiquities at the British Museum between 1894 and 1924. Budge's Egyptological discourse was characterised by a marked Christian inflection. Notably, his work presents what I have termed an Osiride Christology, where Osiris is presented as a type of Christ the Redeemer—Christ in an Atef crown.[12]

In his *Egyptian Magic* (1901), Budge observes that Osiris 'was of divine origin, but had lived upon the earth, and had suffered a cruel death at the hands of his enemies, and had risen from the dead, and had become the God and king of the world which is beyond the grave.'[13] This idea, then, amongst others, was directly adopted by Haggard. In addition, Budge conceived of an 'original monotheism' in ancient Egypt: behind the panoply of theriomorphic deities there was a 'hidden monotheism' that the hierocracy concealed from the proletariat—'the One for the wise, the many for the masses.' To this he attributed a Victorian class distinction, stating that the 'educated classes in Egypt at all times never placed the "gods" on the same high level as God, and they never imagined that their views on this point could be mistaken.'[14]

In the 'Author's Note' to *Morning Star*, Haggard in reference to Egyptian theology mentions a 'Divinity, which they worshipped under so many names and symbols.'[15] Here then is his direct identification of Judaeo-Christian monotheism with a speculative 'original monotheism' in Egypt derived from Budge: an appeal to the 'primordial wisdom' of Egypt in support of the truth of the Christian dispensation. Yet, Haggard's metageographical Egypt is also an overtly Old-Testament one—irrespective of chronologies—where the Israelites sojourn in the 'Land of Goshen', and the Nile is named 'Sihor.'

---

9 Haggard 1889, 60.

10 Haggard 1889, 60.

11 Haggard 1921, 15.

12 The Atef crown of Osiris features the crown of Upper Egypt with two ostrich feather plumes. See https://www.ees.ac.uk/the-royal-crowns-of-egypt [accessed 6 January 2021]. On 'Osiride Christology', see Magus 2022, 83-87.

13 Wallis Budge 1901, xiii.

14 Wallis Budge 1900, 84.

15 Haggard 1910, x.

In a number of his romances, Haggard focuses specifically on the actual historical monotheism of the Pharaoh Akhenaten during the Amarna period, the so-called 'Amarna heresy.' The Pharaoh Akhenaten famously abandoned the pantheon of Egyptian gods in favour of the worship of the solar disc, the Aten. In drawing on this 'Atenism', Haggard conflates a historically confirmed monotheism with Budge's speculative 'original monotheism.' In his autobiography, Haggard writes that Akhenaten was known for 'the heresy of the worship of the Sun's disc, by which, I take it he symbolised the one Almighty God who made the world.'[16] As David Gange argues, this Judaeo-Christianisation led to 'Akhenaten's reign—in reality pretty brutal—[being] glorified as a brief period of Christian virtue in its most Victorian, bourgeois, form.'[17]

These notions all reflect the reality of Victorian Egyptological agendas. It is often assumed that during the second half of the nineteenth century in particular, Egyptology was establishing itself as an empirical archaeological science; but archaeology increasingly took sides with the defenders of biblical narratives against the rise of Darwinism and higher biblical criticism (*die höhere Kritik*) emanating from Germany.[18] Many Egyptologists were searching in Egypt for evidence of the route of the Exodus.

We can summarise, then, the fundamental Egyptosophical components of Haggard's oeuvre: an 'original monotheism' conflated with an explicit Atenism, and (again reprising Budge) an Osiride Christology. For Haggard, there is a hidden, proto-Christian God behind all the menagerie of the Egyptian pantheon. He is appealing to the 'primordial wisdom' of Egypt, and there is little of the imperialist here—it has more to do with Church than State.

Occult truth and the Romantic Isis

Thus far, we have seen how Haggard's Victorian Egyptology was coloured by Christian agendas of archaeological exploration. In this section I shall consider the aspects of Romanticism, closely aligned with and interpenetrating the esoteric ideas that influenced Haggard. I shall consider the notions of the Romantic imagination, the goddess Isis as Nature, and the theme of the Quest.

Haggard employs a series of ironic literary devices by means of which he conveys a nimbus of occult authenticity. In *She,* for example, he poses as the 'Editor', thus losing the author-novelist: he adds copious 'academic' footnotes and includes 'uncial Greek' texts. He uses genuine artefacts such as the 'scarabeus' (fig. 2) and deliberately commissioned forgeries, both featuring as what has been called 'text-objects.'[19] By means of this sleight of mind, the perichoresis (reciprocal inherence) of the real and the imaginary, the Egyptological and Egyptosophical—already complicated by the Christian inflection—is further elaborated. Such text-objects act as 'intermediaries' from the everyday world to the world of both the author and the reader's imagination.

Haggard's realm of the imagination is a liminal zone between the microcosm and macrocosm, the human and the divine. This notion of the imagination as a spiritual, noetic organ receptive to concealed truth is central to Haggard's oeuvre and is a form

16 Haggard 1926, II, 82.

17 Gange 2006, 1094.

18 The German concept of 'higher criticism' refers to the analysis of historical origin, dates, and authorship of various books of the Bible as opposed to the 'lower criticism' concerned with an analysis of the various manuscripts and codices, i.e. textual criticism. See Mackay 1863.

19 Meyer 2008.

Figure 2. H. Rider Haggard, *She* (1887), with the image of the scarabeus on the front cover. It reads 'Suten se Ra', 'The Royal Son of the Sun'. Image courtesy of Recepto Indablog.

Figure 3. Ursula Andress as Ayesha in *She* (1965), Hammer Films Productions Ltd. Image Scala Florence/Heritage Images.

of heightened intuitive faculty , involving a non-sensory perception of ultimate reality.[20] For Haggard, the imagination represents the 'still small voice' calling from the Infinite,[21] and indicates the source to which his spiritual striving is directed. It is the pursuit of this ultimate spiritual goal in opposition to the merely empirical and corporeal that is paramount. Haggard personifies this dichotomy as an 'eternal war', a contest for mankind between the goddesses Isis and Aphrodite. Man is seduced by the sensuality of Aphrodite, and rejects the wisdom of Isis. Thus, in *Cleopatra*, Harmachis the priest poisons the queen in vengeance for her deception and the shunning of his desire. Both are punished in the end for their sensuality and materiality.

This eternal war of flesh and spirit is a central theme of the Ayesha series of romances.[22] Ayesha's Promethean hubris leads her to undergo an alchemical transmutation in the 'Flame of Life' which fixes her in a preternaturally extended corporeality—virtually a material stasis, which was anathema to Haggard. Commenting on her demise at the end of *She*, Gerald Monsman has contended that it is unlikely that 'the gruesome ending of Ayesha, as a force that threatens British control, is an allegorical reestablishment of male imperial authority.'[23] She is not being punished as a dangerous exotic queen (fig. 3), a menacing

20 Haggard's concept of the imagination is akin to S. T. Coleridge' *secondary imagination*. See Chapter XIII: 'On the Imagination, or Esemplastic Power', in Coleridge 1907, I, 202.

21 Haggard 1926,II, 258. Haggard is referring to 1 Kings 19: 12, where Elijah communes with God: 'And after the earthquake a fire; but the LORD was not in the fire: and after the fire a still small voice.'

22 The Ayesha series comprises four romances: *She: A History of Adventure* (1887); *Ayesha: The Return of She* (1905); *She and Allan* (1921), and *Wisdom's Daughter: The Life and Love Story of She-Who-Must-Be-Obeyed* (1923).

23 Monsman 2009, 32.

foreign power, or an avatar of the Victorian 'New Woman.' It is not her femininity that is punished on her return to the Flame, but her *materiality*.

Haggard's work foregrounds a soteriological theme, with the backdrop of the conflict between flesh and spirit. Love—spiritual love or *agápē*—is seen as an agent of redemption. In the Egyptian romances, this Pauline dualism of the material versus the spiritual, the flesh versus the spirit, assumes a philosophical dimension implying the opposition of Western and Eastern thought, although Haggard's metageography of Egypt necessarily problematises this dichotomy.[24] Haggard portrays the seduction of the West by materialism, which he associates with the invasion of 'pagan' rationalist philosophy: a Western civilisation and empire lost to spiritual bankruptcy—as opposed to the 'Wisdom of the East' and the veiled Isis of his occultism.

The 'Veil of Isis' and the trope of unveiling in Romantic idealism are important influences and sources of literary motifs for Haggard. In Chapter XXIII of *She*, 'The Temple of Truth' is clearly an explicit reference to a 1795 poem by the German Romantic poet Friedrich von Schiller (1759–1805), *Das verschleierte Bild zu Sais* ('The Veiled Statue at Saïs'). It tells of an impetuous youth who pursues 'Truth': he lifts her veil only to suffer melancholia, involution, and an early death. Here he sees the statue for the first time:

> They stood within the temple's silent dome,
> And, as the young man paused abrupt, his gaze
> Upon a veil'd and giant IMAGE fell:
> Amazed he turn'd unto his guides —'And what
> Towers, yonder, vast beneath the veil?'
> 'THE TRUTH,'
> Answered the Priest.[25]

In *She*, the travellers behold a statue. Holly asks who it is and Ayesha replies: 'Where then is thy imagination? It is Truth standing on the World, and calling to its children to unveil her face.'[26]

Schiller's poem and Haggard's reprise illustrate the heritage of eighteenth-century esotericism in a number of ways. Firstly, behind the veil of official Egyptian polytheism there is a single monotheistic divinity. Secondly, as we have described, this divinity equates to Jehovah, the God of Mosaic monotheism. Thirdly, this common divinity can be understood as an all-encompassing Sublime, corresponding to a Spinozan *Deus sive*

---

24 This problem of what constitutes 'East' and 'West' has become a topic of some importance in Western esotericism as an academic discipline in recent years, but it is not a new issue. As early as 1950, Raymond Schwab commented:
Sometimes qualified by 'Near' or 'Far', sometimes identified with Africa or Oceania, when not identified with Russia or Spain, the concept of 'the East' has come full circle. As Sylvain Lévi put it, since the world is round, what can this word mean? The term originated with the Roman empire which, true to its Hellenistic heritage, placed two blocs in opposition, 'our world' against some vague Asia. It appeared in Virgil's Aeneid in the first century before Christ: 'The people of the dawn, ... Egypt and every power of the East.' During the first century of the Christian era this res orientales [*sic*] reappeared in the Historiarum Philippicarum of Trogus Pompeius, and Oriens appeared in Tacitus' Germania. Thus the separation of the continents had become official.' See Schwab 1984, 1.

25 This is Edward Bulwer-Lytton's translation and Haggard's likeliest source. See Bulwer-Lytton 1847, 50–2.

26 Haggard 1887, 265.

Natura—although Haggard's own brand of Anglicanism eschews the pantheism that was commonplace among the Romantics.

Isis is considered to represent the *anima mundi* and *natura naturans*. Yet the veiled Isis simultaneously represents 'Truth'—explicit in Haggard's *She*—the truth about Nature and her ontological and eschatological relationship to God and mankind. But this is a truth 'so hideous that one can no longer live after having known it.'[27] In Haggard's *Cleopatra*, the priest Harmachis experiences this terrifying yet fascinating mystery and *does* die—to experience a *palingenesis*, a rebirth in Isis.

Conclusion

In this contribution I have marshalled evidence for the importance of Egyptianising esoteric themes—both Romantic and occult—in the works of H. Rider Haggard. Whilst I have focused for the purposes of brevity on the Egyptian *topos*, British forays into Egypt, India and Tibet led to a counter-invasion of religious and philosophical ideas that engendered a phenomenon peculiar to the nineteenth century, an occultism of Empire. In this paper we have considered the two pervasive intellectual currents of Christian Egyptosophy and Egyptian Romanticism; Haggard's Egypt is white, pre-Islamic and proto-Christian. He interweaves archaeological, biblical, and imaginal narratives. His romances demonstrate that where Western esotericism is concerned, the dichotomy between fact and fiction is not always what it appears.

Bibliography

Assmann, J., 1997, *Moses the Egyptian: The Memory of Egypt in Western Monotheism*, Cambridge MA.

Bulwer-Lytton, E., 1844, *The Poems and Ballads of Schiller: With a Brief Sketch of the Author's Life*, Leipzig.

Coleridge, S. T., 1907, *Biographia Literaria*, 2 vols, Oxford.

Gange, D., 2006, 'Religion and Science in Late Nineteenth-Century British Egyptology', in *The Historical Journal*, 49, 4, 1083–103, Cambridge.

Gilbert, S. M., Gubar, S., 1989, *No Man's Land: The Place of the Woman Writer in the Twentieth Century*, 3 vols, New York.

Hadot, P., 2006, *The Veil of Isis: An Essay on the History of the Idea of Nature*, Cambridge MA and London.

Haggard, H. R., 1889, *Cleopatra: Being an Account of the Fall and Vengeance of Harmachis, The Royal Egyptian, as Set Forth by his Own Hand*, London.

Haggard, H. R., 1926, *The Days of My Life*, 2 vols, London.

Haggard, H. R., 1910, *Morning Star*, London.

Haggard, H. R., 1887, *She*, London.

Haggard, H. R., 1921, *Smith and the Pharaohs*, New York.

Hornung, E., 2001, *The Secret Lore of Ancient Egypt: Its Impact on the West*, Ithaca and London.

Katz, W., 1987, *Rider Haggard and the Fiction of Empire*, Cambridge.

Mackay, R. W., 1863, *The Tübingen School and its Antecedents: A Review of the History and Present Condition of Modern Theology*, London.

27 Hadot 2006, 271.

Lewis, M. W., Wigen, K. E., 1997, *The Myth of Continents: A Critique of Metageography*, Berkley.
Magus, S., 2022, *Rider Haggard and the Imperial Occult: Hermetic Discourse and Romantic Contiguity,* Leiden and Boston.
Meyer, D., 2008, *Reading Maps, Sculptures, and Ancient Pottery: Text-Objects in Late Victorian Novels of Empire* (unpublished BA thesis), Massachusetts.
Monsman, G., 2009, 'Who Is Ayesha? An Allegory of Isis Unveiled', in Zulli, T. (ed.), *She: Explorations into a Romance, Studi di Anglistica*, 20, 15–35, Rome.
Schwab, R., 1984, *The Oriental Renaissance: Europe's Rediscovery of India and the East, 1680–1880,* New York.
Wallis Budge, E. A., 1901, *Egyptian Magic*, London.
Wallis Budge, E. A., 1900, *Egyptian Religion: Egyptian Ideas of the Future Life*, London.

Online sources

The Royal Crowns of Egypt, published on https://www.ees.ac.uk/the-royal-crowns-of-egypt (accessed: 6/1/2021).

About the author

Dr Simon Magus is a psychiatrist practising in London. He studied medicine at what is now the Imperial College of Science Technology and Medicine, and holds an MA and PhD in Western Esotericism from the University of Exeter. He has recently published the book of his doctoral thesis *Rider Haggard and the Imperial Occult: Hermetic Discourse and Romantic Contiguity,* which is volume 31 in the ARIES Book Series *Texts and Studies in Western Esotericism*, Brill Publishers, Leiden.

Figure 1. The parting of the Red Sea, illustration of the Old Testament, end of 19th century, engraving by Bequet, Delagrave edition, Paris. Image A. Dagli Orti/NPL-DeA Picture Library/ Bridgeman Images DGA520172.

The Pillar of Fire and the Sea of Reeds

Identifying the Locations along the Route of the Exodus

Huub Pragt

Introduction

Innumerable books and articles have been written about the fascinating Bible story of the Israelites' exodus from Egypt. Since the beginning of Egyptology, with the decipherment of the hieroglyphic script in 1822 by Jean-François Champollion, several linguists have devoted themselves to the search for possible connections in the Egyptian writings with the stories from the Old Testament. Before that time, the knowledge of ancient Egypt in academia was mainly based on texts handed down from Classical Antiquity. Pharaonic Egypt was also known from Bible stories such as those about Joseph, the viceroy of Egypt, and Moses and the exodus from Egypt. These stories became a regularly discussed topic in the new field of Egyptology. To this day, there is no consensus on the content of the biblical account of the exodus. Scholarly opinions differ widely about the historical circumstances. When we try to determine whether the exodus from Egypt actually took place, at some points the Bible seems to contain a few contradictions. This makes the subject of exodus a common feature in alternative theories on ancient Egypt.

This paper does not address the historical or chronological discussions, nor will it delve deeper into the religious aspects of the biblical narrative. The purpose, however, is to provide the most plausible identification of the places mentioned in the Bible, from the starting point at Raamses until the Israelites reached the bitter spring of Marah.

Departure from Raamses

According to the Book of Exodus, Pharaoh employed the Israelites as slave labourers to build the store cities of Pithom and Raamses. 'So they set taskmasters over them to oppress them with forced labour; and they built garrison cities for Pharaoh: Pithom and Raamses.'[1] The New Jewish Publication Society of America translation notes that others translate the

1 The New Jewish Publication Society of America (NJPS), Philadelphia, 1985, Exodus 1:11.

in Van den Bercken, B. J. L. (ed.), *Alternative Egyptology: Critical Essays on the Relation between Academic and Alternative Interpretations of Ancient Egypt*, Leiden, pp. 166–179.

Hebrew words ערי מסכנות Arei Miskenot with 'store cities'. It is generally accepted that the biblical place name Pithom refers to the Egyptian site of *pr-ỉtm*, usually translated as Pi-Atum, 'House of Atum'. This city, consecrated to the creator-god Atum, was situated near present-day Tell Retabah in the centre of Wadi Tumilat. Raamses or Rameses is the Hebrew designation for *pr-Rꜥ-ms-sw*, usually translated as Pi-Ramesses, 'House of Ramesses'. Pi-Ramesses was the new Egyptian residence, mainly built under Ramesses II. The exodus started in this city, present-day Qantir, located on the east bank of the Pelusiac Nile branch in the eastern Delta.

The Bible describes how God decided not to lead the Israelites by the most logical route. That would have been in north-eastern direction along the traditional Way of Horus, passing several Egyptian military checkpoints.[2] The reason for taking an alternative route is given: the Israelites would end up in the territory of the Philistines along the northern border of Sinai. This would inevitably lead to unwanted skirmishes.

> Now when Pharaoh let the people go, God did not lead them by way of the land of the Philistines, although it was nearer; for God said, 'The people may have a change of heart when they see war, and return to Egypt.' So God led the people round about, by way of the wilderness at the Sea of Reeds. Now the Israelites went up armed out of the land of Egypt.[3]

The statement that they would circumnavigate by way of the wilderness refers to the first stretch from Raamses to Sukkot which is mentioned as such in the Bible text: 'The Israelites journeyed from Rameses to Sukkot, about six hundred thousand fighting men on foot, aside from noncombatants.'[4]

This implies that the Israelites wandered due south, most likely through the sandy stretch of desert to reach Wadi Tumilat. From there Moses wanted to continue in an easterly direction. I suppose that his intent was to eventually pass the smallest of the Bitter Lakes, known today as Lake Timsah,[5] directly along its south side. If Moses succeeded in his plan, the way would have been open to take the ancient Shur route through Sinai.[6] It would appear that this more southerly route to the Way of Horus was not properly defended by the Egyptians.[7]

Sukkot

The first encampment was set up in the form of huts and simple booths built from plant material at a place they called Sukkot. For well over a century, Egyptologists have recognised that the Hebrew word סכות sukkot, corresponds with the Egyptian toponym *ṯkw*, Tjeku. Tjeku is generally identified with Wadi Tumilat or a specific location in this

---

2 Hoffmeier/Moshier 2013.

3 NJPS, Exodus 13:17–18.

4 NJPS, Exodus 12:37.

5 I surmise that Lake Timsah, filled with brackish water, in ancient times was called *š-ḥr*, Lake of Horus. The text from the third year of Merenptah, Papyrus Anastasi III recto 2, 8–9 reads: 'The Lake of Horus yields salt.' Three lines further it is said: 'The reed-swamps come to it (Pi-Ramesses) with papyrus, and the Lake of Horus with rushes.'

6 Hoffmeier/Moshier 2013, 486.

7 Hoffmeier/Moshier 2013, 485.

area, likely a military fort by the same name. The biblical reference to Sukkot could be understood similarly. Sukkot means 'covering', hence booth or hut.[8] Most likely this first camp site can be located approximately 30 kilometres to the south of Qantir, a few kilometres east of the current ruin mound of Tell el-Kebir. This area marks the beginning of the fertile Wadi Tumilat, which continues over more than 50 kilometres in an eastward direction. The Israelites stayed at Sukkot for only a short period of time. 'They set out from Sukkot, and encamped at Etham, at the edge of the wilderness.'[9]

Etham/Pithom

About 20 kilometres east of Sukkot the Israelites arrived at Etham. In Egyptian texts the prefix *pr-* was occasionally omitted when giving a place name.[10] In my opinion Manfred Görg was right in 1990 when he suggested that Etham is an abbreviation for the Egyptian *pr-ỉtm*, that is Pithom from Exodus 1:11.[11] Hoffmeier rejects this assumption.[12] The location of Etham/Pithom, however, has been the subject of much debate. The Swiss biblical scholar and archaeologist Édouard Naville believed he had identified the biblical town of Pithom in 1883 as the archaeological site Tell-el-Maskhuta.[13] This site lies to the east of Wadi Tumilat. A granite group statue representing Ramesses II flanked by the gods Ra-Horakhty and Atum was already found at the site in 1799 by the French engineer Jacques-Marie Le Père.[14] Naville found two inscriptions naming *pr-ỉtm* or per-item, 'House of Atum',[15] and storehouses made of mudbrick. Excavations carried out between 1978 and 1985 by the Wadi Tumilat project of the University of Toronto, directed by John S. Holladay Jr., have shown that Tell el-Maskhuta dates only from the end of the seventh century BC, and may have been built by Pharaoh Necho II from the 26th Dynasty.[16] Although it was known as Pithom until Roman times, it was clearly not the Pithom of the Bible.[17]

The identification with Tell-el-Maskhuta was first challenged by Sir Allen Gardiner,[18] who identified Pithom with Tell er-Retaba.[19] This identification was accepted by William F. Albright.[20] In 1999 Kenneth Kitchen endorsed the identification of Pithom with Tell er-Retaba.[21] Archaeological data show the presence of a major stronghold at the site during the Ramesside period, and little or no occupation elsewhere in the wadi.[22] Excavations carried out by the Polish-Slovak archaeological mission at Tell er-Retaba have uncovered a robust fortress made of mudbrick. This construction dates from the time of Ramesses II. The

8 Hoffmeier 2005, 65–66.
9 NJPS, Exodus 13:20.
10 Caminos 1954, 220.
11 Görg 1990.
12 Hoffmeier 2005, 69.
13 Naville 1885, 4.
14 Le Père 1822, 295.
15 Naville 1885, 4 and pl. 4.
16 MacDonald 1980, 49–58.
17 Seters 2001, 261–62.
18 Gardiner 1918, 268.
19 Also known in the spelling Tell er-Retabah, Tell Rotab, or Tell er-Rebata.
20 Albright 1948, 15.
21 Kitchen 1999, 270.
22 Rzepka et al. 2013, 273.

uncovered area consisted also of courtyards with rounded silos surrounded by rather thin, curved enclosure walls.[23] It is not unlikely that these are the storage areas of biblical Pithom.

Turning back

When the Israelites had reached Etham, the Bible then describes something remarkable. God said to Moses: Tell the Israelites to turn back and encamp before Pi-hahiroth, between Migdol and the sea, before Baal-zephon; you shall encamp facing it, by the sea.'[24]

The Israelites suddenly left Etham by 'turning back'. The verb וישבו veyashuvu can also mean 'to return'. This would mean that they went in north-west direction towards their starting point, the city of Raamses. This implies that the Israelites passed through the desert area north of Wadi Tumilat, the biblical 'wilderness of Etham'. This desert has the shape of a triangle. It has the entire east flank of the fertile Nile Delta on its north-west side, Wadi Tumilat on its south side and the Bitter Lakes on its east side. The west point is the present-day city of Abou Hammad. The north-east point is at El-Qantara and the south-east point at Ismailia. As we shall see, the military fortress Baal-zephon, present-day Tell-Defenneh, also lay at the north-east edge of this sandy desert.

An explanation for God's decision not to let the Israelites move further east, towards Sinai, is provided in the biblical narrative:

> Pharaoh will say of the Israelites, 'They are astray in the land; the wilderness has closed in on them.' Then I will stiffen Pharaoh's heart and he will pursue them, that I may gain glory through Pharaoh and all his host; and the Egyptians shall know that I am God. And they did so. When the king of Egypt was told that the people had fled, Pharaoh and his courtiers had a change of heart about the people and said, 'What is this we have done, releasing Israel from our service?' He ordered his chariot and took his force with him; he took six hundred of his picked chariots, and the rest of the chariots of Egypt, with officers in all of them. God stiffened the heart of Pharaoh king of Egypt, and he gave chase to the Israelites.[25]

The pillar of fire

According to the Bible text, God guided the Israelites through the wilderness of Etham by means of a pillar of cloud during the day and a pillar of fire during the night: 'יהוה went before them in a pillar of cloud by day, to guide them along the way, and in a pillar of fire by night, to give them light, that they might travel day and night. The pillar of cloud by day and the pillar of fire by night did not depart from before the people.'[26]

The phenomenon of the pillar of fire during the night can be explained in physical terms. When the sun is optically below the horizon in the north, this can cause a so-called sun pillar if hexagonal ice crystals are present in the atmosphere. Such a sun pillar takes on the colour of the sun and can hence appear white at one time and yellow or fiery red at other times. This rare physical phenomenon can be observed throughout the night, especially as the sun approaches the Tropic of Cancer (that is during the spring period of

---

23 Smoláriková 2019, 22.
24 NJPS, Exodus 14:1–2
25 NJPS, Exodus 14:3–8.
26 NJPS, Exodus 13:21–22.

Figure 2. Sun pillar at Fensfjorden, Norway, on 26 May 2018. Image Thorod CC BY-SA 4.0 via Wikimedia Commons.

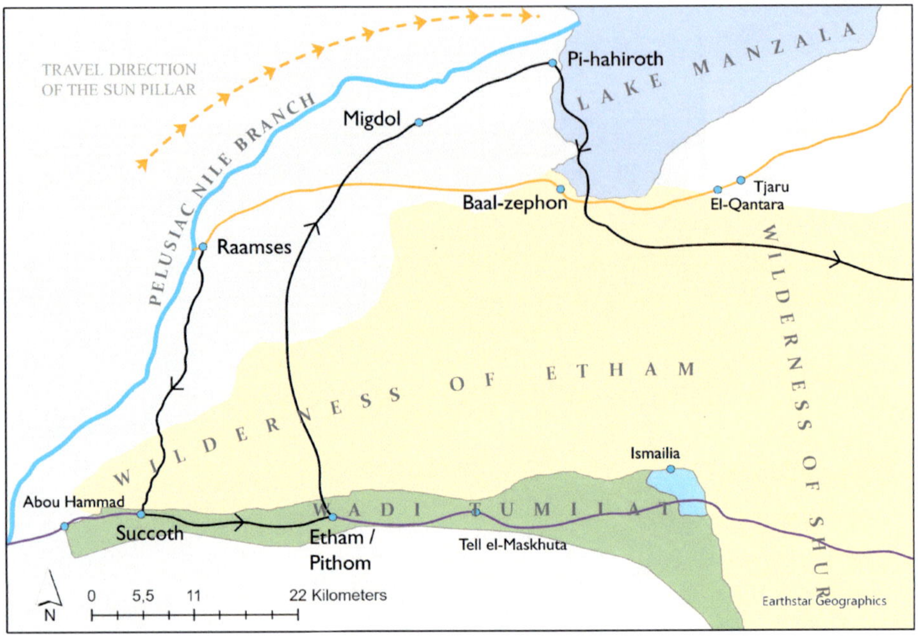

Figure 3. The route from Etham to Migdol and the sun pillar. Map produced by Bart Staats with ArcGIS Pro 2.9.0. World Imagery Data: Earthstar Geographics.

the northern hemisphere). Optically, such a light beam travels slowly from west to east during the night. When the Israelites continued to follow a sun pillar, they may have maintained a northbound track that slightly curved from west to east. This explains their arrival at Pi-hahiroth, the peninsula at the shore of the northernmost of the Bitter Lakes, Lake Manzala. If it was indeed a sun pillar that the Israelites followed through the night, this physical phenomenon was still visible at sunrise: 'At the morning watch, God looked down upon the Egyptian army from a pillar of fire and cloud, and threw the Egyptian army into panic.'[27]

Migdol

In Exodus 14:2 it is said that the Israelites would 'encamp before Pi-hahiroth, between Migdol and the sea'. *Migdol* is not necessarily a toponym: it is a Hebrew term used for an elevated stretch of land that can be used as a military lookout. Often in the ancient Near East a watchtower was built at such a strategic point. James Hoffmeier suggested that the 19th-Dynasty fort Migdol located two kilometres south-east of Tell el-Borg could well be the Migdol of Exodus 14:2.[28] In my opinion, however, Migdol most probably does not refer to a military lookout but to one of the sandy elevations in the area north-east of the Delta. A suitable candidate for this would be Tell el-Ginn. It is located 24 kilometres north-east of Qantir, the biblical Raamses, and two kilometres east of the modern town of Minshat Abu Omar. The appearance of this archaeological site is that of a great sandy

27 NJPS, Exodus 14:24.

28 Hoffmeier 2005, 94-105.

hillock amid cultivated fields. Archaeological research at the site of Tell el-Ginn revealed material characteristic of the Naqada IId2–IIIc1 period, around 3400–3000 BC. It also shows that this elevation in the landscape was uninhabited during the Late Bronze Age (*c.*1200 BC).[29] This fact makes a scientific basis for identification very difficult, but not impossible. Egyptian farmers call this kind of geological formation *gezira*, 'island'. English-speakers call it 'turtleback'. The hillock of Tell el-Ginn is around five meters higher than the surrounding fields and is approximately 900 metres long by 600 meters wide. Tell el-Ginn basically looks like a sand dune running from west to east. Seen from a vantage point to the south, Pi-hahiroth then lies indeed between Migdol and הים *hayam*, the (Mediterranean) Sea.

Pi-hahiroth

After their long walk during a day and a night, the Israelites encamped near Pi-hahiroth. 'They set out from Etham and turned about toward Pi-hahiroth, which faces Baal-zephon, and they encamped before Migdol. They set out from Pene-hahiroth and passed through the sea into the wilderness; and they made a three-days' journey in the wilderness of Etham and encamped at Marah.'[30]

It should be noted that the English Standard Version provides the following translation for Numbers 33:7: 'And they set out from Etham and turned back to Pi-hahiroth, which is east of Baal-zephon, and they camped before Migdol.'

This translation is incorrect, because the Hebrew words על פני בעל צפון al pnei Baal-zephon mean 'which faces Baal-zephon'. The Egyptian military fortress that I would like to equate to Baal-zephon lies on the southern shore of former Lake Manzala. The peninsula of Pi-hahiroth faces Baal-zephon, which is about 12 kilometres to the south.

The etymology of the nam פי החירות Pi-hahiroth, which is apparently Egyptian, has been subject of much speculation. Hoffmeier suggested that it derived from either a genuine Semitic expression or a Semitic popular etymology of an Egyptian toponym that sounded close to pi-ha-hiroth, meaning 'the mouth of the canal'.[31] This could well relate to the estuary of the Pelusiac Nile branch, immediately north of the location. Another translation for the Hebrew Pi-hahiroth could be 'the mouth of freedom', because the Israelites had been freed from bondage.

In my opinion the biblical place name Pi-hahiroth seems to be a corruption of *pr-ḥry-š=f* Per-Heryshef probably pronounced by some as Pi-Haryshof, meaning 'House of Heryshef'. Even the spelling Pene-hahiroth as in Numbers 33:8 can easily be explained as derived from *pr-n-ḥry-š=f* Per-en-Heryshef, also meaning 'House of Heryshef'. The name of the god Heryshef means 'He who is over his lake'. In the time of Ramesses II Heryshef was seen as a creator and fertility god who was born from the primordial waters. His main cult was centred in the Nile valley in Middle Egypt, in ancient *nny-nsw* Neny-nesu, better known as Heracleopolis Magna, modern Ihnasiyyah el-Medina. West of the city of Neny-nesu a shallow lake stretched out during the New Kingdom, over which Heryshef was thought to reside. He was pictured as a ram or as a man with a ram's head. The temple of Heryshef in Neny-nesu was expanded by Ramesses II, who added huge granite columns with palm-leaf

---

29 Watrin 2003.

30 NJPS, Numbers 33:7–8.

31 Hoffmeier 2005, 105.

capitals. It is very conceivable that at the same time in the north-east of the Nile Delta a new temple was built for Heryshef on the shore of the vast and shallow bitter lake Manzala. This place was also referred to with its long name,  *pr ḥry-š=f nb nny-nsw* Per-Heryshef-neb-Neny-nesu, meaning 'House of Heryshef, lord of Neny-nesu'. Later, its Graeco-Roman name would be Heracleopolis Parva. Presently this site is called Tell Belim. In the spring of 2002, an excavation was carried out by Jeffrey Spencer for the British Museum. He has identified a temple from the 26th Dynasty, although it was almost destroyed. The date of part of a temple enclosure older than that from the 26th Dynasty is uncertain. As the base of this older wall lies deep in the subsoil water, it was not possible to search for dating evidence below it. Fragments of pottery and many pieces of hard stone lie on the surface of the archaeological site, including numerous basalt blocks, one with the hieroglyphs *nsw-bỉty* and the beginning of a Ramesside cartouche, *Wsr-[Mꜣꜥ.t]-Rꜥ*. This makes the existence of an original temple from the Ramesside period plausible.[32]

The Sea of Reeds

One of the most pictorial descriptions in the Book of Exodus is of the Israelites' crossing of the Sea of Reeds. Traditional Bible translations speak of the splitting of the Red Sea. The translation with 'Red Sea' was first used in the Septuagint in the third century BC. At that time, 72 rabbis from Alexandria translated the Hebrew words ים סוף Yam Suf not with the literal 'Sea of Reeds', but with 'Red Sea'. When the Bible indicated that the Israelites crossed a considerable amount of water on Egypt's eastern border, the rabbis associated it with the water they knew as the Red Sea. The translators of the Septuagint thus gave a historical interpretation, based on their geographic knowledge of that time. Hoffmeier states with certainty that the Hebrew word סוף *suf* derives from the Egyptian word *ṯwf* or *ṯwfy*.[33] This is usually translated with 'papyrus plants' or 'papyrus marsh'. If we consider Yam Suf as a generic name for an area, it can refer to any swampy area where water plants grow such as papyrus, reeds, or bulrush. This means that 'Sea of Reeds' can apply to at least five different lakes on the eastern border of the Nile Delta, roughly corresponding to the Isthmus of Suez.[34] Before the Israelites' departure from Egypt, the Sea of Reeds is already mentioned in Exodus 10:19. The text refers to the ninth plague of Egypt: 'יהוה' caused a shift to a very strong west wind, which lifted the locusts and hurled them into the Sea of Reeds; not a single locust remained in all the territory of Egypt.'

From this it can be concluded that the Sea of Reeds was located on the eastern side of Egypt. It is very likely that the swampy areas in the Isthmus of Suez are meant, not the Mediterrean Sea or the Red Sea. That also explains why Lake Timsah could be referred to as Sea of Reeds in Exodus 13:18, when Moses still intended to reach the Shur route by crossing Wadi Tumilat. I will explain a little further why I think that Lake Manzala could be meant in Exodus 15:4, where it is said that the officers of Pharaoh are drowned in the Sea of Reeds.

In the continuation of the description of the Exodus, I see two more remote wetlands that are referred to as Sea of Reeds. The second Sea of Reeds is mentioned after the

32 Spencer 2002.

33 Hoffmeier 2005, 81.

34 North to south: Lake Manzala, El-Ballah Lake, Lake Timsah, Great Bitter Lake, Small Bitter Lake.

Israelites left the camp site Elim.[35] This could well be identified as present-day Bir er-Rashaydah. This former lake has become a geological *playa*, it has almost completely dried up. This plain can be found immediately to the south-east of the town El-Hassana in the centre of the Sinai. I see the third Sea of Reeds as the swampy area of the Araba region between Eilat and the Dead Sea.[36] This elongated rift running north-south is not equally filled with water everywhere, and in some places, there is insufficient water for reeds or other shallow-water plants throughout the year. When Moses proclaims the laws and regulations to the Israelites at Mount Horeb, he mentions the borders of the promised land for the first time. There he mentions the third Sea of Reeds, most probably meaning the swamps in the northern part of the Araba, just south of the Dead Sea.[37] In my opinion the same area is referred to when the Israelites set out from Mount Hor by way of the Sea of Reeds to skirt the land of Edom. [38]

Crossing the first Sea of Reeds

The event of crossing the Sea of Reeds is described in Exodus 14:9–30. A remarkable fact, however, is that in this specific Bible passage only the Hebrew word הים *hayam*, 'the sea' is used to refer to the body of water through which the Israelites would proceed. There is a possible explanation for the apparent discrepancy with other passages in the Bible, where the same event is referred to as crossing the Sea of Reeds. During the New Kingdom Lake Manzala stretched 30 kilometres further north, as far as the current barrier beach separating the Manzala lagoon from the Mediterranean Sea. When we consider such a vast expanse of water on the north side of the Delta, it is quite conceivable that this vast shallow lake could also have been taken for a sea by the Israelites. Since the construction of the Suez Canal in the nineteenth century, Lake Manzala has decreased in size by 80%, partly due to drainage work. In ancient times, Lake Manzala held brackish water and was between 1.20 and 1.50 metres deep. The bottom of the lake consisted of fat river clay, an ideal environment for the shallow-water plant bulrush to grow on its banks. The Nile branch that passed the city of Pi-Ramesses ended in Lake Manzala. That is why I suppose that Pi-hahiroth was located on a natural mound on the eastern side of the estuary. And I assume Lake Manzala to be the wetland area where the crossing of the Sea of Reeds took place.

When the Israelites saw the Egyptian soldiers with their chariots ready to attack, God ordered Moses to lift his staff and stretch out his hand over the sea. A very strong east wind cleared a path. 'Then Moses held out his arm over the sea and יהוה drove back the sea with a strong east wind all that night, and turned the sea into dry ground. The waters were split, and the Israelites went into the sea on dry ground, the waters forming a wall for them on their right and on their left.'[39]

This phenomenon of temporary natural water impoundment is extremely effective in shallow water with rush vegetation. Scientifically it is called wind-tidal and can occur in several oligohaline (brackish) rush marshes around the world. Smooth cord grass, for instance, is a species that occurs in marshes of eastern North America. This water plant is

35 Numbers 33:10–11.

36 Numbers 14:25, Deuteronomy 1:40 and 2:1, I Kings 9:26, Jeremiah 49:21.

37 Exodus 23:31.

38 Numbers 21:4.

39 NJPS, Exodus 14:21–22.

known to hold back water during a wind tidal.[40] Criticism of this assumption may arise from the fact that mention is made of how the waters formed a חומה *choma*, 'wall' for them on their right and on their left. An obvious explanation could be that the walls are seen as a metaphor for two natural obstacles, the bodies of water that should not be entered. It is also possible that the Hebrew word חומה *choma*, in this case refers to an independent form of the adjective חום *choom*. It then takes on the meaning of 'a darkened, dark brown or black area'.

It is well conceivable that over the temporary land bridge in a north-south direction the Israelites fled to the south. According to the biblical description, Pharaoh followed them with his army. After the last Israelite reached the other side, the wind died down and the waters closed. Pharaoh and his army drowned. After this key event many references are made to this crossing of the Sea of Reeds.[41]

When they were safe, the Israelites started a song. An excerpt from it reads: 'The deeps covered them; they went down into the depths like a stone.'[42] This passage in the song is most likely based on a metaphor. The dramatic form was chosen to indicate that the Egyptians had been conclusively defeated. When this passage is taken literally, it is understandable that the crossing of the Sea of Reeds was thought to have taken place from the shores of a deep water such as the Red Sea.

Baal-zephon

The closest visible strip of land across the peninsula of Pi-Haryshof, the biblical Pi-hahiroth, lay to the south, where an Egyptian fortress along the Way of Horus was located. Opinions differ about the name given to this fortress during the New Kingdom. The identification with the ancient place called Tjeben(et) is strongly rejected by Leclère and Spencer.[43] Many centuries after the New Kingdom, in the time of the prophet Jeremiah, around 580 BC, this place was referred to as Tahpanhes.[44] Later the Greeks called the place Daphnai. Presently the archaeological site is known as Tell Defenneh. In 2003 David Rohl proposed identifying this military stronghold with the biblical location of Baal-zephon.[45]

What makes things complicated is that Baal-zephon actually is a designation for the Canaanite storm god Baal in his role as 'Lord of Mount Zaphon'. Mount Zaphon lies on the border between present-day Turkey and Syria. Nevertheless, the Hebrew name for this Egyptian fortress can be explained, as it was inhabited by Egyptian soldiers and their families. In the north-east of the Delta, the Egyptian god Seth was worshipped as a protector of Egypt, and equated with the Canaanite god Baal. Although there is no archaeological evidence for this yet, it is conceivable that a cult of Seth was maintained in the fort's enclosure.

The wilderness of Shur

In their attempt to get out of Egypt as quickly as possible after they had crossed the Sea of Reeds, the Israelites most likely would have chosen to land on the east side of the Egyptian

---

40 Lagomasino et al. 2013, 1165–80.

41 Exodus 15:1-21 and 15:22, Numbers 33:8; Deuteronomy 11:4; Joshua 2:10, 4:23, 24:6; Isaiah 10:26 and 11:15–16; Psalms 106:7–11, 106:22, 114:3, 124:3–5, 136:13–15; Nehemiah 9:9–11.

42 NJPS, Exodus 15:5.

43 Leclère et al. 2014, 34 notes 45–47.

44 Jeremiah 43:7.

45 Rohl 2003, 185–189.

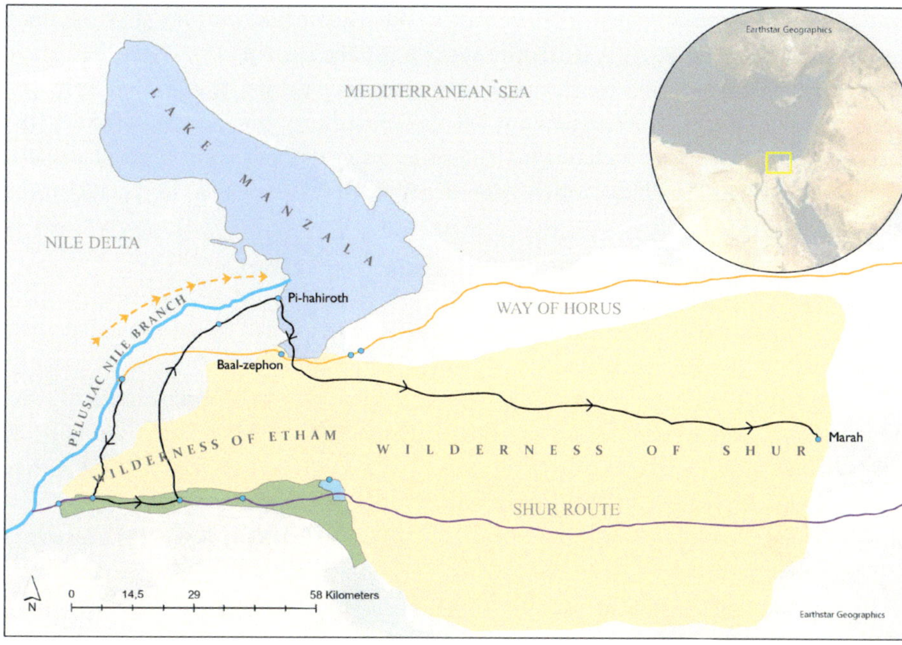

Figure 4. The route to and through the wilderness of Shur. Map produced by Bart Staats with ArcGIS Pro 2.9.0. World Imagery Data: Earthstar Geographics.

fortress Baal-Zephon. They must have crossed the Way of Horus from north to south and then moved on. The route they chose ran east towards the Sinai. In the Book of Numbers, it is said: 'They set out from Pene-hahiroth and passed through the sea into the wilderness; and they made a three-days' journey in the wilderness of Etham and encamped at Marah.'[46] The mention of a three-days' journey in the wilderness of Etham is logical. As indicated before, the Egyptian fortress lies on the northern edge of this triangle-shaped desert. If we look at the parallel text from the Book of Exodus, however, there seems to occur a contradiction at this point: 'Then Moses caused Israel to set out from the Sea of Reeds. They went on into the wilderness of Shur; they travelled three days in the wilderness and found no water.'[47] There is a good explanation, though. When the Israelites landed near Baal-zephon, they re-entered the wilderness of Etham. At that moment they began their three-day trek. Once they passed the Isthmus of Suez into the desert region of Sinai, the area was called the wilderness of Shur. In later biblical texts the same place is referred to as Shur[48] or Shi-hor.[49] The name for the wilderness of Shur may have been derived from *š-ḥr* 'Lake of Horus'. The exact location of this lake has never been determined. In my view, however, it could well relate to Lake Timsah. The eastern border of Lake Timsah forms the starting point of the eastbound ancient Shur route towards Canaan. The point where the Israelites entered the wilderness of Shur lies immediately south of present-day El-Qantara, about five kilometres south of the next Egyptian military fortress Tjaru,

46 NJPS, Numbers 33:8.
47 NJPS, Exodus 15:22.
48 I Samuel 15:7 and 27:8.
49 Joshua 13:3, Isaiah 23:3, I Chronicles 13:5.

current Tell el-Heboua I.[50] It had already been decided not to take the Way of Horus along the north border of the Sinai. A southern route along Lake Timsah to reach the Shur route would from this point be a considerable and dangerous detour. It is not unlikely that Moses therefore decided not to follow any existing route, but to travel due east through the desert plain for three days. I assume that after traversing this vast plain of the wilderness of Shur they reached the bitter well of Marah, present-day Bir el-Malhi in the hills of the Bedouin village El-Maghara.

Conclusion

In their attempt to flee Egypt, the Israelites unexpectedly turned back toward Raamses, present-day Qantir. This was the starting point of their exodus. This occurred at the second stopping point of Etham, present-day Tell Retaba. Day and night they moved north from Wadi Tumilat. They were guided by a pillar of cloud during the day and a sun pillar at night. At one point they could not go on. Near Pi-hahiroth, present-day Tell-Belim, they were hemmed in on the west by the branch of the Nile and on the north and east by Lake Manzala. After a strong easterly wind had picked up, part of the lake dried up. The Israelites took the opportunity to cross south toward Baal-Zephon, present-day Tell-Defenneh. From there they continued their journey eastward into Sinai, through the wilderness of Shur, for three days without interruption.

Bibliography

Abd El-Maksoud, M., 1998, *Tell Heboua, 1981–1991: Enquête archéologique sur la deuxième période intermédiaire et le nouvel empire à l'extrémité orientale du delta*, Paris.

Albright, W. F., 1948, *Exploring in Sinai with the University of California African Expedition. Bulletin of the American Schools of Oriental Research*, 109.

Caminos, R. A., 1954, *Late-Egyptian Miscellanies*, London.

Gardiner, A. H., 1918, 'The Delta Residence of the Ramessides', in *Journal of Egyptian Archaeology*, 5, 127–138.

Gardiner, A. H., 1920, 'The Ancient Military Road between Egypt and Palestine', in *Journal of Egyptian Archaeology*, 6, 99–116.

Görg, M., 1990, 'Etham und Pithom', in *Biblische Notizen*, 51, 9–10.

Hoffmeier, J. K., 2005, *Ancient Israel in Sinai: The Evidence for the Authenticity of the Wilderness Tradition*, New York.

Hoffmeier, J. K., Moshier, S. O., 2013, '"A Highway out of Egypt": The Main Road from Egypt to Canaan', in *Desert Road Archaeology in Ancient Egypt and Beyond, Africa Praehistorica*, 27, 485–510.

Kitchen, K. A., 2003, *On the Reliability of the Old Testament*, Grand Rapids.

Kitchen, K. A., 1999, *Ramesside Inscriptions, Translated and Annotated Notes and Comments, vol. II: Ramesses II, Royal Inscriptions*, Oxford.

Lagomasino, D., Reide Corbett, D., Walsh, J. P., 2013, 'Influence of Wind-Driven Inundation and Coastal Geomorphology on Sedimentation in Two Microtidal Marshes, Pamlico River Estuary, NC', in *Estuaries and Coasts*, 36, no. 6, November 2013.

Leclère, F., Spencer J., 2014, *Tell Dafana Reconsidered, British Museum Research Publication*, 199, London.

50 Abd El-Maksoud 1998.

Le Père, J.-M., 1822. 'Mémoire sur la communication de la mer des Indes à la Méditerranée par la mer Rouge et l'isthme de Soueys', in *Description de l'Égypte: ou, Recueil des observations et des recherches qui ont été faites en Égypte pendant l'expédition de l'armée française*, l'État moderne vol. 11, Édition Panckoucke, 1822, Paris, 37-370.

MacDonald, B., 1980, 'Excavations at Tell el-Maskhuṭa', *The Biblical Archaeologist*, 43, issue 1, 49–58.

Naville, É., 1885, *The Store-city of Pithom and the Route of the Exodus*, London.

Rzepka, S., Nour el-Din, M., Wodzińska, A., Jarmużek, Ł., 2013, *Egyptian Mission Rescue Excavations in Tell el-Retabah. Part I: New Kingdom Remains. Ägypten und Levante 22/23*, Wien.

Rohl, D., 2003, *From Eden to Exile: The Epic History of the People of the Bible*, Arrow.

Seters, J. van, 'The Geography of the Exodus', in *The Land That I Will Show You: Essays in History and Archaeology of the Ancient Near East in Honor of J. Maxwell Miller*, Sheffield, 2001, 255–276.

Smoláriková, K., 2019, 'Fortified Delta: A Case Study from Tell el-Retaba', *Asian and African Studies*, 28, no. 1, 19–112.

Spencer, J., 2002, 'The Exploration of Tell Belim, 1999–2002', in *Journal of Egyptian Archaeology*, 88, 37-51.

Watrin, L., 2003, 'Projet Tell el-Ginn', in *Bulletin du GREPAL* no.1, Paris, 10–17.

About the author

Huub Pragt (1961) studied Egyptology at Leiden University. For ten years he worked at the National Museum of Antiquities in Leiden, where he was engaged in education and public activities. In January 2001 he founded his proprietorship Huub Pragt Egyptoloog. In the years that followed, he specialised in teaching courses on Egyptology for institutions and individuals. In the Netherlands and Flanders, he is often asked to give lectures. Pragt also leads tours and short excursions in the field of ancient Egypt.

Figure 1. Plate 13 from *Description de l'Égypte*, vol. V: *Antiquités-Descriptions (Pyramides de Memphis)*, showing the Gallery in the pyramid of Khufu. Image Allard Pierson, OL 63-1000.

Epilogue

Willem van Haarlem

When the date of my retirement was slowly approaching, I started to consider options for marking this occasion. Eventually, I thought it appropriate to organise a symposium about a subject that has fascinated me for a long time: alternative or 'fringe' Egyptology. Fortunately, my colleague and successor Ben van den Bercken agreed to participate in the organisation of this event.

Although we did not pretend to cover all alternative theories in our final programme, a representative selection was achieved nevertheless: pyramidology, the Curse of the Pharaoh, the exodus of the Israelites, Amarna-related matters, the Orion theory, the role of aliens, ancient Egyptian wisdom; cults such as Freemasonry, the Rosicrucians and the Hermetic Order of the Golden Dawn, and Afrocentrism. It was also quite illuminating to hear about non-Western viewpoints from China and Latin-America.

Alternative and mainstream Egyptology are two branches on the same tree that have grown more and more apart, and can be compared to such cases as astrology and astronomy or alchemy and chemistry. Aidan Dodson's contribution has clearly shown this.[1]

Some of the more extreme theories however can hardly be taken seriously: the role of aliens in ancient Egypt, for instance, and the theories involving audio waves, kites or sails to move stones for building the pyramids. It is nevertheless true that we are still not absolutely certain as to how, for example, the pyramids were constructed. There remain uncertainties in Egyptian chronology as well, to mention another issue.

If alternative theories inspire 'mainstream' scholars to re-examine their previous assumptions, that is not a bad thing in itself. For example, the subject of Afrocentrism deserves special attention. As it is potentially politically sensitive, its claims require especially careful and critical consideration, but certainly no off-hand dismissal.

In general, I think mainstream Egyptology should not ignore the less extreme 'alternative' factions, but address them seriously and, if necessary, refute them (or not) with clear arguments—hopefully to the benefit of both sides.

---

1 The contents of this contribution were published after the symposium in Dodson 2022, 137–42.

Bibliography

Dodson, A., 2022, *Tutankhamun, King of Egypt: His Life and Afterlife*, Cairo.

About the author

Willem van Haarlem graduated in Egyptology at the University of Amsterdam and obtained his PhD at Leiden University. Between 1990 and 2014 he worked as field director of the excavations at Tell Ibrahim Awad. From 1999 to 2003, he was assistant-director of the Dutch-Flemish Institute in Cairo. Van Haarlem is the author of a number of publications on ancient Egypt. He retired from his post as curator of the Egyptian Department of the Allard Pierson (University of Amsterdam) in 2021.